Colonial America on Film and Television

Colonial America on Film and Television

A FILMOGRAPHY

by

BERTIL O. ÖSTERBERG

McFarland & Company, Inc., Publishers

Jefferson, North Carolina, and London

Library of Congress Cataloguing-in-Publication Data

Österberg, Bertil O., 1943–
    Colonial America on film and television : a filmography / by Bertil
O. Österberg.
       p.   cm.
    Includes index.   ∞
    ISBN 0-7864-0862-6 (illustrated case binding : 50# alkaline paper)
    1. United States—In motion pictures.   2. Historical films—
United States—Catalogs. I. Title.
PN1995.9.U64O78   2001
016.79143'658—dc21   00-56835

British Library cataloguing data are available

Cover photograph: *Lafayette* (Copernic/Cosmos, 1961). The Marquis de Lafayette
(Michael Roger) at Yorktown.

Manufactured in the United States of America

McFarland & Company, Inc., Publishers
 Box 611, Jefferson, North Carolina 28640
  www.mcfarlandpub.com

To Camilla,
and to all frontiersmen and women,
colonials, Native Americans, patriots, loyalists,
Coureurs de Bois, Redcoats, Yankees,
authors, film producers, and reenactors
who help me to keep this interest alive.

Table of Contents

Introduction

To a European, the history of North America from its colonization may seem short indeed. It is, however, rich in exciting events and dramatic conflicts.

No other continent has its history reflected on the film screen as frequently as North America. Movies and television have been extensively utilized to retell the story of America, and no resources have been spared in filling it with drama and adventure.

The place and period most frequently covered is the American West in the 1840s–1890s. Since the beginning of motion picture history, moviegoers have shown a tremendous interest in westerns. For generations audiences have lined up in front of the box offices for these tales of the "old" West. Many of the major production companies have also used westerns as bread and butter products to finance bigger and more serious ventures. During the 1930s and '40s a considerable number of so called B westerns were released, which were produced in short time and on limited budgets. This pattern was later repeated during the early years of the television era.

To the genre of western movies are commonly assigned those movies which deal with the North American past before the settlement of the West. With a certain degree of generalization this time of American history can be referred to as the colonial period. This book covers movies, TV films, and TV series dealing with the colonial period of America's history from the time when the first Europeans set their feet on its soil to explore the continent, throughout the colonial wars until after the War of 1812.

This is a long time span—more than 300 years if you begin with Columbus—yet the number of films is relatively small. This book covers just over 160 film and TV entries, of which about 40 are from the silent movie era. Compare this number with the several thousand western movies that have been produced. During the 1930s and '40s, dozens or perhaps hundreds of western "cliffhangers" series were released. During the same period, only *one* was made with motifs from the colonial period, Mascot's **Last of the Mohicans** (1932).

It is hard to understand why so few films depict the colonial period, especially when it has great historical interest and should be a treasure chest of film ideas. Perhaps part of the explanation can be found in the words of famous director John Ford (in Peter Bogdanovich's book *John Ford*): "There have been very few pictures about the American Revolution—

I think because actors are afraid of wearing those wigs." Darryl F. Zanuck said tersely: "Pictures about American history never make a nickel."

Nevertheless, famous directors have occasionally tackled the subject of colonial America. John Ford himself directed one of the most well-known and popular of all colonial movies, **Drums Along the Mohawk** (20th Century–Fox, 1939). In 1924, D.W. Griffith produced and directed the silent epic **America** (United Artists), and in 1947 Cecil B. DeMille rewrote history in his **Unconquered** (Paramount).

A favorite subject of colonial film stories is the hardship the first settlers faced when they were battling the American wilderness; their struggle to survive, living under rough conditions, often threatened by starvation in a wild and unfriendly environment. These films also focus on the conflicts the settlers faced in their ambition to gain land from the Native Americans.

A number of films address the opposition which was raised between different European nationalities as a result of the political situation in Europe leading up to the American phase of the Seven Years War, the so called French and Indian War. Further, they depict the growing dissatisfaction of the colonists against the ruling British, the victors of the French and Indian War, which led to the Revolutionary War and the creation of America's independent states, and later, when the defeated British tried to recapture their authority, to what is usually called the War of 1812.

These film stories frequently tell us how the hard life on the frontiers created strong and resolute men and women, individualists like Daniel Boone and Davy Crockett, but also profit-hungry adventurers and renegades.

Unlike many westerns, colonial film stories often have a direct historical link, even if the history is rather significantly rewritten and many of the characters are fictional. Commonly appearing, though often only as side figures, are men who came to play important roles as politicians and statesmen, but who first won admiration as brave fighters on the battlefields in the wilderness. Names like Sir William Johnson, George Washington and Andrew Jackson should be familiar in this respect. Also famous from history are those men who led the exploration of the western part of the continent, people like Captain Meriwether Lewis and Lt. William Clark.

Native Americans play important roles in these movies, even if they frequently are pictured as faceless, brutal murderers who make life complicated for the settlers. There is, however, room also for famous Indians from history, like Pontiac, Thayendanegea (Joseph Brandt) and Tecumseh, as well as familiar fictional natives like Hiawatha, Chingachgook and Uncas.

The connection to American classical literature is also obvious in these movies. Longfellow's poem *The Song of Hiawatha* (1855) has served as a basis for several films. His *The Courtship of Miles Standish* also found its way to the movies, as did Nathaniel Hawthorne's classic novel *The Scarlet Letter*, about a woman accused of adultery in a Puritan New England settlement. This novel has been filmed several times throughout the years.

More recent novels appearing on the screen include Elizabeth Madox Roberts's *The Great Meadow*, Elizabeth Page's best seller *The Tree of Liberty,* Howard Fast's *April Morning* and *Rachel,* and Kenneth Roberts's epic *Northwest Passage.*

The author whose work by far most frequently has been used as sources for colonial movies is James Fenimore Cooper. His *Leatherstocking* novels (*The Deerslayer, The Pathfinder, The Last of the Mohicans, The Pioneers,* and *The Prairie*) have been filmed several times.

The research for this book produced some evidence that more films of colonial history once existed. Several short films were shot during the early silent film period. Unfortunately many of these films are lost today, and on some of the titles very little or no information is available. This lack of information is reflected in the spare coverage of some titles.

It has been encouraging to see how the success of Michael Mann's recent production of **The Last of the Mohicans** (Morgan Creek, 1992) has created a new interest in the subject, with quite a few productions dealing with colonial America being released in the years since. The fact that Native Americans are treated with increased respect in the new productions is also encouraging.

All of us who love early American history on film can only hope that this trend will continue and that we can expect many more productions in the genre for the future.

American Colonial History on Film: An Overview

The Early Frontiers

The oldest known account of contact between Europeans and the North American continent is when Leif Ericsson's brother Thorwald, in the year of 1006, explored somewhere along the northeast coast of the New World.

Accepted by historians, is the discovery of Florida by Juan Ponce de León in 1513. To secure the new discovered land against the French, who were exploring further north, the Spaniards in 1526 made an attempt to create a settlement somewhere on the Carolina coast, under the leadership of Lucas Vásquez de Ayllón. The whole colony, however, disappeared without a trace, probably exterminated by hostile Indians.

Further Spanish attempts to colonize the continent were made, and in 1540 Francisco Vásquez de Coronado led an expedition to locate the mythical Seven Cities of Cibola. Coronado failed in his mission but during his expedition in the Southwest he introduced the horse to the Indians, which animal later was adapted by Comanches, Apaches and Utes.

About the same time another expedition headed by Hernando de Soto set out for the Southeast to find riches. The expedition proceeded through parts of what at present are known as Georgia, South and North Carolina, Tennessee, Alabama, Mississippi and Arkansas. In 1542 the survivors of the expedition made their way through Texas to Mexico. On their way the expedition met with numerous Indian tribes, such as Creeks, Cherokees, Chickasaws and several others.

The French also made attempts to settle in the Southeast but were dislodged by the newly arrived Spaniards, who then exerted complete control of the region.

Coronado's failure in the Southwest resulted in a temporary loss of interest in the area. Later, however, various expeditions were sent out and in 1610 a permanent Spanish capital was established in Santa Fe. The event was used for a story in the movie **Kiss of Fire** (Universal, 1955).

Of the early exploration of North America by the Spaniards, the film industry has shown very little interest, although Coronado's search for the Seven Cities of Cibola gave the impulse for the story in **Seven Cities of Gold** (20th Century–Fox, 1955). The film does not relate Coronado's expedition in 1540, but a later attempt to locate the expedition in California.

In **Mission to Glory** (Western World, 1980), Father Francis "Kino" Kin, a priest in California, fights Indians and Conquistadors in the defeat of his people in the 17th century.

The further exploration of North America by the Spaniards continued in the Southern area during the 1600s, but the Spaniards never extended thereafter much beyond the Rio Grande. Other nationalities entrenched themselves further north on the continent.

Attempts were also made by the British to explore the Southwest. In 1577 during his sea travels and raids against Spanish treasure ships, the famous Sir Francis Drake and his band of English pirates landed in California and named the country New Albino, according to the story in the Italian film **Seven Seas to Calais** (Adelphia Compagnia/MGM, 1963). Not only Europeans tried to settle the North American continent. In **Kings of the Sun** (United Artists, 1963) a Mayan Indian tribe emigrates from Mexico to settle in Texas.

The French explored the Northeast coast and in 1534 Jacques Cartier, during his exploration of the Gulf of St. Lawrence, realized the fur trading possibilities with the Algonquin Indian tribes. This resulted in a growing French interest in the area and several French traders arrived and started fur trading with the natives. The new trade market with the Europeans, however, created problems with the trade privileges among the different Indian tribes, which resulted in war between them and the whites. In the early 1600s,

for example, Samuel de Champlain, who later gave name to Lake Champlain, and some of his men participated on the Hurons' side in violence against the Mohawk Indians. The action resulted in long-lasting resentment against the French by the Mohawks and other Iroquois tribes.

In **Black Robe** (Alliance Entertainment, Samson production, 1991), Iroquois Indians attack and capture a French missionary (Lothaire Bluteau) and his Algonquin guides on a journey into the Canadian wilderness, where they intend to reinforce the troubled Jesuit mission to the Huron tribe. The story takes place during the mid–17th century and is based on a novel by Brian Moore. Another story about a French "Black Robe," who goes to teach Christianity to the Indians during this period, was filmed by Kalem in **A Priest of the Wilderness: Father Jogue's Mission to the Iroquois** (1909).

In the late 1500s the different Northern Iroquois tribes had settled their suicidal differences, and legend says that a Huron named Daganawidah and a Mohawk chief and shaman named Hiawatha founded the confederation of the five Iroquois nations of New York about 1570. The confederation was one of the few republics the world has known, and there is some evidence that this influenced the founding fathers while they were modeling the young American republic.

In 1855 Henry W. Longfellow, inspired by an earlier American ethnologist who had translated the story of the real Hiawatha into a series of myths and identified Hiawatha as a Chippewa chief, compounded the error and wrote of them in *The Song of Hiawatha*. Longfellow's poem inspired the film industry to five film versions: **Hiawatha** (Charles Urban Trading Co., 1905); **Hiawatha** (Independent Moving Picture Co., 1909) directed and played by William Ranous as Hiawatha and Gladys Hulette as Minnehaha; **Hiawatha, the Indian Passion Play** (State Rights, 1913) directed and produced by Frank E. Moore; **Hiawatha** (Monogram, 1952) with Vincent Edwards as Hiawatha and Yvette Dugay as Minnehaha; and a made for TV version, **Song of Hiawatha** (Hallmark Home Entertainment, 1997).

Other Europeans settled on the Atlantic coast, and the Dutch founded in 1609 their colony, New Amsterdam, that later would be known as New York.

To the south along the Atlantic coast on Roanoke Island, the outer island of North Carolina, a British colony was settled in 1587 under the leadership of Governor John White. White, who had returned to England for supplies, one year later came back to find that all the members of the colony had vanished. The reason for the disappearance of the colony has never been solved.

The mysterious disappearance of the Roanoke settlement was dramatized in a three part TV mini-series in 1986, **Roanoak** (Public Broadcasting System).

The first permanent English settlement in America was established north of Roanoke Island, at Jamestown, Virginia. One of the settlers was an adventurer by the name of Captain John Smith. A strong Indian, Powhatan, who was chief of a confederacy of Algonquin tribes, ruled the region. Many of the settlers, ill suited for the new life, died of diseases and sporadic hostilities by the Indians. In later years John Smith in his *The General History of Virginia, New England and the Summer Islands*, related how when Indians captured him he was saved from death by Pocahontas, Powhatan's daughter. Whether the story is true or not has never been verified. Pocahontas later married one of the colony's leading men, John Rolfe, whom she accompanied to England, where she died of smallpox in 1617.

Of the story of John Smith and Pocahontas the film industry has made seven movie versions. In 1908, Edison Company released **Pocahontas—A Child of the Forest,** and in 1910 a new version with the title **Pocahontas** was issued by Thanhouser. Further versions were released: **Jamestown** (Chronicle of American Pictures/Pathé, 1923) with Dolores Cassinelli as Pocahontas and Leslie Austin as John Rolfe; **Pocahontas and John Smith** (Universal, 1924) a one-reeler comedy; and in 1953 Eclipsa/United Artists produced **Captain John Smith and Pocahontas,** which was also released with the title **Burning Arrows.** Two Pocahontas films were released in 1995. In one version children also have their share of the story in Walt Disney's heavily advertised cartoon feature **Pocahontas** (Buena Vista). The other was **Pocahontas, the Legend** (Good Times Entertainment).

The conflict in bringing Native Americans to Europe in the early 1600s is dealt with in two recent productions. In the Canadian TV mini-series **Shehaweh** (Les Prod. de CERF/Telefilm Canada/Canadian Broadcasting Corp., 1992) an Indian girl is captured and brought to France. In Walt Disney's movie **Squanto: A Warrior's Tale** (1996), a young warrior experiences the same fate and is brought to England. They both return to North America to find their tribes wiped out in the contact with the European colonists.

The tobacco that the English colonists were planting in Virginia had developed a rich market in England. This resulted in pressure by the settlers on the Indians for more land to grow the crop. The friction between the whites and the Indians led to a long war, and when the hostilities ended in 1664 the Indian confederacy had been smashed.

In 1620, a group of English Calvinists living in Holland who had been suspended from the British Church because of their religion, departed on the ship *Mayflower* to settle in the New World. These "Pilgrims" sailed from Plymouth and landed on the Massachusetts coast, where they decided to settle and adopt their own religion. During their first winter in the new country more than half of them died of cold and scurvy. The next summer, however, they raised good crops and later new settlers arrived from overseas, and they were successful in their resolution. On film, the story of the Pilgrims' journey across the Atlantic, the landing at Plymouth, and the hardships of the first year, were told in **The Courtship of Miles Standish** (Charles Ray Productions, 1923) and in **Plymouth Adventure** (MGM, 1952).

The Dutch in New York managed to get along well with the Indians in the area. In 1626 a party of Dutch led by Peter Minuit bought Manhattan Island for goods at a value of $24 from the Manhattan Indians, members of the Wappinger confederacy. The buying of Manhattan by the Dutch has served as a story in two films: **Buying Manhattan** (Edison, 1909) and **When Broadway Was a Trail** (Shubert/World, 1914) with O.A.C. Lund and Barbara Tennant.

In New England, new colonists arrived and pushed inland, buying and trading land from the Indians. New settlements were established from Maine to Connecticut. At the beginning the newcomers treated the Indians well, but when a group of settlers from Massachusetts Bay in 1636 destroyed a Pequot Indian town, war broke out. The war that followed led to the destruction of the whole Pequot nation. The war, which is known as the Pequot War, was used for stories in two movies: **Priscilla and the Pequot War** (Kalem, 1911) and **Puritans and Indians** (Kalem, 1911).

Puritan and Indian trouble was also brought up in the recent film version of **The Scarlet Letter** (Lightmotive/Allied Stars/Cinergi/Moving Picture, 1995) in which Indians attack Massachusetts settlements. **The Scarlet Letter**, which is based on Nathaniel Hawthorne's classic novel, has previously been done in several film versions. MGM did a silent version in 1926, directed by the famous Swedish director Victor Sjostrom. The first talking version came in 1934 (Darmoun/Majestic), and a German-Spanish coproduction came in 1973; in 1979, PBS produced a four-hour TV mini-series.

To the north in Canada the French had allied themselves with Huron and Algonquin tribes for fur trade. The Iroquois, who had been supplied with guns by the Dutch and now were in the service of the English, turned against their former enemies, the Hurons. After numerous frustrations, a big war party of Senecas and Mohawks made their way into the Huron country and destroyed and burned the principal villages of the Hurons. After the victory over the Hurons the Iroquois launched a series of wars over three decades against various northern Indian tribes.

Some silent movies dealing with the hostilities between the Iroquois and other northern Indian tribes during the period were reflected in **Fighting the Iroquois in Canada** (Kalem, 1910); D.W. Griffith's **A Mohawk's Way** (Biograph, 1910); **Prisoners of the Mohicans** (Pathé, 1911); **In the Days of the Six Nations** (Republic, 1911); **Gathering of the Council of the Six Nations** (1911); and **The Huron Converts** (Reliance, 1915).

When the hostilities between the different tribes declined, the whites continued to push westwards, rebuilding old alliances and seeking new tribes for trading. In 1653 two trappers, Pierre Radisson and Medard Chouart Sieur des Groseilliers, traveled along the Ottawa River to Lake Huron and farther to Michigan. They made their first contacts with Indians on the open plains who were eager to trade for knives, tomahawks and fire arms. More important was their journey to the North the next year, to the Northwest coast of Lake Superior, Lake Nipigon and along the Albany River to the Atlantic

Ocean. At their arrival they were received with little support from the French governor for setting up fur trading relations with the tribes in the North. Instead, they were pressured to pay high taxes. The failure to enlist the French merchants in their operation in the North caused Radisson and Groseilliers to turn to the English for assistance. In 1668, with British partners, they began trading at Hudson's Bay with Indian tribes who brought their furs out of central Canada, and in 1670 the partnership received a royal charter as the Hudson's Bay Company. 20th Century–Fox fictionalized the story for the screen in 1940 in **Hudson's Bay**.

On TV, the story of Pierre Radisson and of adventures of fur trappers around the Hudson's Bay region were dealt with in two Canadian-produced northwoods serials: **Tomahawk** (CBC, 1957-58) and **Hudson's Bay** (North Star, 1959).

In New England the settlers visited numerous injustices upon the Indians. A Wampanoag Indian, Metacom, known to the colonists as King Philip, tried to form an alliance among the New England tribes; for many years war threatened and finally in 1675 it broke out.

In the beginning of the war, known as The King Philip's War, the Indians were successful in their raids against the settlements: 51 were attacked and several were completely destroyed. In 1676, however, luck for the Indians turned and Philip suffered serious defections. With the help of an Indian informer, Philip was killed and one by one the Indians were wiped out and the war came to an end in New England.

In **Scarlet Letter** from 1995, King Philip and his Wampanoag warriors attack the "New Jerusalem" settlement in Massachusetts. The attack came just in time to save Hester Prynne (Demi Moore) from being hanged for witchcraft by the Puritans.

Also in the Southwest, trouble between whites and Indians arose. The Pueblo Indians pushed the Spaniards out of New Mexico in 1680, but ten years later the Spaniards returned and smashed the Pueblos forever. The subject came up in Kalem's **The Indian Uprising at Santa Fe** (Kalem, 1912).

In Pennsylvania the settlers get along better with the natives. The Quakers, led by William Penn, showed more concern for Indian rights than most settlers did elsewhere. In 1682 Penn made a treaty with the Delaware Indians, who were led by Tamanend, known by the English as Tammy. London-born William Penn's founding of the Quaker movement and the sect's settlement in Pennsylvania were inaccurately biographied in **The Courageous Mr. Penn** (also called **Penn of Pennsylvania**; Esquire Films, Hoffberg/BN, 1941). William Penn's and his followers' fight for religious freedom was also dealt with on film in **The Quakers** (1913).

The French, who could not give up their thoughts of exploring the South, sent in 1680 an expedition led by La Salle down the Mississippi River, and in the spring of 1681 they reached the Gulf of Mexico. La Salle was the first white man who had succeeded in traveling from the Great Lakes all the way down to the mouth of the Mississippi.

When traveling down the river, La Salle took the lands on both sides of the river in possession and declared it as French territory. To secure the new land the French explorers built forts at strategic locations along the way and named the country Louisiana in honor of Louis XIV.

In the North the relations between the French and the English constantly became worse, since 1690 the French and their Indian allies had carried out several attacks on New England settlements. In 1679, at one of those attacks a woman by the name of Hannah Duston was taken prisoner. She, however, managed to escape and brought back with her several Indian scalps, which at that time were paid for with bounty money. Kalem in **Hannah Dustin** filmed the fate of Hannah Duston in 1908.

The arrival of the French in the South alarmed the Spaniards. In 1720, after the French had also begun to probe across Texas, a Spanish expedition marched into Louisiana Territory to reconnoiter the situation, but on the Platte River they ran into a force of French and allied Indians who almost wiped them out.

The French pressed their exploration farther up the Missouri, and in Canada they pushed west. The relations between the French and the English were further worsened, especially as the two countries in Europe were almost continuously at war against each other. In the West the French hurried to build posts at strategic sites along the main routes and soon they were able to intercept much of the British trade.

On the New England frontiers the French and their Indian allies from Canada frequently attacked the English settlers. The frontier wars and the intertribal conflicts over the fur trade had filled the country with displaced Indians, bands of many tribes who were looking for new homes.

From North Carolina, the Tuscarora Indians, who had been beaten by the colonists, moved north and joined the New York Iroquois to form the Six Nations. The Iroquois in general continued to be friendlier to the English, but maintained neutrality and exercised a balance of power between the two sides.

A conflict between the French and English settlers, although resulting in several skirmishes on the frontiers, was not an open war, but soon when the war between England and France broke out in Europe, the conflict would spread resulting in the American phase of the Seven Years' War.

In one of James Fenimore Cooper's well-known novels, *The Deerslayer*, the story takes place on the New York frontier just prior to the outbreak of the war between the English and the French. *The Deerslayer* was filmed in several versions. The first version was issued by Vitagraph in 1913, directed by Hal Reid. In 1920 a German company, Luna-Film, made a lengthy version of the Cooper work called **Lederstrumpf** (Leatherstocking). This film, directed by Arthur Wellin, was issued in two parts: **Der Wildtöter** (**The Deerslayer**) and **Der Letzte Mohikaner** (**The Last of the Mohicans**). The film was released in United States under the title **The Deerslayer** and was trimmed from 12 to five reels.

Pathé produced a series entitled **Leatherstocking** in 1924, although the final product was more a reworking of *The Deerslayer*. It was released in ten chapters, and was directed by George B. Seitz. In 1943, the Republic Studio issued a low-budget version of **The Deerslayer** by Lew Landers. 20th Century–Fox released a color version directed by Kurt Neuman in 1957, and in 1967, a European version was released by Delfa, **Chingachgook—Die grosse Schlange**, directed by Richard Grosehopp. The last version, to date, is a made for TV feature from 1978, starring Ned Romenko as Chingachgook and Steve Forrest as Deerslayer. In this treatment the story was transferred in time from that of the original novel to the French and Indian War, after the death of Uncas.

The French and Indian War

In the early eighteenth century several frontier skirmishes took place between British and French colonists for land possessions in North America.

The French were concerned over the

territorial aims of Great Britain on the continent and while extending their fur trading posts, the French continued their program of construction of new forts. Their purpose was to establish a strong linkage between France's Great Lakes Empire and her colony in Louisiana.

In 1744, the French captured an English island off the Northern Coast of America. This was in the Great Banks area, where both France and England claimed fishing rights. An unexpected attack by the French on Cape Breton, Nova Scotia, was entirely successful. This was the beginning of King George's War, the North American segment of the War of the Austrian Succession.

Thus far it was a sea war, but throughout the frontier both Indians and whites remained poised for either fight or flight. In 1745 in a brilliant campaign laid out by Massachusetts Governor Shirley, the French fortress of Louisbourg was taken. New England militia led by William Pepperrell, along with the English fleet commanded by Peter Warren, put the bastion under siege on May 5. It was surrendered to them on June 17. The event was filmed on location in Louisbourg in the Canadian TV mini-serial **Hudson Frontier** (also titled **The Adventure of a Lady**, HTV Ltd., 1986).

The Treaty of Aix-la-Chapelle in Europe ended King George's War. The enmity between France and England, however, remained in America. France claimed all of North America from the Alleghenies to the Rocky Mountains and from Mexico to the North Pole, excepting only the English colonies and some possessions on the borders of Hudson's Bay. All this vast area was known as New France. But the fact remained that the English with their relatively small territory had a population of whites 21 times greater than the French had in all the rest of the continent. To strengthen their forces the French allied themselves with

several Indian tribes—Abnakis, Algonquins, Huron, Nippissi and a fair number of Iroquois in Canada. From the upper Great Lakes they allied with Ottawas, Potawatomis and Chippewas, and from the Ohio country with Wyandots, Shawnees, Delawares and Miamis.

Almost the only Indians allied to the British were the New York Iroquois League, especially the Mohawks. The loyalty of the Iroquois was mainly a result of skillful work by William Johnson, a former fur trader who was in charge of British Indian affairs. Johnson's influence on the Iroquois League comes to life in one of the films in the Turner Pictures Native American series, **The Broken Chain** (Turner Pictures, 1993) with Pierce Brosnan cast as William Johnson.

The British claimed the Ohio Valley area, which the French regarded as their own, having explored it and indeed having built a chain of forts to protect it. In 1753 Governor Dinwiddie of Virginia decided to demand the evacuation of the territory. An expedition led by young George Washington was sent out with the purpose of sounding out the intentions of the French, and possibly persuading them to take their claims elsewhere.

In mid–November they reached Fort Le Boeuf, where the French commander listened to the young envoy with courtesy but replied that the French had no thoughts of moving from the land to which La Salle had laid claim 70 years earlier. Washington returned to Williamsburg in January 1754 and the result of the otherwise unsuccessful expedition was to point up that sooner or later there would be war with the French.

The disagreements about the territorial claims in Ohio led to several skirmishes which became a major war on July 3, 1754, when a mixed force of French soldiers and Indians attacked Fort Necessity, a post in Northwest Pennsylvania which had been erected hastily by the orders of Washington. Vastly out-numbered, inadequately fortified, Washington surrendered Fort Necessity on July 4. Half of his men had been killed.

Washington's expedition to Fort Le Boeuf was part of the screen story in Columbia's **When the Redskins Rode** (1951). The highlight of the film was the attack on Fort Necessity, but as Hollywood always wanted the "good guys" to win, the history was rewritten so that Washington and his men beat off the French attack with the help of Delaware Indians, who in reality fought on the French side. In the MGM/UA TV mini-series **George Washington** (1984), however, Washington, played by Barry Bostwick, lost Fort Necessity to the French in accordance with history. George Washington in military service for the British cause was earlier dealt with in the silent movie **Washington Under British Flag** (Vitagraph, 1909).

The early part of the French and Indian War was also treated in Columbia's **The Pathfinder** (1952), which was based on James Fenimore Cooper's novel with the same name, even though not much from Cooper's story could be recognized in the film version. More faithful to the original story is a recent Hallmark Home Entertainment version of *The Pathfinder* (1996). A German-French TV co-production has **The Pathfinder** as a very free adaptation, according to German Karl May tradition, in one of its episodes, **Das Fort am Biberfluss (The Fort on Beaver River)** in their **Lederstrumpf (Leatherstocking)** series (Aura Film). Other episodes of the production are: **"Wildtöter"** (**"The Deerslayer"**), **"Der Letzte Mohikaner"** (**"The Last of the Mohicans"**), and **"Die Prärie"** (**"The Prairie"**). Even Russia has produced a version of *The Pathfinder* (**Sledopyt**, 1987). Other Leatherstocking productions are: **Leatherstocking** (Biograph Co., 1909), **Lederstrumpf** (Leatherstocking, Luna Film, 1920), and **Leatherstocking** (Pathé serial, 1924).

The Colonies were deeply shocked and distressed at the defeat of Colonel George Washington's army. In England, Brigadier General Edward Braddock was promoted to Major General and ordered to America to take command of all the military forces. Braddock worked out an ambitious plan for a simultaneous attack on four key French fortifications. Braddock himself was to march against Fort Duquesne; Major General Shirley had as his objective the destruction or capture of Fort Niagara. An army of provincials from New York, New Jersey and New England under William Johnson would be sent to Crown Point. Lieutenant Colonel Robert Monckton would lead another force against the French fortress at Louisbourg in Nova Scotia.

The campaign started well for the British, when Monckton in July 1755 captured the French fort of Beausejour in Nova Scotia. The taste of victory became short when Braddock's force on July 9 almost within sight of Fort Duquesne were ambushed by an army of French and Indians. In the awful battle that followed almost the whole British army was wiped out. Out of approximately 1,400 men, the total dead—or wounded—figure was 977! For the French the corresponding figure was only around 50.

Braddock himself fought like a madman; four horses were killed under him. He himself was shot through the lung while on his fifth horse. Among Braddock's officers was Colonel George Washington, who kept his Virginians in hand and held back the enemy while the pitiful remains of Braddock's army raced to safety. Washington, though unhurt, had two horses shot from under him, and his coat had been pierced by four bullets. Assisting Braddock's army was also a 21-year-old sergeant by the name of Daniel Boone.

The defeat of General Braddock's army was dealt with on the movie screen in MGM's **Winners of the Wilderness** (1927), in which Tim McCoy played an Irish officer attached to Washington's Virginians. Washington himself was pictured in **Washington Under the British Flag** (Vitagraph, 1909), directed by J.S. Blackton and with Joseph Kilgour in the role as George Washington. In Braddock's defeat in the TV mini-serial **George Washington** (MGM/UA, 1984), James Mason was cast as General Edward Braddock.

An adventure of the young frontiersman Daniel Boone, just after the defeat of Braddock's army, was presented in **Young Daniel Boone** (Monogram, 1950), in which Boone is helping a little group of settlers to escape from French-allied Indians. Daniel Boone's involvement in the French and Indian War was further dealt with in the Universal series **In the Days of Daniel Boone** (1923), directed by Frank Messenger, with Jack Mower in the role of Boone. Another "In the Days..." silent movie dealing with the French and Indian War was **In the Days of the Six Nations** (Republic, 1911), which is based on James Fenimore Cooper's novels.

Braddock's defeat left the Western frontiers wide open to France's Indian allies, whose raids forced settlers to withdraw to the East as much as 100 miles.

William Johnson, who had some problems assembling and equipping his provincial army, proceeded north with his army toward their destination, Crown Point. At the head of Lake George they ran into an army of French regulars, Canadians and French-allied Indians under the command of Baron Ludwig Dieskau. Johnson, who had trained his provincials to fight wilderness war the Indian way, managed to defeat the French force and capture Baron Dieskau in the battle, which took place on September 8, 1755. Before leaving the arena Johnson's army built a substantial fort, which was named Fort William Henry after one of the king's grandsons.

For General Shirley matters did not go well at all. Because of the lack of men and supplies his campaign against Fort Niagara had to be canceled.

In England, Royal orders were drawn up in January 1756 giving the command of the American force to General Webb, who later would relinquish it to General Abercromby, and Abercromby, in turn, to John Campbell. In France, a new commander was also chosen to replace Baron Dieskau, who had been wounded during the battle with Johnson's army at Lake George. The man selected to fill the post was Louis Montcalm.

On May 11, 1756, Louis Joseph, Marquise de Montcalm arrived in Canada to take charge of French and provincial forces. Less than a week later, on May 17, England officially declared war on France.

The British plan for their summer campaign was to strike against three different French posts—Fort Ticonderoga at Lake Champlain, Fort Frontenac at the mouth of Lake Ontario, and Fort Niagara at the head of the same lake. Rather than wait for a British attack, the French planned to attack and destroy Fort Oswego, which had a strategic location at Lake Ontario.

In July 1756, John Campbell arrived in New York from London. The new commander decided to abandon the plans for striking against Niagara and Frontenac and instead to aim only for Fort Ticonderoga. In the meanwhile, a French army under Montcalm on August 14 attacked and took Fort Oswego. After the capitulation of Fort Oswego, Montcalm destroyed its defensive works as well as two neighboring forts, Fort Ontario and Fort George, by fire. Montcalm's first battle in America had been a signal success. When receiving the message of the British defeat at Oswego, the English General Webb abandoned the two forts, Williams and Bull, on the Mohawk River.

With Montcalm's victory, the British had lost their access to the Great Lakes, and with even Fort William and Fort Bull lost, the road now was opened for the French to strike against the British fortifications in the Mohawk Valley and the Hudson River area, and then against Albany and New York itself. The plans for a British attack on Fort Ticonderoga were put in abeyance in favor of preparing for the defense of Fort Edward and Fort William Henry, which were expected to be the next aim for the French. The French army did, however, not come. Instead, Montcalm had returned his army to Montreal and then with reinforcements proceeded to Fort Ticonderoga to wait for the English attack, unaware of the fact that the English were waiting for him to attack.

The autumn became early winter and the time for considerable campaigns was over for the year. Things looked bad for the English. The successful campaign of Montcalm's army impressed the Indians and a substantial number of tribes were seeking alliance with the French rather than with the British, who had lost their prestige and among the Indians were not considered as men, but as women.

The British commander, General Campbell, directed his attention for the 1757 summer campaign against Fort Louisbourg in Nova Scotia. When the main part of the British army sailed off for Louisbourg, General Webb was left behind as commander of Fort Edward to guard the frontiers. The French showed no concern over the English campaign against Louisbourg as they were certain that this giant fortress could withstand any siege brought against it. Therefore, when the time came for Montcalm to take up the summer offensive, he decided to strike against Fort William Henry and Fort Edward.

On August 2, Montcalm with his army and a substantial number of allied Indians attacked Fort William Henry. For several days the fort was set under siege with a constant bombardment from Montcalm's artillery. The English commander, Colonel Munro, sent several messengers to General Webb at Fort Edward asking for reinforcement, but when he realized that Webb could not march for the relief of Fort William Henry, he had to surrender the fort to Montcalm. On August 9, the capitulation document was signed which allowed the British troops to leave with the honors of war with French escort to Fort Edward. During the departure of the English troops, however, Montcalm could not control his Indians, who massacred and captured many of the British. Perhaps as many as 1,500 soldiers, women and children were massacred or taken prisoner; certainly more than 200 men were killed. Père Roubaud, missionary to the Abnakis, ordered his charges not to participate in the ritual cannibalism the Ottawa practiced on their victims.

The struggle for Fort William Henry and the Indian massacre of the defeated British was depicted in several of the film versions of *The Last of the Mohicans*, based on James Fenimore Cooper's novel, most notably so in the 1920 version directed by Maurice Tourneur (Associated Producers), United Artist's version from 1936 which was directed by George B. Seitz, and the most recent box office success from 1992, directed by Michael Mann (Morgan Creek International). The 1992 film was partially based on Philip Dunne's screenplay for the 1936 version.

Tourneur's **Mohicans** is one of the best translations of Cooper's novel to the screen of the many film versions. In 1911 there were two films of *The Last of the Mohicans*, each one reel long (Powers and Thanhouser were the releasing companies). The Thanhouser version was filmed at Lake George, New York, and the actual arena of the story. Another version was released in 1914 and in 1920 the German Film Company, Luna-Film, released a two part film based on Cooper's work of which the second was **Der Letzte der Mohikaner (The Last of the Mohicans)**. It was directed by Arthur Wellin and even though filmed in Germany, it had the authentic look of Upper New York. The first talkie version of *Last of the Mohicans* came in 1932 when Mascot released a 12-episode cliffhanger with the starring team Harry Carey and Edwina Booth.

In 1947, Columbia released a mediocre color version, which takes great liberty with Cooper's novel, called **Last of the Redmen. The Iroquois Trail** (United Artists, 1950) was loosely based on *The Last of the Mohicans*, but for some reason the story was transferred in time from 1757 to 1755 and instead of the attack on Fort William Henry, Montcalm and his troops in this version attacked Fort William on the Mohawk River. In reality, no such attack occurred; in fact in 1755 Montcalm had not yet arrived in America. Two European versions were produced in 1965. One in Italy, **L'ultimo dei Mohicani**, and the other in Germany, **Der Letzte Mohikaner** (International Germania-Balcazar).

In 1956, a syndicated TV series was filmed in Canada by producer Sigmund Neufeld, called **Hawkeye and the Last of the Mohicans**, and issued to TV in 39 episodes. Most of the serial was directed by Sam Newfield and had John Hart in the title role as Hawkeye and Lon Chaney as Chingachgook. In 1962 four features were made from segments of the serial and issued to TV by International Television Corporation. They were: **Along the Mohawk Trail, The Redmen and the Renegades, The Long Rifle and the Tomahawk** and **The Pathfinder and the Mohican**. In England the BBC produced in 1971 another TV series, **The Last of the Mohicans**, which was very faithful to Cooper's original work, and in 1977 a TV feature starring Steve Forrest and Ned Romano was released by NBC. Hanna & Barbara produced an animated film special, **The Last of the Mohicans**, for CBS in 1975.

The box-office success of Michael Mann's 1992 film of **The Last of the Mohicans** (Morgan Creek), with Daniel Day-Lewis in the role of Hawkeye, gave inspiration to a 21-episode TV series, **Hawkeye, The First Frontier** (Stephen J. Cannell, 1994).

After Montcalm's victory at Fort William Henry, he decided not to further press the attack against Fort Edward. This decision was based on a variety of reasons. Most of the Indians left after the successful battle, supplies were short, and General Webb's force at Fort Edward had been substantially reinforced. Montcalm burned Fort William Henry and returned to Montreal via Ticonderoga and Crown Point.

The disaster for the English was not ended with the loss of Fort William Henry. General Campbell's campaign in Nova Scotia failed, without even having gotten within firing distance of Fort Louisbourg. General Campbell was relieved of his command of the British forces in America and recalled to England. His designated successor was his second-in-command, General James Abercromby.

For the British it was essential to cut the vital link between Canada with France, and this could only be done with the taking of Louisbourg and Quebec and the establishment of a powerful naval blockade on the St. Lawrence. Further lost ground had to be recovered: Fort Duquesne had to be taken, as well as Fort Niagara and Fort Ticonderoga. To cut the supply route to the French interior forts, Fort Frontenac had to be destroyed.

In 1758, Sir Jeffrey Amherst, second-in-command to Abercromby, was to go by sea to take the Louisbourg bastion at the mouth of the St. Lawrence. General Forbes would lead a campaign against Fort Duquesne and General Abercromby himself would strike against Ticonderoga.

With a force of well over 15,000 men, Abercromby in July went against Montcalm's defense force at Fort Ticonderoga of 3,600 men. The British held a position above the fort, Mount Defiance, which made the defenses of the post vulnerable to artillery. That Abercromby was incompetent as a military leader was proved when instead of using his artillery against the ill-constructed fort, he ordered an all-out frontal attack with muskets alone. Outnumbered, Montcalm had been prepared to retreat. Instead, he easily mowed down the charging enemy. The strategy was a disaster for the British and Abercromby lost his nerve and ordered his army into full retreat, and thus the most incomprehensible defeat in English history became fact.

Against odds, supporting Abercromby during the attack on Fort Ticonderoga, were Sir William Johnson (Pierce Brosnan) and Mohawk chief Joseph Brandt (Eric Schweig) in **The Broken Chain** (Turner Pictures, 1993).

For three years now the English had suffered defeat after defeat; what was needed desperately was a victory of some kind. At last they got it when the French on July 27 had to surrender the Louisbourg fortress after a 49-day bombardment from Amherst's fleet. More good news for the British was the capture and destruction of Fort Frontenac, on the north side of Ontario, giving the British control of the lake; also in December 1758 General John Forbes with his army cut across the Pennsylvania wilderness and captured Fort Duquesne which the English renamed Fort Pitt. General Abercromby's failure at Ticonderoga resulted

in his recall to England and Major General Jeffrey Amherst was appointed military commander in America.

The English now rode their luck in turning the war their way. In the plans for the summer campaign of 1759, General James Wolfe, second-in-command, was to advance with a fleet up the St. Lawrence, take Quebec and then move against the principal French-Canadian city, Montreal. At the same time, the main British army, under Amherst, was to strike against Fort Ticonderoga and Fort St. Frederic and then northward through Lake Champlain and join with Wolfe for the attack on Montreal. Amherst further sent Colonel John Prideaux and Sir William Johnson with a force, first to rebuild Fort Oswego and then to strike against Fort Niagara.

After having left a small force under Colonel Frederick Haldimand to rebuild a fort on the ruins at Oswego, Prideaux and Sir William continued with the main part of their army to Fort Niagara, which they set under siege. An artillery accident killed Colonel Prideaux, and Sir William Johnson once again was in command of an English army. On July 25, he led his army to a stunning victory over the French and took Fort Niagara. Consequently, Pierce Brosnan as Sir William Johnson with Brandt and his Mohawks were also successful in their Niagara campaign in **The Broken Chain**.

The news of Johnson's taking of Niagara spread throughout America. It was a gigantic step for the English because a vital French link across the continent was severed. Afraid that William Johnson with his army would follow up with more attacks on Western forts, the French themselves burned Fort Machault, Fort Le Boeuf and Fort Presque Isle and marched to Fort Detroit to take refuge there and await the coming of the English. General Amherst with his army in the meantime had advanced against Fort

Ticonderoga, which was easily taken as the French only had left a small detachment for its defense. After the capture of Fort Ticonderoga, Amherst proceeded north and occupied Fort St. Frederic at Crown Point, which had been abandoned by the French.

Amherst's taking of Fort Ticonderoga was depicted in Edison's **The Capture of Fort Ticonderoga** (1911), and in Columbia's **Fort Ti** (1953).

Rogers' Rangers was a famous company of colonial woodsmen led by the colorful Major Robert Rogers from New Hampshire, who had trained his men in guerrilla fighting and how to survive in the wilderness. Rogers's company, which was much appreciated by General Amherst, did a lot of scouting and carried out important raids behind the French lines. The Rangers were well recognized in their characteristic green buckskin dresses and Scottish caps. Major Rogers's main life dream was to blaze a trail across unmapped America and find a route to the Pacific. In 1759, Rogers led his company into Canada and destroyed a village of French-allied Abnaki Indians at St. Francis, in revenge for their raids on white settlements in the British colonies.

The Rangers' raid on the Indian village at St. Francis is the main event in the King Vidor film **Northwest Passage** (MGM, 1940), based on Kenneth Roberts's novel with the same title from 1937. The film version of Roberts's long novel, with Spencer Tracy in the role as Robert Rogers, deals only with the first part of the book and does not touch on Major Rogers's attempts to raise support and funds for his life mission to find the Northwest Passage. The film did well but wartime economies were one reason why MGM backed away from filming the second part of the book. In the 1950s, however, MGM made a 26-episode TV series of **Northwest Passage** which was freely based on Kenneth Roberts's novel, which

contained scenes from Vidor's 1940 film version. In 1959, three feature films were released from segments of the TV series. They were: **Frontier Rangers** (from the three TV episodes: "The Gunsmith," "The Bond Woman," and "The Burning Village"), **Fury River** (TV episodes: "The Vulture," "Stab in the Back," and "The Fight of the River") and **Mission of Danger** (TV episodes: "The Red Coat," "The Break-Out" and "The Secret of the Cliff").

General James Wolfe with his army of 9,000 men had sailed up the St. Lawrence and on June 26 the siege of Quebec began. The French forces at Quebec, under the command of Montcalm, amounted to some 15,000 men and 1,000 Indians—mostly Ottawas, Chippewas, and Potawatomies under Chief Pontiac. For the next two months, Wolfe probed Quebec's defenses without success. Failing to penetrate, Wolfe turned to terrorism against the civilians, bombarding the city day and night, concentrating his fire on residential rather than military targets.

After a siege of 80 days, the final battle took place on the Plains of Abraham on September 13, 1759. During the battle General Wolfe was mortally wounded, but the English won the decisive battle. Montcalm fought brilliantly but his efforts cost him his life.

Two movies dealing with the battle of Quebec have been released: **Wolfe, or The Conquest of Quebec** (Kalem, 1914) directed by Kenean Buel, and **Wolfe and Montcalm** (The Chronicles of American Picture Corp., 1924).

Within one year from the time of the fall of Quebec, the whole of Canada was in British hands. In September 1760, Amherst with an army of 17,000 English soldiers surrounded and took Montreal. With the loss of Montreal the French regime in Canada was ended.

The war now had come to an end,

even if it took until 1763 before the Treaty of Paris was signed, which ended the French and Indian War in America and the Seven Years' War elsewhere. By one of the treaty's terms France lost Canada to England. From Spain, which became allied with the French in the war, England received Florida. The American continent from the Atlantic to the Mississippi River now was British.

Pontiac's Rebellion

After the French defeat in the French and Indian War, British troops moved into surrendered French forts on the Western frontiers. In November 1760, an English force, under Major Robert Rogers, came sailing up Lake Erie and raised the British flag over Fort Detroit.

All over the Western frontiers, forts were rebuilt and strengthened: Fort Pitt at the Forks of the Ohio, Fort Stanwix on the Mohawk River and the strongest of them all, Fort Niagara. During the war, the British had promised the Indians that these and other such installations would be destroyed or turned over to the Indians as soon as they no longer were needed against the French. These promises, however, were not fulfilled.

When English agents like Sir William Johnson and George Croghan tried to reassure and win the loyalty of the former French allied Indian tribes, the tribes remained suspicious, unable to believe that the French were going for good. They believed that French soldiers from New Orleans and Eastern Canada soon would appear to continue the war against the English enemy. The struggle of the Indian agents to win over the Indians was further aggravated because of the commander-in-chief of the British forces in North America, Sir Jeffrey Amherst. Amherst had an arrogant contempt for Indians,

whom he regarded as inferior people and who were best handled by strong discipline. His Indian agents had more understanding of native background and traditions, but Amherst gave them their orders and expected them to obey him.

During their alliance with the French, the Indians had been used to being supplied with gifts, provisions and ammunition for their summer hunting. The Indians appreciated this policy of the French but Amherst had no understanding of the French method of encouraging the Indians. Colonel Henry Bouquet, commandeering forces in Pennsylvania, protested to Amherst that ceasing this action would have disastrous effects, but Amherst refused to listen to such criticism. The changes confused the Indians. The Senecas were the first to become restive, sending war belts to other tribes—invitations to join them in a war against the English. In the summer of 1761, the Western Indians were, however, not willing to risk an uprising against the frontier forts suggested by a deputation of New York Senecas at a council in the Detroit area.

In Europe, the war between England and France continued and in January 1762, Spain entered the war as an ally of France. In America rumors spread among the Indians that French and Spanish troops might come up from New Orleans to retake Canada. Throughout the year of 1762 conditions grew steadily worse, which gave the Ottawa war chief Pontiac the opportunity to organize an Indian alliance against the British. In the alliance were tribes of Ottawas, Chippewas, Hurons, Potawatomis and other Great Lakes tribes, as well as Shawnees, Wyandots and Delawares from Western Pennsylvania and Ohio.

Set during this time period is a recent film, **Keeping the Promise** (Atlantic Films, 1997). This film does not, however, deal with Pontiac's Rebellion, but touches upon Abnaki Indian dissatisfaction against

British settlers in Maine in 1763. The Ab-naki sided with the French during the French and Indian War.

In 1762, Pontiac was about 42 years of age. He was probably born in an Ottawa village on the Detroit River and it is assumed that either his father or mother was Chippewa or Miami. As a young brave he gained prominence in war parties during the French and Indian War participating on the French side in raids against the British in upstate New York, and either as a warrior or leader of an Ottawa band when General Braddock's army was defeated in Western Pennsylvania in 1755.

On the movie screen, Pontiac's involvement in Braddock's defeat was dealt with in MGM's **Winners of the Wilderness** (1927), which had Chief John Big Tree in the cast as Pontiac.

On the 27th of April 1763, Pontiac summoned a secret council of Ottawa, Huron and Potawatomi warriors and chiefs on the banks of the Ecorse River about ten miles below Fort Detroit. At the council, a decision was made to strike against Fort Detroit. Pontiac made up a plan to get his braves inside the post, pretending they came on a friendly visit and then striking from inside and taking the fort by surprise. The British commander, Major Henry Gladwin learned about Pontiac's plan and the attack failed. Failing to take Detroit by surprise, Pontiac organized a siege of the fort and with his allies he struck at farms in sight of the fort.

The siege of Detroit started a general Indian uprising in the Great Lakes area. On May 16, a band of Ottawa and Hurons surprised and captured the British Fort Sandusky on Lake Erie and killed the small fort's 15-man garrison. On May 25, Potawatomis took Fort St. Joseph on Michigan and killed or captured its garrison. A few days later another war party forced the surrender of

Fort Miami on the site of present day Fort Wayne, Indiana.

Further east, Delaware and Mingo Indians joined the uprising and swept up Pennsylvania's Monongahela Valley, attacked and massacred settlers and began a siege of Fort Pitt.

Now the entire Western frontiers were suddenly aflame. On May 28, a supply fleet for Detroit, under the command of Lieutenant Abraham Cuyler, was ambushed and captured. More than 50 of the 96 complements were killed. On June 1, the Indians forced the surrender of Fort Ouiatenon on the Wabash River at present-day Lafayette, Indiana. Far to the north, Chippewas and Sauks surprised and butchered the garrison of Fort Michilimackinac, by pretending to play a game of lacrosse between Chippewas and Sacs on the plain outside the post.

The Senecas and Shawnees, in the East, also entered the war and on June 16 a party attacked Fort Venango and killed the entire 15- or 16-man garrison, except for the commandant. Two days later the same party captured Fort Le Boeuf and burned it, killing about half of the 13-man garrison. On June 19, Senecas, Ottawas, Hurons and Chippewas attacked and took Fort Presque Isle on the present site of Erie, Pennsylvania. Thirty soldiers surrendered on the pledge that they would be given safe conduct to Fort Pitt. Despite their promise, the Indians, however, divided up the defeated men among the tribes as prisoners.

In the Far West, the Indians on June 21 forced the abandonment of Fort Edward August at Green Bay, Wisconsin. In less than two months, the British had lost all their Ohio Valley and Great Lakes posts except for Detroit and Fort Pitt, both of which were under siege.

The British commander in New York had difficulties in understanding what was happening on the Western frontiers. Gradually he realized the seriousness of the situation and decided to send a reinforcement of 260 men to Detroit, under the command of his aide, the young Captain Dalyell. On June 28, Captain Dalyell with his reinforcements arrived at Fort Detroit. Two days later the self-confident Dalyell, with Major Gladwin's hesitant approval, marched his troops to beat Pontiac at his village. Pontiac, however, had learned about the British plans and set up an ambush for the troops. The British troops were taken by surprise and were forced to withdraw to the fort, after having lost several of the men. In the battle, Captain Dalyell was shot dead.

The movie **Battles of Chief Pontiac** (Jack Broder/Realart, 1952) had Pontiac's siege of Fort Detroit as its base story. In the film, the reinforcement troops sent to Detroit and later against Pontiac's village were for some reason not lead by Captain Dalyell but by a fictional Hessian officer by the name of VonWeber, who was a notorious Indian hater. In this film VonWeber commits an act of germ warfare by disseminating smallpox among the Indians using contaminated blankets as gifts to the Indians. In reality this incident occurred during the siege of Fort Pitt when General Amherst ordered the fort commander to summon Delaware chiefs to the fort for a parley and presented them with blankets from the fort's smallpox-ridden hospital. This was later reported to cause an epidemic spread of the disease in the Delaware tribes.

Also set during the time of Pontiac's Rebellion is the beautifully photographed Canadian TV series **Marguerite Volant** from 1996.

After the death of her parents, young Marguerite (Catherine Senart) is struggling to maintain her family's manor outside Quebec when British occupation troops arrive after the French defeat by England. In the background of the story, the political impact of Pontiac's uprising against the British is seen from the French point of view. French Canadians, who have difficulties in accepting the French loss to the British, are supplying Pontiac's troops with arms.

In the East, Shawnees, Delawares, Mingos and Senecas were spreading panic among the frontier settlements from New York to Virginia. The terror and bloodshed the Indians spread caused the colonists to organize special Colonial forces that were thrown against the Indians, and more British troops began to appear in the West.

British-allied Iroquois Indians, under the leadership of Joseph Brandt, attacked a Delaware town for revenge in **The Broken Chain** (Turner Pictures, 1993). As a war trophy, Joseph Brandt brings home a Delaware woman who would become his wife.

In August, Colonel Bouquet with an army of about 460 men, including Royal Americans and a unit of the regiment Highlanders called the Black Watch, set out for the relief of Fort Pitt. When they were within 30 miles of Fort Pitt, a force of Delawares, Shawnees, Hurons and Mingos intercepted Bouquet. Bouquet, who had learned fighting in backwoodsman fashion, fooled the Indians, who abandoned their guerrilla tactics of forest warfare and rushed into an ambush of Bouquet's defense line. The Indians were beaten. Losses were equal in numbers on both sides; for Bouquet it was 50 men killed and 60 wounded. The Indians having lost two chiefs gave up a decisive battle. After the Battle of Bushy Run, named after a stream beside Bouquet's camp, Bouquet with his army relieved Fort Pitt.

Indian warfare on the Pennsylvania borders and the siege of Fort Pitt were dealt with in Cecil DeMille's **Unconquered** (Paramount, 1947). Robert Warwick played Pontiac's role in **Unconquered**. The Indian uprising in Pennsylvania was also brought up in RKO's **Allegheny Uprising** (1939), in which renegade traders were supplying Indians with liquor and firearms. The basic story of the picture, however, depicts the first revolt of Pennsylvania colonists against British soldiers—an event in the American history that prefaced the Revolution.

Fort Niagara endured the Seneca siege but was never taken. September the 18th became, however, the bloodiest day in the war for the English. A wagon train was attacked by more than 300 Senecas at the Devils Hole, a narrow passage on the road between Fort Schlosser at Lake Erie and Fort Niagara at Lake Ontario. Only a few of the white soldiers managed to escape for Fort Niagara. There were 72 officers and men slaughtered.

In spite of the many successful raids by the Indians, the final victory over the whites seemed no closer as time passed. Week after week the siege of Fort Detroit continued without apparent loss of strength and spirit of Gladwin and his garrison. Many of the Indian chiefs who had been fighting with Pontiac realized that French troops would never appear from the South. One by one the different Indian bands announced that they were abandoning the war and went for their homelands. When Pontiac realized that he was losing his hold he made attempts to win small but daring victories that would convince the restless tribes of a final Indian victory. A relief schooner, *Huron*, from Fort Niagara with supplies for Detroit was attacked on September 2, but the assault failed. Many of the attacking Indians were killed and the defeat further weakened Pontiac.

Throughout September and October dissension spread rapidly across the Indian country. On October 29, Pontiac's dream of a free Indian Territory was smashed. A French officer arrived from the South with a letter to him from the French commander of Fort de Chartres on the Mississippi River. In the letter Pontiac was told that the peace treaty between France and England had been signed and that he should no longer strike the British but bury the hatchet with them as the French King had. The siege of Fort Detroit was broken and in mid–November Pontiac traveled to the French-held Illinois country to find out why the French had abandon their Indian allies.

Back East the Delawares, Shawnees, Senecas, Wabash and many of the Hurons were still continuing the conflict, and although the French commander at Fort de Chartres refused to support him, Pontiac appealed to the Illinois tribes and the tribes down the Mississippi to join the hostilities. Through the fall and winter of 1764 he traveled from tribe to tribe to win allies for a new uprising. But the initiative had now passed into the hands of the British and they were pacifying tribes more quickly than Pontiac could stir them up. A force under Colonel John Bradstreet traveled among the tribes around the Great Lakes and signed with many of them a permanent peace. A short time later Colonel Henry Bouquet marched out of Fort Pitt with 1,500 men to strike against the Indians who were still raiding on the Ohio and Pennsylvania frontiers. His show of force caused the capitulation of most of the tribes. In the peace treaty, at Fort Stanwix, it was agreed that the Indians should surrender all their white captives. This created some unexpected difficulties when many white children and youths refused to leave their adoptive Indian parents.

The Walt Disney movie **The Light in the Forest** (Buena Vista, 1958) centers on a young white boy who has lived most of his life with the Indians, and who rebels when his real parents try to reacquaint him with their way of life. The story is based on a novel by Conrad Richter. The theme of problems for Indian captives after the treaty at Stanwix was also illuminated in the East German film **Blauvogel (Blue Bird)** from 1979.

The final peace treaty between the Indians and the British was signed in July 1766 at Fort Ontario. After the negotiations, Pontiac returned home to the West and settled among his own people on the Maumee River. Later, both Indians and French tried to persuade Pontiac to raise the hatchet once more against the British, but Pontiac was now taking the side of the British, and counseling peace. Pontiac's pro–British attitude caused many of the Indians to turn against him and on April 20, 1769, when he visited a small trade store in Cahokia, an old French village on the east side of the Mississippi River opposite St. Louis, he was murdered by a Peoria Indian.

The War for Independence

The year of 1763, when the Treaty of Paris was signed ending the French and Indian War, is usually regarded as the beginning of the American Revolution, because in this year the British ministry determined to raise revenue from the colonies.

Not too unreasonably England decided that as the colonists would benefit from the protection of British troops, they should somehow contribute economically to their maintenance. The British attempt to enforce such measures upon the colonists as well as a proclamation issued by the king in 1763 forbidding any further encroachment by individuals or private land enterprises on the territory west of the Alleghenies caused irritation among the colonists. A series of different legal acts were issued; the Trade and Navigation Act; the Sugar Act of 1764 which was the one that pinched the hardiest; the Stamp Act of 1765; and the Townshend Duties of 1767.

The uproar these acts caused in the colonies was almost unanimous. In Wil-liamsburg, Virginia, Patrick Henry made a passionate speech against the Stamp Act. Patrick Henry's speech before the Virginia House of Burgesses was featured in the 1917 movie, **The Spirit of '76** (Continental Production Company).

By initiative of Massachusetts, delegates from all the colonies met for a congress in New York. The congress stated in a Declaration of Rights and Grievances that "only colonies could levy taxes on the colonists."

The opposition in the colonies to British rule grew and there were outbreaks of mob violence. Later this changed to open rebellion. In June 1772 patriots burned the British vessel *Gaspec* in Providence, and in December 1773 colonists disguised as Indians boarded three ships bearing tea cargo in Boston and dumped the tea into the harbor. To bring the recalcitrant Bostonians to terms, British troops entered Boston harbor in July 1774.

On September 5, 1774, the first Continental Congress met in Philadelphia with delegates representing 12 of the 13 colonies. The Congress decided to forbid the importation of British goods and purposed the prohibition of colonial exports to England.

The conflict could not be put off any longer. In April 1775, a detachment of British soldiers had been sent to Concord to confiscate firearms and ammunition. Minutemen, who had been warned by Paul Revere on his famous ride, fired on them in Lexington. The British returned the fire and killed eight colonists.

Some movies from the silent period with sequences about Paul Revere's famous midnight ride and the Battle of Lexington are: **The Pride of Lexington** (Republic, 1911); **Washington at Valley Forge** (Universal, 1914); **The Spirit of '76** (Continental Production Company, 1917); **Cardigan** (American Releasing, 1922); **Janice Meredith** (MGM, 1924); and D.W. Griffith's **America** (United Artists, 1924).

Johnny Tremain (Buena Vista, 1957), originally filmed as a two-part program for the Disney TV show, released as a feature movie is a fictional treatment of the events leading to the Revolutionary War, including Revere's Ride.

The colonists' stand at Lexington Green as observed through the eyes of a teenaged boy can be seen in the well-crafted TV feature **April Morning** from 1988, adapted from the 1961 novel by Howard Fast.

"The shot heard around the world" in Lexington served to mobilize a colonial militia of 20,000 to 30,000 farmers who came running to Boston. The news of the outbreak of hostilities greatly influenced the Second Continental Congress. George Washington, one of the Virginia delegates, was appointed commander in chief of the Colonial Army.

In the siege of Boston the Americans occupied Bunker Hill, just opposite the town, and were threatening Boston from the north. The British, under the command of General Howe, decided to dislodge the Americans from the hill.

A frontal attack was conducted in three separate assaults. The hill was finally taken but the British lost almost half of the men used in the action. The Battle of Bunker Hill was beautifully photographed in Griffith's great epic of the Revolutionary War, **America**, from 1924.

An important key to the invasion route between Canada and the colonies was Fort Ticonderoga on Lake Champlain. On May 10, 1775, an American force led by Connecticut Colonel Benedict Arnold surprised and defeated the garrison of the fort. Important to the Americans were the British artillery pieces there. To secure the rebel defenses in Boston, 50 heavy artillery guns were sledged eastward the next winter. This probably hastened the British departure from Boston.

The capture of the cannons at Ticonderoga was in the story of **"The Rebels"** (Universal, 1979), the second installment of young Philip Kent's adventures in Revolutionary America, based on the novel *The Rebels* by John Jakes, part of his *Kent Family Chronicles*. Other parts of the TV mini-series were **"The Bastard"** (1978) and **"The Seekers"** (1979).

The Americans pressed their forces further north to conquer Canada in two columns. The main column, led by Richard Montgomery, went up the St. Lawrence River while Benedict Arnold's men followed another route. After exhausting marches and partial successes the two armies joined in sight of Quebec. The attack on the town failed, however, and the death of Montgomery on December 1, 1775, marked the end of the undertaking.

In the spring of 1776, Washington pushed his force against Boston and opened bombardment from all parts of his lines. General Howe withdrew by embarking his troops on ships and the siege of Boston was broken.

When the British evacuated Boston, Washington felt assured that New York, already threatened, would be the next objective and therefore concentrated in and about it his whole disposable force.

As the revolutionary movement spread there was an increased sentiment among the colonists for a complete dissolution of all political connection between the colonies and Great Britain.

Richard Henry Lee, one of the Virginia delegates of the Congress in Philadelphia, introduced a resolution declaring that the colonies ought to be free and independent states. The Congress set up a draft committee and on July 4, 1776, after three weeks' work on the document, mostly by Thomas Jefferson, the Congress passed a Declaration of Independence.

With the help of few song and dance

numbers Thomas Jefferson (Ken Howard), John Adams (William Daniels) and Benjamin Franklin (Howard Da Silva) persuaded the Congress to ratify the Declaration of Independence in the movie musical **1776** (Columbia, 1972), based on the Tony Award–winning Broadway musical.

The signing of the Declaration of Independence was also featured in **The Spirit of '76** from 1917, a film that ran into political problems, accused of being anti–British.

For the British the capture of New York was essential. It was not only an important harbor, but control of the Hudson River would provide a vital link of the route to Canada.

In August 1776, a British force under General Sir William Howe attacked New York. The Battle of Long Island was fought on August 27 and lost by the Americans, who suffered 1,000 causalties.

The battle of Long Island was also fought in the MGM/UA TV mini-series **George Washington** (1984), casting Barry Bostwick as George Washington.

The defeat of the American Army on Long Island was a heavy blow to the patriot cause and on November 16, Washington was forced to abandon New York state and retreat to New Jersey after the fall of Fort Washington, where he lost 3,000 men. During Washinton's retreat to New Jersey his army melted away to almost nothing. The New York and New England militia deserted in great numbers.

Al Pacino, acting as a fur trapper, was against his will drawn into the fighting of the Brooklyn Heights in the British movie **Revolution** (Goldcrest-Viking, 1985). Enlisted as a scout on the American side, he participated in different war skirmishes, including a Canadian campaign, Valley Forge, and the final surrender of Cornwallis at Yorktown in 1781.

General Howe established a chain of posts in New Jersey at Newark, Amboy, New Brunswick, Princeton and Trenton before himself leaving for New York. In spite of his weakened force, Washington, who had moved his army to the Pennsylvanian side of the Delaware River, recrossed the river on December 26 and surprised the British-allied Hessian troops who were encamped at Trenton. At the Battle of Trenton, the Hessians were caught by total surprise. The attack lasted less than 45 minutes and was a complete victory for the patriots. The surprise attack at Trenton by Washington can be seen in the previously mentioned **George Washington** MGM/UA TV serial. In **Janice Meredith** (MGM, 1924), it was one of the highlights of the story.

Determined on revenge for the defeat at Trenton, British commander Lord Cornwallis, with forces much more powerful than the Americans, moved his troops from New York toward Washington, whose troops almost were trapped, but managed to slip out and routed the British force at Princeton. After Princeton, Washington marched his troops to Morristown, where he went into winter quarters.

In the spring of 1777, the British planned to have General Burgoyne's army invade from Canada with the help of Tories and Indians. Sir William Howe was to proceed along the Hudson River Valley to meet with Burgoyne in Albany.

Burgoyne's army was divided in two columns. The main column, under Burgoyne, came down along Lake Champlain and Lake George. A smaller force, under French and Indian War veteran Lieutenant Colonel Barry St. Leger, was given a diversionary mission to the frontiers. St. Leger would leave Montreal, and proceed up the Saint Lawrence River to Lake Ontario to attack from the West in order to open up to Albany.

The main force under Burgoyne sailed down from Canada on Lake Champlain and captured without meeting any resistance the American fort at Ticonderoga, which was supposed to protect against invasion from the North.

St. Leger with 900 Redcoats, Tories and Iroquois advanced via Lake Ontario and the Mohawk Valley. When the force reached Fort Stanwix, St. Leger decided on a siege of the fort. An American militia relief column, under Brigadier-General Nicholas Herkimer, was sent to support the garrison of the fort.

When St. Leger's scouts brought him word that Herkimer's force was on the march, he sent Joseph Brandt, the Mohawk chief, and 400 Indians, with John Butler's Tory Rangers to ambush the Americans at a place near Oriskany. In the ambush half of the Americans were killed, wounded or taken prisoner. Considering the numbers of men engaged at Oriskany, it was one of the bloodiest and most bitterly fought battles of the Revolution. Herkimer died soon after the battle, and the survivors made their way back to Albany the best they could.

The British siege of Fort Stanwix failed largely because reinforcements under General Benedict Arnold were sent for relief. When Arnold arrived, the enemy had gone, because the Indian allies to the British fell for an American ruse that Arnold's men were as numerous as the leaves on the trees. They decamped so suddenly that St. Leger had no other alternative than to abandon the mission and return to Montreal.

In John Ford's **Drums Along the Mohawk** (20th Century–Fox, 1939), General Herkimer (played by Roger Imof) dies in the house of Mrs. McKlennan (Edna Mary Oliver) after having his injured leg amputated. The main topic of the film deals with the struggles inflicted on the settlers in the Mohawk Valley by Indians, provoked by British Rangers. Another movie on the same theme is Edward L.

Alperson's **Mohawk** (20th Century–Fox, 1956), in which stock footage from **Drums Along the Mohawk** is used.

The Americans' loss in the Battle of Oriskany was touched upon in the recent cable-TV feature **The Broken Chain** (Turner Pictures, 1993), which mainly deals with the life of Mohawk Chief Joseph Brandt and the tearing apart of the Iroquois Confederacy during the French and Indian War.

After the capture of Fort Ticonderoga, on their way south, things went badly for General Burgoyne and his army. American General Gates with 9,000 men met Burgoyne in a battle at Freeman's Farm on September 19. Pounded by the American forces, Burgoyne retreated into the fort at Saratoga, 30 miles north of Albany. In vain he awaited assistance from Howe's Army in the South, because General Howe was working along different campaign instructions. Burgoyne had to surrender to the Americans on October 17. This capture of some 5,000 men was the greatest victory of the American Army so far.

In the **Devil's Disciple** (United Artists, 1959), "Gentleman Johnny" Burgoyne, who is on his way south with his army to join with Howe's forces, gets involved in suppressing rebellions against the British in New England. The story is an adaptation to the screen of George Bernard Shaw's satiric play, and has Laurence Olivier in the role as General Burgoyne. Burt Lancaster and Kirk Douglas both go the patriot way against the British.

Burgoyne's defeat had far-reaching consequences. At one stroke nearly one fourth of Britain's effective troops in America were lost. For the British things went better with General Howe's Army.

Because of lack of communication Howe moved against Philadelphia instead of Albany. The British army did not have far to go to Philadelphia but

Washington was determined to be more successful than he had been when covering New York. He decided to block Howe at Brandywine Creek about halfway to Philadelphia. In the battle, which took place on September 11, Howe defeated Washington's forces, but it was by no means a decisive victory. The American Army was still ready to fight again. On October 4, the two armies met again at Germantown. Although the Americans once again were defeated, Washington and his men were still very much in contention and were not in flight.

Howe evacuated Germantown in order to shorten his defensive circuit around Philadelphia. The British now had another important position to defend and Howe called for help from the Royal Navy to open the Delaware River for supply ships. Washington finally had to retreat but not before costing the British losses in ships and men.

When the armies turned to their winter quarters, Howe settled in for a comfortable winter in Philadelphia, which Congress had hastily abandoned. Washington settled his men at a cold comfort at Valley Forge, a few miles outside Philadelphia. Thanks to Washington's caution and the fighting skills of American soldiers there had been no decisive British victory in 1777.

The winter in Valley Forge was rough on the American troops. Not only was there a lack of clothing and food, but it was also bitterly cold. Of the 11,000 men who arrived in December barely 6,000 remained: some 2,500 had died and 2,500 had deserted.

Amid all the hardship and suffering at Valley Forge, one piece of good fortune was the arrival of Baron Friedrich Wilhelm August von Streuben, a Prussian army volunteer who came to serve the Continental Army in the cause of liberty. Von Streuben had served in the army of Frederick the Great. It was important to train the Continentals so that they could confront the British on the battlefield without having to rely on defensive positions. Baron von Streuben was the one person to perform such an act, and he drilled the troops in bayonet practice and in battlefield maneuvers. Von Streuben reworked Prussian army drills to fit the American Army needs.

In spite of the difficulties, Washington's Army was better disciplined and better trained than ever before when the spring came.

The suffering of the Continental Army at Valley Forge has attracted several scriptwriters to replay the history on the movie screen in the productions **Washington at Valley Forge** (Universal, 1914); **The Spirit of '76** (Continental, 1917); **America** (United Artists, 1924); **The Howards of Virginia** (Columbia, 1940, based on the novel *The Liberty Tree* by Elizabeth Page); **"The Rebels"** (**Kent Family Chronicles**, Universal, 1978); **George Washington** (MGM, 1984); and **Revolution** (Goldcrest-Viking, 1985).

Baron von Streuben's drill of Washington's army at Valley Forge was dealt with in both **"The Rebels"** and the 1984 **George Washington** TV mini-series.

Early in 1778, the patriot army had a series of discussions on different strategies. Some of the generals supported a plan to recapture Philadelphia, while others suggested an attack on New York. American allied foreign generals, Lafayette, Von Streuben and Duportail, advised Washington to make no offensive moves until his army had been substantially strengthened or the British had disclosed their own intention.

British commander Clinton intended to evacuate Philadelphia by moving his army by land across New Jersey to New Brunswick. With his 10,000 men, and his long wagon train extended over 12 miles, Clinton's flanks invited an attack from

Washington's army. The Continental Army overtook the slow-paced enemy at Monmouth on July 28. Washington ordered General Lee, who was placed in command of 5,000 men, to attack the British rear. However, the British rearguard, under Cornwallis, was stronger than anticipated and Lee probably did the correct thing and withdrew his men. An angry Washington reprimanded Lee and lined up his army on defense on a hill ridge.

Encouraged by the retreat of Lee, Clinton sent reinforcements to his rear and tried to drive Washington from his ground. The weather was not helpful for the British and their attack on Washington's defense was repelled. Night ended the conflict and both parties slept on the ground which they had occupied. At midnight Clinton withdrew his troops and resumed his march to Middletown. The retire was so silent that on the morning of the 29th the Americans were surprised to find themselves alone on the field.

After resting his men for a few days, Washington marched to the North River, and Clinton embarked for New York. The Battle of Monmouth was the last major engagement fought on Northern soil during the Revolution. The Americans had 229 killed and wounded, the British over 400.

Washington's criticism of Lee resulted in Lee's one-year suspension from the army, a humiliation Lee rejected; he asked the Congress to remove him from service. The dispute between Washington and General Lee and the Battle of Monmouth is thoroughly covered in the 1984 MGM/UA TV mini-series **George Washington**.

On February 6, 1778, France and United States signed a treaty of alliance, which placed a whole new aspect on the war. The war was now extended into a world war. The French-American alliance pushed naval considerations into the war

scene and a shift of geographical focus to the West Indies took place. For the British the war in North America took second place. This was mainly marked by the fact that the British troops largely stopped coming.

The French, under Admiral d'Estaing, provided troops, ships and supplies to their new ally in North America. In July 1778, Admiral d'Estaing and his fleet, together with American troops under Major-General John Sullivan, struck the British at Newport. A British fleet under Lord Howe came to relieve the French-American pressure on British General Robert Pigot and his army.

Scottish-born John Paul Jones was one of the greatest American naval heroes of the war. Early in the war he distinguished himself while operating from American ports. He won several sea battles and raided the coastal region of Nova Scotia. It was in the European Theater, however, that Jones won his lasting acclaim. The naval hero's story was put on film in the big production **John Paul Jones** (Warner Bros., 1959) with Robert Stack cast as Jones.

D'Estaing sailed out to engage Lord Howe's fleet but a fierce storm broke over them, damaging and scattering both fleets. The need to repair his ships led d'Estaing to abandon Rhode Island. The American siege was thereby weakened and Sullivan with his army evacuated Rhode Island and the Americans' hopes of taking Newport collapsed.

During the Rhode Island campaign the gallant young officer Marquis de Lafayette served under General Sullivan. Lafayette had come to North America at his own expense earlier to serve in any capacity and the Congress had made him Major General.

Lafayette's involvement in the American Revolution was pictured in the international spectacle **Lafayette** (Copernic/Cosmos, 1961). Lafayette also turned up in **Washington at Valley Forge** (Universal, 1914) and the TV series **The Young Rebels** (ABC, 1970-71). The story of the series was set in 1777 and dealt with members of the fictional Yankee Doodle Society. They were based in Chester, Pennsylvania and their goal was to harass the British behind their lines and to serve as spies for the Americans. In the series, Lafayette, a 20-year-old French nobleman, was a frequent ally who often came to the young rebels' aid. Other TV appearances of Lafayette during the American revolution are in the Kent TV saga, "The Rebels" and the TV mini-series **George Washington.**

On the Revolutionary frontiers, settlers suffered from hostilities by British allied Indians. On the New York frontiers, Mohawk chief Joseph Brandt and the hated Tory, Colonel John Butler, led a mixed British and Indian force on hit-and-run raids during 1778 and 1779. Butler's Rangers and Indians massacred Wyoming Valley, Pennsylvania, on July 3, 1778.

On September 12, 1778 Joseph Brant with his Indians destroyed the settlements at German Flats in the Mohawk Valley. This event played an important role in John Ford's **Drums Along the Mohawk.** In this one the Iroquois were led by British captain Caldwell, played by John Carradine.

In November 1778, it was the turn of Cherry Valley on the frontiers of New York. In D.W. Griffith's **America**, Captain Walter Butler, played by Lionel Barrymore, together with Brandt's Iroquois performed the massacres of Cherry Valley and Fort Sacrifice in the Mohawk Valley. Other movies with stories about the Indian struggles in the Mohawk Valley are: **The Pride of Lexington** (1911) and **The Spirit of '76** (1917). In **Cardigan** (1922) American patriots' ally themselves with Cayugas against the British allied Indians in the Mohawk Valley. The mas-

sacre in Mohawk Valley was also brought up in **Mohawk** from 1956 and in **The Broken Chain** (Turner, 1993).

On the frontiers perhaps Kentucky suffered the most. Daniel Boone, born a Pennsylvanian, came to symbolize the American frontiersman. As a hunter and scout Daniel Boone had first penetrated into Kentucky from the Cumberland Gap in 1769. In April 1774, Boone founded Boonesborough, a settlement in the wilderness. In 1775 he was hired by a land speculator to survey and lay out roads there.

Boone's reputation spread in Kentucky. Though he had been fighting Indians since he was a teenager, including during the French and Indian War, it was a Shawnee siege of Boonesborough during the American Revolution that became the most celebrated of his many battles. In 1778, Boone was captured by the Shawnee chief Blue Jacket and was later adopted into the Shawnee tribe.

There are several films which deal with Daniel Boone's adventures and life on the Kentucky frontiers: **Attack on Fort Boonesborough** (American Mutoscope & Biograph, 1906); **Daniel Boone or: Pioneer Days in America** (Edison, 1907); **Daniel Boone's Bravery** (Kalem, 1911); **In the Days of Daniel Boone** (Universal, 1923), a series dealing with the French and Indian War, with Jack Mower as Boone); **Daniel Boone Thru the Wilderness** (Sunset, 1926, with Roy Steward as Boone); **Daniel Boone** (RKO, 1936, with George O'Brien as Boone); **Young Daniel Boone** (Monogram, 1950, David Bruce as Boone); **Daniel Boone Trail Blazer** (Republic, 1956, Bruce Bennet); **Daniel Boone** (Disney, 1960-61 TV series, Dewey Martin); **Daniel Boone** (Disney, 1964–70 TV series, Fess Parker); and **Young Dan'l Boone** (Fox-TV, TV series 1977-78, Rick Moses).

Other movies with motifs from frontier life in Kentucky during the Revolutionary War are the MGM epic **The Great Meadow** from 1931, based on the novel with the same name by Elizabeth Madox Roberts, and **Follow the River** (Hallmark, 1995), in which frontier settlements are raided by Shawnee Indians. The story is based on a 1981 novel by James Alexander Thom.

While Daniel Boone struggled on the Kentucky frontiers, a 25-year-old surveyor, George Rogers Clark, obtained authorization from Kentucky's parent state, Virginia, to raise a force to overwhelm the key points of British influence north of the Ohio. The objectives were to take Kaskaskia and Cahokia in the Illinois country and to the east, Vincennes on the Wabash. Eventually Clark hoped to seize Detroit, where British Lieutenant Governor Henry Hamilton ("The Hair Buyer General") terrorized the Americans by sending British-led Indian raiding parties to destroy the American back settlements.

Clark set off down the Ohio with less than 200 men. Early in July 1778, the hamlets of Kaskaskia, Cahokia and Vincennes fell to Clark without bloodshed. General Hamilton led a force from Detroit to retake the key post Vincennes and to restore royal authority throughout the Illinois Country. The small American garrison of Vincennes surrendered. Refusing to accept the British rule of Vincennes, Clark again set off with some 180 men on a terrible winter march, sometimes in shoulder deep ice water to retake Vincennes.

In February 1779, Hamilton surrendered Vincennes to Clark and his frontiersmen, who under cover of darkness dispersed themselves in such manner as to exaggerate their numbers.

Clark's brilliant conquest of the Illinois Country was of great psychological importance to the Americans in a war where clear-cut American victories were scarce. Clarke wanted to pursue his am-

bitions against Detroit but he failed to receive reinforcement from Virginia. During the last years of the war Clark was on the defensive along the Ohio River fighting Indians. After the war the nation never made much of Clark's talent and he was quickly forgotten. Most people, however, know about his brother, William Clark of Lewis and Clark fame.

Having failed in the North, the British turned to the South. Their plan was to seize Georgia, which was weak, and move northward. In the closing days of 1778 they took Savannah and in 1779 they occupied interior areas of Georgia and South Carolina. On November 2, 1778 Congress instructed Benjamin Lincoln, who was appointed commander in the South, to invade East Florida in order to destroy the threat by the British garrison in St. Augustin. Lincoln was, however, provided with little support and he was shut up in Charleston.

In December, British Lieutenant-Colonel Archibald Campbell landed near Savannah. Led by a slave through a swamp to a weak point in the city defense he took the city with only minor casualties.

General Augustin Prevost, arriving in Savannah, took command of the combined British force there and sent messengers to the Tories of South Carolina, urging them to take up arms and cross the Savannah River at Augusta, to join forces with a strong detachment under Campbell to seize this patriot stronghold.

The British reached Augusta on January 29, 1779, and occupied the town. With the capture of Augusta the whole state had been secured for the British with disconcerting ease. The British found Augusta not so easy to control, and because of patriot militia raids, Campbell retired from Augusta.

General Prevost measured the abandonment of Augusta as a temporary loss, and when American General Lincoln advanced toward Augusta to occupy the city, Prevost countered by crossing the Savannah River and moved his army toward Charleston. Lincoln hurried to rescue and saved the city. After fierce fighting at Stony Ferry below the town, Prevost returned to Savannah.

Southern patriots appealed for help to French Admiral d'Estaing, who had remained in the Caribbean during the summer. D'Estaing arrived on the Georgia coast on September 1 with 20 ships and a line of 5,000 troops. General Lincoln rushed south from Charleston, but his march was slowed because of poor roads. On the 16th Lincoln arrived near Savannah. Prevost, reinforced by troops from Port Royal, rejected a summons to surrender and a regular siege of the city began.

In early October the bombardment of the town started. On October 9, the combined American-French force attacked. The attack was a disaster for the allies. The outnumbered British held off their opponents. Almost one-fifth of the American and French troops were killed or wounded compared to minor British losses. Disagreements between the allies slowed progress of operations, and the threat of Atlantic storms forced d'Estaing to call them off. He set sail for France. The attack on Savannah was the last major encounter of the year.

Although the American troops suffered from hardship during the war, remarkably few of Washington's subordinates abandoned him or went over to the enemy. The only highly placed soldier to commit treason was Benedict Arnold. Arnold has repeatedly quarreled with state and congressional officials and the Congress had sacrificed him on the promotion lists. Washington had designated him as a commander of the forces in Philadelphia in 1778. Through all Arnold's troubles with Pennsylvania offi-

cials, Washington stood staunchly behind him.

In the fall of 1779, Arnold entered into treasonable correspondence with British officer Sir Henry Clinton. The result was that Arnold would join the enemy and also would turn over the strategic fortress of West Point. The possession of West Point would give the British the opportunity to control the Hudson River.

Arnold started different maneuvers to become commander of West Point and in August 1780 Washington ordered him the command. Not to raise any suspicion of treachery, Arnold started to strengthen the post and put it in good order.

Arnold's plot to deliver West Point to the British failed. The details of the conspiracy were exposed when the intermediary Major John André, Clinton's adjutant, who was sent to make the final arrangements with Arnold, was captured on September 23. Arnold fled from West Point, escaping to the British, but André was hanged as a spy according to military custom, to the great distress of Clinton. During the rest of the war Arnold sided with the British even if they never had real trust in him.

In **The Scarlet Coat** (MGM, 1955), Cornel Wilde plays an American officer who deserts to the British in order to unmask a traitor who turns out to be Benedict Arnold. Robert Douglas plays Arnold. The treachery of Arnold is also well covered in the 1984 **George Washington** TV mini-series. Stephen Macht appears in the role as General Benedict Arnold.

The success at Savannah encouraged the British to press ahead with a plan for an attack on Charleston. In May 1780, the British captured General Lincoln and his 5,000 men and the principal Southern seaport together. It was one of the heaviest blows of the Revolution for the patriots. The American commander, the "Hero of

Saratoga," Horatio Gates, was sent south to stay the tide.

The principal British magazine for an intended campaign in North Carolina and Virginia was established at Camden, 100 miles or so from Charleston. It was therefore to Camden that Horatio Gates directed his army. His army of 3,000 men, half of it raw militia, was crushed by Lord Cornwallis at Camden, August 16. Gates lost more than half his force in the battle and he did not halt in his flight until he had covered nearly 200 miles. However, the British hope of detaching the South from the American cause was foiled by their mishandling of the situation and by guerrilla fighting against which they were helpless.

The new American commander in the South, Nathanael Green, turned the luck for the Americans with the help of leaders of partisan bands, Francis Marion, Thomas Sumter and Andrew Pickens.

The few movies which deal with the operations in the South during the Revolution are concentrated on the American Revolutionary hero and guerrilla fighter Francis Marion, "the Swamp Fox." Two movies from the silent period are **General Marion, the Swamp Fox** (Champion, 1911) and **Francis Marion, the Swamp Fox** (Kalem, 1914), with Guy Coombs as Marion. In Walt Disney's TV serial **The Swamp Fox** (1959–61), Francis Marion, played by Leslie Nielsen, operates around Charleston, South Carolina, in 1780. With hit-and-run tactics Marion and his band struck and harassed the British forces around the Carolina swamps.

After Camden, Cornwallis planned to conquer North Carolina in order to cover the Southern states. He needed support from Loyalists and was convinced that they would only rise if his army advanced into North Carolina.

Cornwallis, however, encountered more problems. Delayed by malaria and yellow fever, his sick army struggled northward from Camden only to find out that people in North Carolina were more hostile to England than any others in America. Cornwallis's army experienced constant harassment from American guerrilla fighters. Fighting in this manner was far more effective for the patriots than fighting Redcoat veterans in close rank formation.

Cornwallis's left wing with Loyalist militia under Major Patrick Ferguson was designed to counter any activities from the rebel raiders. Ferguson's mission failed, however, and on October 7 at King's Mountain, 30 miles west of Charlotte, Ferguson's entire force was killed or captured when attacked by frontiersmen. Ferguson lost his life, over 300 of his men were killed or wounded and nearly 700 were captured.

After the disappointment at King's Mountain, Cornwallis withdrew his army from North Carolina and made winter quarters at Winnsborough below Camden.

Horatio Gates's position had been weakened by intrigues of some Southern politicians and a new American commander, Nathanael Green, took charge of the American Southern Department. Green found himself obliged to rely on support from partisan bands under such leaders as Francis Marion and Thomas Sumter.

In early 1781, Green and Cornwallis met in a battle at Guilford Courthouse. Green was defeated in the battle but withdrew his army intact. Green showed astonishing skills in long and rapid marches. Even if he in nine months lost four important battles, he wore the British troops out. Aided by fighters such as Marion, Morgan and Anthony Wayne, Green pressed the British. This in combination with the hostility of the inhabitants finally forced the British back into Charleston and Savannah.

The development in the South persuaded Cornwallis to withdraw, and in the spring of 1781 he left Cape Fear and moved north with his troops to join the traitor Benedict Arnold in Virginia.

Cornwallis arrived in Virginia in May 1781 and took command of the forces of Arnold and Phillips. Cornwallis's presence, with a combined army of 7,200 men, terrified Virginia authorities. However, after an ineffectual pursuit of American forces under Lafayette, Cornwallis was under constant pressure from guerrilla bands. Lafayette received a 1,000-man contingent of Pennsylvania Continentals as reinforcement from the North under General Anthony Wayne. Cornwallis fell back through Richmond and down the peninsula, closely followed by Lafayette. On July 6, at Green Spring near Jamestown, the Americans fought a fierce but indecisive skirmish, after which Cornwallis retired to Yorktown at the mouth of the York River. Cornwallis established his base in Yorktown and began erecting fortifications.

In August 1781, General Washington received information that French Admiral de Grasse with 28 ships and additional troops had left the French West Indies. The French Admiral offered his cooperation and together with Washington's army of some 6,000 men near New York and French General Rochambeau's about 5,000 men at New Port, Rhode Island, a combined American-French army of some 16,000 men moved against Yorktown.

Cornwallis had the British fleet protecting his rear. When the French fleet arrived a confusing naval battle took place. When the smoke cleared, the French controlled Yorktown harbor and Cornwallis's troops were cut off from escape by sea. A heavy bombardment from the American artillery battered down the British inner defense and on October 19, Cornwallis was forced to surrender.

Several movies noted earlier have scenes from the defeat of the British and Cornwallis surrender at Yorktown: **The Spirit of '76**; **America**; **The Howards of Virginia**; "**The Rebels**" (Kent TV-Saga); and **George Washington** (TV). In Hugh Hudson's **Revolution**, Al Pacino makes up with his British enemy officer, played by Donald Sutherland, during the siege at Yorktown.

The war was now practically ended; the English evacuated Charlestown and Savannah and remained inactive in New York for two years. King George stubbornly refused to acknowledge defeat for some time but in 1783 a peace treaty was signed which ended the war.

The Old Northwest and the War of 1812

In the peace treaty of 1783, the British made generous terms. The situation for the British was more favorable than one might have expected. The British fleet had won a decisive victory over the French in the West Indies, and there were still British troops in New York. During the war the patriots had occupied land north of Ohio in what is now Indiana, Illinois and Michigan. Most of this wild country was, however, recaptured by the British during the end of the war.

The British abandoned to the new republic all the country from the Alleghenies to the Mississippi, with the northern boundary against Canada. The Americans were also given extensive fishing rights off the Canadian coast. France, although America's ally, wished its protégée to remain a convenient satellite, not to become a sovereign nation that one day might span the continent. France had her own view of postwar arrangements; Spain was granted sovereignty over Florida and the Gulf Coast all the way to

Mississippi. The expected natural expansion of the American republic was westward and had the British decided to hold on to the Northwest, a constant political friction with the Americans would have been the result.

In order to contribute to the creation of a national government, the Articles of Confederation had been adopted in 1781, which gave the basis for setting up a congress. This system, however, proved to be wholly unsatisfactory and inadequate because no national sovereignty was given to the central government.

In the peace treaty with England, the 13 colonies were listed as 13 states. In the Declaration of Independence there was no stated union among the 13 independent colonies but there was a friendship tie among them during the course of the war. When the war was over this tie was practically dissolved. The national crisis came to a climax in 1786. Hard money was scarce and growing scarcer. Seven states turned to issuing paper currency, a simple means of paying debts and taxes, but also a controversial issue separating debtors from creditors. There was no real governmental rule; the states were quarreling over boundary lines and other internal and foreign matters. So disorderly was the situation that men spoke about the possibility of war between some of the states.

The financial depression these crises led to created an intense antagonism between poor and wealthy. In Massachusetts dissatisfaction about taxes levied to pay the Revolutionary debt gave rise to a revolt led by Revolutionary War veteran Daniel Shays. Shays' Rebellion was stopped, but the brief crisis deeply alarmed conservatives all over the nation. A revolutionary movement toward the left was to be prevented.

The lack of strength of the state government induced distress among groups whose livelihood was dependent upon some measure of central rule. There was a lack of uniform currency among the states, which complicated terms for merchants. Exporters regretted the lack of protection for their enterprise to market American goods abroad. It also proved to be difficult to reestablish the old commercial relations with the British Empire and commercial links between Britain and America revived strongly after the conflict. Spain had closed the Mississippi River to American commerce.

The Southern states and some of the small Northern states, with little of their own manufacturing, were dependent upon imported goods which conflicted with the interest of certain states which laid tariffs on all imports to prevent dumping of European goods on their markets.

The demands for a functional national authority arose also from other groups than merchants and manufacturers. Many officers and soldiers had received land warrants as payment for their service during the war. Together with land speculators, who had bought up land at cheap rates, they wanted a government which was strong enough to protect their interests.

To improve the situation a convention of all the states was called in Philadelphia in March 1787. In the meeting 55 delegates from 12 states met to discuss the Articles of Confederation. The purpose was to make certain necessary alterations in the Articles. Because the document was so unrealistic in principle the convention took the giant step, after only five days discussion, of scrapping the Articles. A complete new document was prepared which fashioned the Federal Constitution, which established a new and far stronger national government.

In June 1788 the new constitution was ratified by the member states and declared the fundamental law of the United States. The next step was to elect a president. In February 1789, the former commander in chief, George Washington, became the unanimous choice as the candidate for president. His leadership for the new government was the only one that really appealed to the people. During the first National Congress, which was held in April 1789, the electoral vote selected George Washington as president and John Adams as vice president.

The election of Washington for president and the ratification of the American Constitution were dealt with in a sequel the **George Washington** TV mini-series: **George Washington—The Forging of a Nation** (MGM/UA, 1986).

After the American Revolution, the Americans sought to force the Indians to realize their defeat and to ally with the victorious colonials. But neither the Iroquois Confederacy nor the Western tribes accepted American assertions of their defeat and subjection. Although their British ally was defeated, the Indians still regarded themselves as independent. The Miami chief Little Turtle, who was allied with the British during the Revolutionary War, became most aggressive against the hordes of white settlers pouring into the Northwest Territory. Between 1783 and 1790, he and his allies were responsible for the deaths of about 1,500 settlers.

Shawnee warfare on the Ohio frontiers in 1790 was brought up in **Many Rivers to Cross** (MGM, 1955), in which Robert Taylor, cast as a trapper, is trying to escape a wedding-hungry Eleanor Parker. Shawnee Indians are also raiding settlers William Holden and Robert Mitchum in Ohio during the same period in **Rachel and the Stranger** (RKO, 1948). A TV mini-series **The Awakening Land** (Bensen-Kuhn-Sagal, 1978) was based on a trilogy of novels by Conrad Richter and tells the haunting story of pioneering life in Ohio during the late part of the 18th century.

In 1790 the new president responded to the crises on the frontiers by sending an American army—militia plus a few regulars under General Josiah Harmar—into the Indian country against Little Turtle and his force of Miamis, Shawnees, Potawatomis and Chippewas. Harmar exercised little control over his troops and he had no experience in fighting Indians. Little Turtle and his warriors ambushed Harmar's force and killed 183 soldiers. The general retreated, and unnaturally Little Turtle let him extract his battered command.

Harmar claimed victory, but Washington knew better and turned over the command of the campaign to General Arthur St. Clair, governor of the Northwest Territory. An ex–Revolutionary War veteran, like Harmar, St. Clair was wholly ignorant of Indian warfare.

In October 1791, he went blundering off into the wilderness with an ill-prepared army of 2,000 men, including 600 regulars. With his force, which was reduced to about 1,400 because of desertions, St. Clair managed to establish Forts Hamilton and Jefferson and picked his base at the high ground of the Wabash River about 50 miles from the later site of Fort Wayne, Indiana, where he hoped to make a stand.

Little Turtle with some 1,100 warriors attacked and scattered St. Clair's militia. St. Clair launched several bayonet charges, but the enemy faded back into the woods. At last, with more than half his army down and completely surrounded, St. Clair ordered a retreat. Of St. Clair's army, 623 officers and men died, along with 24 civilians. The Indians lost 21 warriors and had 40 wounded. In proportion to the number of men fielded that day, it stands as the worst loss the American Army has ever suffered.

In 1794, President Washington had better luck when he chose General Anthony Wayne as commander of the campaign against Little Turtle and his allies. "Mad Anthony," as he was called, was a soldier with a very fine record in the Revolution. Being a stern disciplinarian he made sure to get the army in good shape for the campaign. Wayne marched his men to winter quarters in Fort Greenville on the Maumee. In the spring of 1794 he erected Fort Recovery farther west on the site of St. Clair's defeat. Little Turtle tried an assault on the fort and was repulsed.

At the end of July, the bulk of the American forces, 2,200 regulars and 1,500 Kentucky militiamen, arrived at Fort Recovery. Little Turtle assessed the strength of Wayne's army and advised the Indians to negotiate for peace. The other chiefs overthrew him and made Turkey Foot their new war chief, who brought his warriors against Wayne's army. The battle took place at a spot, once hit by a tornado, called Fallen Timbers on August 20, 1794. Wayne beat them soundly at a loss to himself of only 33 men killed. The Indians' losses were unknown, but large. "Mad" Anthony Wayne's victory over the Indians at Fallen Timbers was brought up in the **"The Seekers,"** part III of the **Kent Family Chronicles** (Universal, 1978). This part of the series, built on John Jakes's best-selling American Bicentennial book series of the Kent Family saga, also covers the pioneering of family members on the Western frontiers.

After the Battle of Fallen Timbers, the Old Northwest was generally quiet for the first time in many years. Like George Washington, Thomas Jefferson, who succeeded John Adams as president of the United States in 1801, believed in westward expansion. In Europe Napoleon had made a secret treaty with Spain that gave Louisiana, which France had lost in the peace treaty of the French and Indian War, back to the French. The territory included 800,000 square miles between the Mississippi and the Rockies. For a sum of $15 million, Jefferson bought the Louisiana Territory from the French in 1803. To discover how much land he in fact had bought he sent two young explorers, Meriwether Lewis and William Clark, on an expedition west.

Lewis and Clark departed on their famous expedition from St. Louis in March 1804. The expedition followed the Missouri into the interior, and their trek westward would take them as far as the Columbia River in modern-day Washington.

On their journey the expedition met with friendly Oto and Mandan Indians. The only time they had come to real danger was from potentially hostile Teton Sioux. During the winter a key member was added to the expedition, the Shoshoni girl Sacajawea, who would help in guiding the expedition. The Mandans had kidnapped Sacajawea as a child. Just how much Sacajawea contributed to the expedition's success has been disputed.

When Lewis and Clark returned to St. Louis from their expedition in September 1806, they had traveled nearly 8,000 miles. If they had failed to find the Northwest Passage, they brought extensive knowledge about the Far West that was important for the westward migration now becoming a permanent part of American life.

The adventures of Lewis and Clark on their expedition to the West were filmed by Paramount in **The Far Horizons** (1955), with Fred MacMurray as Meriwether Lewis and Charlton Heston as William Clark. **The Prairie** (Screen Guild, 1948) is a lose adaptation of James Fenimore Cooper's novel with the same name from 1827, and centers on a family that moves into the newly opened Louisiana Territory. A similar pioneering story is told in **The Pioneers** (Monogram, 1941), which also was inspired by one of Cooper's novels, *The Pioneers*, from 1823.

The new time with the expansion

west also had impacts on the "old" frontiers. In **Big Jack** (MGM, 1949), Wallace Beery, contradicting his notable role as Magua in **The Last of the Mohicans** (Associated Producers, 1920), made his last film performance as a more sympathetic villain in this picture. Set in the backwoods of Virginia and Maryland in the year of 1802, the story deals with problems of old backwoodsmen (and women) adjusting to the new epoch in Colonial America.

Indian resistance toward white advances into the Northwest continued in the early years of the new century. A Shawnee chief, Tecumseh, began to preach unity to tribes to inspire them to resist the westward movement of the new Republic.

Tecumseh was born in 1768, near present-day Dayton, Ohio. Tecumseh fought alongside the British in the Revolution, and he later stood with Little Turtle against Harmar and the following year against St. Clair. He led raids against border settlements and during Anthony Wayne's campaign he lost a brother in the Battle of Fallen Timbers.

A turning point for Tecumseh came from a vision of his brother Tenskawatawa, called the Shawnee Prophet, which demanded that the tribes abandon all the white man's ways and return to ancient tribal traditions. Tecumseh and Tenskawatawa started to work toward an intertribal alliance that would liberate the Indians from the necessity of white contact.

Tecumseh's strategy was to buy time with the threat of war, time in which he traveled around to engage border nations from the deep South of Florida to the North of the upper Missouri River, his object being to hold the Ohio River as a permanent border against the whites. He visited tribes like the Sioux in the West, and went south to the land of the Chickasaws, Choctaws and Creeks. Only as a unified sovereign state, Tecumseh reasoned, could the Indians resist being absorbed by the whites.

Tecumseh and his brother established their headquarters—The Prophet's Town—on the Wabash River near its confluence with the Tippecanoe River in the Indian Territory. Tecumseh was successful enough in his efforts in uniting the different Indian nations that eventually General William Henry Harrison, governor of the Indiana Territory, became alarmed. In 1811, Tecumseh's followers spread terror along the frontiers. In July, Potawatomis killed some Illinois farmers. Harrison chose to believe that the murderers were followers of Tecumseh and his brother.

In late summer of 1811, Tecumseh undertook a new recruiting expedition among the Chickasaws, Choctaws and Creeks—together a potential source of 50,000 warriors. General Harrison decided to take advantage of Tecumseh's absence and strike against the confederacy headquarters at Prophet's Town. Harrison moved his army of 1,000 men up the Wabash and on November 7, they went into camp on Burnt's Creek, three miles from the mouth of the Tippecanoe River.

Although Tecumseh had told his brother to avoid a fight until he returned from the South, with Harrison's army just a few miles away, Tenskawatawa decided on a secret sneak attack. The Indians attacked before dawn on November 7 with such ferocity that Harrison's force at first fell back. But Harrison rallied his men, who at last held their ground. At dawn the soldiers launched a bayonet charge against the Indians. Always reluctant to face this cold steel, the Indians broke and ran. The Indians became so demoralized that they did not even defend their own town. Harrison entered Prophet's Town and after taking all supplies, he burned the town.

It was an indecisive, painful victory, losses on both sides were heavy—60 Americans killed and at least 120 wounded with casualties approximately the same on the Indian side. When Tecumseh returned early in 1812, he publicly rebuked his brother. Tenskawatawa drifted west and soon dropped into obscurity.

Tecumseh and his conflict with Tenskawatawa, the Battle at Tippecanoe and the burning of Prophet's Town, all come to life in Sam Katzman's **Brave Warrior** (Columbia, 1952).

After the Battle of Tippecanoe, the Potawatomis, Winnebagos and Sacs and Foxes, though shaken, remained loyal to Tecumseh. The Wyandots also adhered to the cause. But among he Delawares, Miamis and even the Shawnees, there were wholesale defections. The Battle of Tippecanoe was a terrible psychological defeat for Tecumseh, and a serious setback to his efforts to unite the Indian tribes against the whites.

Thomas Jefferson, the new president, favored a more democratic policy than his predecessors. He planned to adopt a new set of policies, later carried on by his successor, James Madison. This put the United States on a collision course with Great Britain and ultimately led to a new "Revolutionary War."

In Europe France initiated a great commercial war against Britain. In spite of the strong position of Napoleon after his military triumph at Austerlitz in 1805, he could not invade England because her great naval victory at Trafalgar gave Britain sea control.

Jefferson used federal authority in an attempt to maintain American neutrality during the struggle between Great Britain and France. America in British eyes was a weak, inconsequential nation that could be pushed around with impunity.

The conflict in Europe struck heavily on American commerce. The British cut off American ships with products for France and France ordered a seizure of any American vessel bringing goods to British ports.

To win the war against France, Britain was dependent on building up its navy. One of its problems was to recruit crews to its war ships because sailors were so ill-paid, ill-fed and ill-handled. Many sailors deserted and found refuge on more pleasant and safer American ships. The conflict between America and Great Britain was triggered by the British policy of waylaying American ships in international waters to seize sailors to be forced to serve in the British Navy. In the summer of 1807, the American frigate *Chesapeake*, with a large number of suspected British sailors among its crew, was fired upon and boarded by the British warship *Leopard*. The *Chesapeake* affair stirred public outrage throughout the United States.

British and French decrees on cutting off trade for their opponent rendered trade for America virtually impossible. If American ships complied with the French decrees, the British subjected them to seizure. The losses under the British and French regulations were heavy. Between 1807 and 1812, France and Britain and their allies seized about 900 American ships.

Combined with a growing Indian threat to the frontier settlements from the league of Indian tribes formed by Tecumseh, stirred up by British agents in Canada, a growing number of congressional members began to talk about war. Land-hungry Westerners ably represented in the Congress and abetted by the Southerners wished to grab all of Canada. All this formed the basis for President Madison declaring war on Great Britain in 1812.

Westerners were eager to invade Canada, and Michigan Territory governor William Hull, who had attained the rank of colonel in the Revolution, was placed in command of American forces north of Ohio—300 regulars and 1,200 Kentucky and Ohio militia. With the objective of taking Fort Malden, which guarded the entrance of Lake Erie, Hull crossed the Detroit River into Canada, but the old man was infirm and inept, he failed in his mission and began the war by surrendering Detroit without firing a shot. Disaster then followed disaster, and the American invasion of Canada ended in general failure. The day before Hull caved in, the garrison at Fort Dearborn (present-day Chicago) surrendered to the British and their Indian allies. Again the West was now open to Indian massacre and British invasion.

With 1,100 men General Harrison marched to recapture Detroit, and on his way he built Fort Meigs, near the site of the Battle of Fallen Timbers, as a base to attack Detroit and nearby Fort Malden in Canada. British General Proctor and Tecumseh, now a brigadier general in the British Army, with a force of 900 regulars and militia and 1,200 Indians, attacked and laid a two week siege on Fort Meigs in April 1813, which Harrison defended at great costs. Proctor finally broke the siege, after many of his Canadian militia and Indian allies had drifted away. The United States had suffered 320 killed and wounded; British losses (excluding Indians) were only about 100. Still, the British had been unable to capture the fort, largely because it was so well built.

The American campaign in the East did not go much better. The War Department selected a militia officer, Major General Stephen Van Rensselaer, to direct the operations on the Niagara front. Van Rensselaer shared his command with the regular army officer, General Alexander Smyth. The war plan was to seize Queenstown Heights on the British side of the Niagara River and Smyth was to attack Fort George six miles to the north.

But Smyth, unwilling to take orders from a militia officer, refused to cooperate. By October of 1812, more than 6,000 American troops faced a force of perhaps 2,000 British and Indians across the Niagara River.

In spite of outnumbering their enemy the Americans could not resist the assault from the enemy. The American troops had to surrender. In all, around 900 Americans were captured at the Canadian side of the river. Local Republicans—never reconciled to General Van Rensselaer's command—blamed him for the defeat.

After the disaster, the War Department replaced Van Rensselaer with Smyth as commander, unaware of Smyth's shortcomings. Smyth planned to launch an attack on Fort Erie at the south end of the Niagara River. The attack was, however, given up when Smyth's officers voted it down. The abandonment of the attack on Fort Erie brought the fighting on the Niagara front to an end.

The third and most important thrust in the American war campaign was supposed to be against Montreal. An old Revolutionary War veteran, Henry Dearborn, was elected to head this operation. In November Dearborn, with an army of 6,000 to 8,000 men marched from Albany to Plattsburgh on Lake Champlain. The American militia, however, refused to cross the border to Canada and the whole army soon retreated, and Dearborn had to give up his half-hearted attempt on Montreal. Thus the American invasion of Canada in 1812 failed on all three fronts. The principle reason for America's failure was poor leadership. The basic story in a Canadian made-for-TV feature, **Chronicle of 1812** (Emmeritus Productions) concerns espionage activities to reveal Dearborn's war plans against Kingston and Montreal.

By the end of 1813 the American position seemed to improve. Benjamin

Howard, governor of the Missouri Territory, led a successful invasion of the Illinois country, and William Clark, who succeeded him as governor, mounted an offensive against Prairie du Chien.

In August 1813, William Henry Harrison had rebuilt his army, fielding some 8,000 men. In October Harrison defeated retreating British and Indians, who had abandoned Fort Malden after being cut off from waterborne support. The battle took place on the Thames River where Tecumseh had persuaded British General Proctor to take a stand. No one knows who actually killed Tecumseh, but he died that day.

Films with motifs from Tecumseh's life include a European production, **Tecumseh** (Defa, 1972) with Gojko Mitić in the role of Tecumseh, and **Tecumseh, the Last Warrior** (Turner, 1995), a teleplay from TNT based on the book *Panther in the Sky* by James Alexander Thom. **Ten Gentlemen from West Point** (20th Century–Fox, 1942) also deals with warfare of Tecumseh and his Indian allies, with Noble Johnson in the cast as Tecumseh. The main story of the film is about the early history of the United States Military Academy.

The war at sea also went much better for the Americans. The navy, systematically built up under Washington and Adams, even if numerically small, was effective because it was blessed with great organization. The nation also had a rich maritime tradition. Officers and men alike were excellent seamen and skilled with cannon and small arms. Most of the officers had seen action in the Quasi-War (1798–1801) or in the Tripolitan War (1801–1805). In a series of naval actions, like that of the *Constitution* and *Guerrière* and the *United States* and *Macedonian*, the Yankee captains consistently defeated British vessels. On the Great Lakes, too, the American proved their merits. Captain Oliver Hazard Perry built

a fleet on Lake Erie and attacked and boarded small British vessels. Yet in the end the stronger British navy established full command of the seas and kept a close blockade of the American coast.

Naval activities of the American fleet during the war are covered in the third part of the TV mini-series of the Kent Family saga, **"The Seekers"** (Universal, 1979). So also in **Mutiny** (United Artists, 1952), in which an American ship runs the English blockade to collect gold bullion from France.

By the time the campaign of 1814 opened, the initiative in the war had shifted to the British. Europe was at peace. The United States now was alone against Great Britain.

In the early autumn of 1814 some 13,000 veterans had reached Canada, bringing British troop strength to near 40,000. The American Army had also improved steadily by experience. The new secretary of war, John Armstrong, continued to push capable young officers ahead. New recruits were enlisted and by early 1815 the total of men in uniform was close to 45,000.

The United States still held the advantage in the West. America controlled Lake Erie and its supply lines to the West. The Americans decided to make another drive on Canada. The plan was to destroy posts on Lake Huron, drive the British from the Niagara frontiers, and then seize other posts on Lake Ontario. If this campaign was successful, then Kingston and Montreal might be attacked.

In accordance with American strategy, the navy prepared to attack Fort Mackinac on Lake Huron in the summer. The undertaking failed for the Americans and this ended America's naval presence on Lake Huron until the end of the war. On Lake Ontario the Americans had to give up Fort Oswego after a British offensive lead by General Gordon Drummond.

The heaviest fighting on the Northern

frontier took place along the Niagara River. The Americans crossed the river into Canada to seek out the enemy. In a series of battles, the American commander, Jacob Brown, continued to demonstrate that American troops could hold their own against British troops. But Brown's invasion had little of strategic importance.

Although the heaviest fighting took place on the Niagara front, the British concentrated most of their troops farther East. It was in upper New York that they launched their only major offensive on the northern frontier. Sir George Prevost, governor-general of Canada, crossed into the United States in August 1814 with a plan to march down the western side of Lake Champlain in order to attack Plattsburgh. When Napoleon's forces were defeated in Spain, the British were able to reinforce their armies heavily. Wellington veterans drove into New York at Plattsburgh on Lake Champlain.

A naval and land contest took place on Lake Champlain in September. The American fleet decisively defeated the British fleet on those waters, and the British were forced to retreat. When Prevost learned about the defeat he ordered a retreat of the British land troops. The battles on Lake Champlain and at Plattsburgh closed out the fighting on the Northern frontiers in 1814. The fighting in Canada continued to be indecisive. Neither side could claim any significant conquests, and control of the lakes was divided.

Demoralizing to the Americans was the British invasion of Chesapeake. In the summer of 1814 a British army of fewer than 5,000 men landed near Washington and met a similar sized American force at Bladensburg. The unheroic defenders gave way for the British force and retreated. British troops fired on the Capitol and the White House and later subjected Fort McHenry near Baltimore to bombardment, but not much was accomplished.

The Battle of Thames had reversed the course of the War of 1812, but did not end white–Indian hostilities. Many of the Creeks living in Alabama and Georgia remained neutral when the War of 1812 broke out, but not all remained neutral during the course of the war. Red Eagle of the Red Sticks Creek, who had been impressed by Tecumseh's message, attacked Fort Mims, on the lower Alabama River on August 30, 1813, and slaughtered 400 settlers.

When the word of the massacre reached Tennessee, an army under Major Andrew Jackson was authorized to suppress the Creeks. With 5,000 Tennessee militiamen Jackson marched into the Red Sticks' country in November 1813. Learning that 200 Creek warriors were staying in the village of Tallushatchee, Jackson sent 1,000 men against the Indians, among them a rangy frontiersman named Davy Crockett. In the ambush, 186 Indians were massacred.

Andrew Jackson and General William Claiborne unsuccessfully pressured Red Eagle for the next two months. It was not until March 1814, after having destroyed every Red Stick town, that Jackson brought an end to the Indian uprising in the South, known as the Creek War, by attacking at Horseshoe Bend. In the attack about 750 of the 900 Red Stick warriors were killed.

Andrew Jackson's campaign against the Creek nation was pictured in MGM's **The Frontiersman** (1927), which had Tim McCoy in the lead role as a captain in Jackson's Tennessee militia. The frontier legend Davy Crockett's involvement in the Creek Indian War can be seen in the Walt Disney movie **Davy Crockett, King of the Wild Frontier** (Buena Vista, 1955), with Fess Parker playing Davy Crockett. The success of this film led to another feature movie based on a combination of two stories from the TV series—**Davy Crockett and the River Pirates** (Buena Vista, 1956), which deals with Davy's and his sidekick, George Russel's (Buddy Ebsen) adventures on the Ohio River in 1810.

In 1988, the Disney Studio once again tried to breathe new life into Davy Crockett in a TV series with episodes as part of *The Magical World of Disney*. Tim Dunigan was selected to play young Davy Crockett; the series dealt with the Creek War of 1812-13. The first episodes had an older Crockett, played by country music star Johnny Cash, looking back on his adventures as a young member of Andrew Jackson's militia. The series never generated much interest and only four hour-long episodes were filmed.

Other movies about Davy Crockett (not including "Alamo" films, which are beyond the scope of this book) are: **Davy Crockett—In Hearts United** (Bison, 1909); **Davy Crockett** (Selig, 1910); **Davy Crockett Up-to-Date** (Superba, 1915); and **Davy Crockett** (1916).

The War of 1812 was officially over at the close of 1814, but its bloodiest and most senseless battle was fought a fortnight after the peace treaty was signed. Wellington's brother-in-law, Sir Edward Parkenham, led 8,000 troops in an ill-timed and badly planned frontal attack against Andrew Jackson's army near New Orleans. Jackson's collection of American regulars, militia, Indians and bayou pirates smashed the assault, killing or wounding some 2,000 British soldiers. Parkenham himself was killed. This was January 8, 1815, after the peace treaty was signed, but before the Americans knew it.

The Battle of New Orleans had no real military significance. It made, however, the fiery, imperious Jackson a national hero, which contributed to his later election as president. The story of Andrew Jackson's life was told in the bio-graphic film **The President's Lady** (20th Century–Fox, 1953), which had the Battle of New Orleans as an adjacent story. Charlton Heston played Andrew Jackson. In **The Buccaneer** (Paramount, 1958), Yul Brynner was cast as pirate *Lafitte*, who comes to aid General Andrew Jackson (again played by Charlton Heston) when the British attack New Orleans. The film was supervised by Cecil B. DeMille, who himself directed the first version of **The Buccaneer** (Paramount, 1938), which had Fredric March in the role as Jean Lafitte, and Hugh Sothern as Andrew Jackson. The sea adventures of pirate Lafitte after the British had been driven from New Orleans is told in a cheerful low-budget swashbuckler movie, **The Last of the Buccaneers** (Columbia, 1950).

Returning from the Battle of New Orleans with his Kentucky militia regiment, John Wayne in **The Fighting Kentuckian** (Republic, 1949), detours his regiment to help French exiles in Alabama settle terms in their struggle with local rivermen in 1819. In this movie Wayne has Oliver Hardy as his sidekick.

In its military and naval campaigns, the record of the United States during the war was decidedly mixed. There was some success—most notably on the Northern lakes and at New Orleans—and some failures, particularly in Chesapeake Bay and on the Canadian frontiers. America's success came at the peace-negotiating table in Ghent in Belgium.

For the first time the United States was taken seriously in Europe, although the nation was unable to conquer Canada or to achieve any of the maritime goals for which it was contenting. The war also broke the power of the Indians in the Northwest and the Southwest, and contributed to the making of Canada. The British never considered the war more than a sideshow—a footnote in their history.

Filmography

Allegheny Uprising (RKO, 1939)

Produced by P.J. Wolfson. Directed by William Seiter. Screenplay by P.J. Wolfson based on the story The First Rebel by Neil Swanson. Photography by Nicholas Musuraca. Running time: 81 minutes.

Cast: *Janie MacDougle* Claire Trevor, *Jim Smith* John Wayne, *Captain Swanson* George Sanders, *Callendar* Brian Donlevy, *MacDougle* Wilfred Lawson, *Duncan* Robert Barrat, *Professor* John F. Hamilton, *Calhoon* Moroni Olsen, *Anderson* Eddie Quillan, *M'Cammon* Chill Wills, *Poole* Ian Wolf, *MacGlashan* Wallis Clark, *Morris* Monte Montauge, *General Gage* Olaf Hytten and *Governor Penn* Clay Clement.

The story: In Pennsylvania, 15 years before the American Revolution, the trader Callendar is selling liquor and firearms to hostile Indians, which results in the massacre of settlers. Young Jim Smith and his fellow frontiersmen find out about the trade.

Janie MacDougle, daughter of a tavern keeper, is in love with Jim who is hard to flirt.

The frontiersmen make their way after a band of marauding Indians. Jim escapes from captivity with the Indians and goes to Philadelphia to report to the British about the illegal trade. By the command of Captain Swanson, a troop of British soldiers is garrisoned at Fort Loudon for the protection of the settlers.

Callender brings supplies to the fort, but he also continues the trade in firearms with the Indians. The frontiersmen disguise themselves as Indians and raid the trader's caravan and confiscate the illegal firearms. Callender burns government supplies, carried in the same wagon train, and places the blame on Jim and his men. The settlers go to the fort to seek justice on Callender, and when repudiated they attack the fort. The British surrender and leave the fort. Jim sends proof of the illegal trade to Governor Penn. Swanson returns with reinforcements and reoccupies the fort. Jim and his friends once more attack and besiege the fort.

Callender's men murder a settler and place the blame on Jim, who is arrested. During a court martial, at which Janie demonstrates Jim's innocence, a British officer sent by Governor Penn arrives and releases Jim. Swanson is forced to leave for England and Jim and Janie are reunited.

Notes: John Ford's **Stagecoach** from 1939 with John Wayne and Claire Trevor in the leading roles is considered to be one of the best westerns ever produced. To follow up on the successful pairing of Wayne and Trevor, RKO brought them together in another movie, **Allegheny Uprising**, also released in 1939.

The story deals with a colonial uprising, led by Wayne and his "Black Boys," against the ruling British in the early 1760s, one of

starring
CLAIRE TREVOR
JOHN WAYNE
GEORGE SANDERS
BRIAN DONLEVY
WILFRID LAWSON
ROBERT BARRAT
JOHN F. HAMILTON
MORONI OLSEN
EDDIE QUILLAN

Produced by P. J. Wolfson. Directed by William A. Seiter.
Pandro S. Berman in charge of production.
Screenplay by P. J. Wolfson.

Released by
R K O RADIO

the sparks that later would lead to the American Revolution.

The movie was released at the same time as John Ford's **Drums Along the Mohawk** entered the theaters. Compared to the "Master's" film, **Uprising** was less prestigious and produced under a more cautious budget in black and white.

The movie, as did most of movies dealing with American-British conflicts during the Revolutionary War, faced political problems. To depict British as unpleasant during a time when they were struggling against a growing Nazi tyranny in Europe, just before the outbreak of World War II, was not popular. After several cuts the film could be released in England under a new title, **The First Rebel**, the same title which Neil Swanson's book had, and on which the screenplay was based.

In spite of having John Wayne and Claire Trevor in the cast, **Allegheny Uprising** failed to attract audiences on either side of the Atlantic.

"The second Wayne-Trevor vehicle, Allegheny Uprising, was a rather plodding film ... So malapropos did it seem at the time to remind the British ... that they had once fought against America, that it was never released in England."—William K. Everson in *A Pictorial History of Western Film*

Even if not being the successful follow-up to the Wayne-Trevor pairing in **Stagecoach** that RKO had hoped it to be, the film has a touch of enjoyable atmosphere which also has been appreciated by some critics.

"This was a ponderous and dull follow-up of *Stagecoach* as could be imagined.... Nevertheless, it has handsome production values and is proficiently directed by William A. Seiter." —Allen Eyles in *John Wayne and the Movies*

"Besides the buoyant presences of Wayne, Trevor, Sanders and Donlevy, this film does capture an almost forgotten chapter of American history. A colorful fabric of the story plus the array of recreated details of a bygone era make this film very worthwhile viewing."—M. Parish and M.R. Pitts in *The Great Western Pictures*

America (United Artists, 1924)

Produced and directed by D.W. Griffith. Screenplay by John L.E. Pell. Story by Robert W. Chambers. Photography by G.W. Bitzer, Marcel Le Picard, Hendrik Sartov and Hal Sintzenich. Length: 175 minutes.

Cast: *Nathan Holden* Neil Hamilton, *Nancy Montague* Carol Dempster, *Captain Walter Butler* Lionel Barrymore, *Judge Montague* Erville Alderson, *Charles Philip Edward Montague* Charles Emmett Mack, *Samuel Adams* Lee Beggs, *John Hancock* John Dubton, *King George III* Arthur Donaldson, *William Pitt* Charles Benett, *Lord Chamberlain* Downing Clark, *Patrick Henry* Frank McGlynn, Jr., *George Washington* Arthur Dewey, *Richard Henry Lee* P.R. Scammon, *Captain Hare* Louis Wolheim, *Chief Joseph Brandt* Riley Hatch, *Chief Hikatoo* Harry Hemels, *Thomas Jefferson* Frank Walsh, with Charles Emmett Mack, Lee Beggs and Frank McGlynn.

The story: In 1775, there is a growing unrest in the 13 American colonies. William Pitt and Edmund Burke vainly protest the injustice of taxation. The autocratic George III orders British Redcoats into Boston.

An encounter between the British soldiers and a few colonists, among whom is Nathan Holden, in Lexington, results in open war. The Americans have to choose—Rebel or Tory. Nathan develops a love interest in Tory Judge Montague's daughter Nancy.

In June 1776, the rebels fear a British attempt to break out of Boston. In a bold move to stop this, they fortify Bunker Hill. The British attack but are defeated. On July 4, 1776, the Continental Congress passes the Declaration of Independence.

Captain Walter Butler, a renegade

Opposite, top: Allegheny Uprising (RKO, 1939)—Lobby card: McDougle (Wilfred Lawson, *right*) enjoys seeing his daughter Janice (Claire Trevor) take a liking toward Jim Smith (John Wayne) when he and Jim return from the war. *Bottom:* "The Professor" (John Hamilton) in a riverfight with a Delaware Indian.

America (United Artists, 1924)—Nathan Holden (Neil Hamilton) arrives at the Montague home to inform Philip Montague (Charles Emmett Mack) about the British advance against Lexington.

American, is assigned by the British to rally the Indian Confederacy to their cause. Butler promises Montague the loyalty of the Six Nations to the King. He also tries to win Nancy's sympathy. The progress of the war changes in advance of the British. At Valley Forge Washington's Army is suffering through the winter. The next summer Butler and his Indians terrorize the whole of Northern New York state and commit the massacre of Cherry Valley.

Most of the major fighting has moved southward of Virginia, but Butler continues his campaign of pillage and massacre. Washington sends Nathan Holden to the Mo-hawk Valley to deal with Butler. The Americans learn that a war council is about to be held at the Montague home, and Nathan arrives to learn about Butler's plan to raid the Mohawk Valley. The valley people take refuge in Fort Sacrifice. The fort is severely attacked by Butler and the Mohawks, but Nathan arrives with reinforcements and rescues the colonists. His own men kill Captain Butler when he tries to stop them from deserting.

The tide of war changes; gradually American forces gain the upper hand and at Yorktown, Cornwallis surrenders to Washington.

Opposite, top: America (United Artists, 1924)—Nancy Montague (Carol Dempster) in audience with the British governor of Massachusetts, Sir Francis Bernard. *Bottom:* Nancy Montague (Carol Dempster) meets with the notorious British Tory, Captain Walter Butler (Lionel Barrymore).

America—Revolutionary fighter Nathan Holden (Neil Hamilton) at rest.

Notes: America, the last of Griffith's silent epics, was a semi-documentary drama about the American Revolution. Griffith had plans that this would be the first of a series of films about American history. However, he ran into financial problems with the picture and had to abandon his plans for sequels.

The suggestion for doing a movie about the American Revolution came from the Daughters of the American Revolution. At the time this was a strong organization which wanted its point of view to be exposed by the powerful movie medium.

An historian and a novelist, who gave it a mix of history lecture and romantic fiction, wrote the story for the film. The movie is not entirely of a piece, but individual historical parts are very well crafted.

Initially the film ran for 16 reels, and it required an intermission. The battle scenes are spectacles. To direct Griffith used such unusual tools as portable telephones to communicate with his assistants. To do large-scale battle scenes he utilized help from the U.S. Army.

To keep up with the documentary thoughts when doing the movie several historical events were included in the movie's first part: "The shot heard around the world," the battles of Concord and Lexington, Paul Revere's ride, the Battle of Bunker Hill, Washington at Valley Forge

Opposite, top: America—Nancy Montague (Carol Dempster) at the battlefield of Lexington. *Bottom:* Harry O'Neil in the cast as Paul Revere—"the only applicant who could ride the Irish horse Griffith purchased for the production."

America—Captain Walter Butler (Lionel Barrymore) with Mohawk dinner guests.

and the signing of the Declaration of Independence.

Authenticity was important for Griffith in making **America**. For this reason it is said that Griffith chose actor Harry O'Neil to play the role of Paul Revere, only because he was the only applicant who could ride on the expensive Irish horse that Griffith had purchased for the picture. The total outcome of Griffith's work in spite of his care for authenticity has later been criticized.

"Griffith used the drums actually beaten at the Battle of Lexington, Major Pitcairn's pistols, flintlocks, vehicles, farming implements, and even garments of the Revolutionary War period. ... The end result of all these extensive preparations, though, was nevertheless an elaborate fiction."—*The Velvet Light Trap, Nr. 8, 1976.*

As with Goldstein's **The Spirit of '76**, the film had political problems. It is difficult to make a film about the American Revolution without presenting the British as villains. To some extent **America** might be an exception:

"It is curious and unexplained fact that movies about the American Revolution and its legendary heroes have not been popular. D.W. Griffith's 1924 production, **America**, is an exception ... and in its time drew large audiences."— George Mitchell in *American Cinematographer*, October 1990.

Initially **America** was banned in England, but it was possible to bring it to the English market in a heavily reworked version titled **Love and Sacrifice**. The British version presented the story more as a civil war between two groups of Englishmen.

Except for the evil appearance of George III and a renegade American, Captain Butler, who led the Iroquois on in a series of bloody raids against settlers in New York's Mohawk Valley, the Indians were the only group that could be portrayed as villains without entering into political problems. The second part of the film concentrates heavily on the war in Northern New York and the conflict between British-allied Indians and the colonists. Not to paint the British too negatively, the worst possible image of the Indians comes across in **America**.

"The Indians in this movie are ignorant, easily beguiled, arm-folding stoics, or crazy, drunken, torturing fiends."—R.N. Friar in *The Only Good Indian*

"While the British troops had been models of military honor and good conduct, the Indians were barbarous savages ... no one spoke up for the Indians as 'good sportsmen,' and audiences were left with a reaffirmation of their attitudes toward the incorrigibly violent Native Americans."—John E. O'Conner in *The Hollywood Indian*

America premiered on February 21, 1924. It was generally well received by the critics.

"**America** ranks among the three or four truly great films of the cinema's brief history.... The Revolution has been reproduced with such perfection and mood and detail that the spectator feels himself literally experiencing much of the action and sentiment that accompanied it..."—*Movie Weekly*, March 22, 1924

"It pulses with life, and for the beauty, **America** has no equal."—*Theater Magazine*

Later reviews prized the photographic quality of the movie and have raised America as a forgotten classic:

"Scene after scene of breathtaking beauty unfolds: Paul Revere's ride, Bunker Hill seen through the rigging of the British Man of War, the American flag, carried for the first time at the Battle of Johnson Hall..."—*American Cinematographer*, October 1990

"...in many ways one of Griffith's best films, showing that he had lost none of his cunning in staging and sustaining mass action sequences."—William K. Everson in *The American Silent Film*

"...the evocation of the successive battles—Lexington, Bunker Hill, snow-bound Valley Forge—has characteristic grandeur, combining misty impressionism and realistic detail into formalized heroic images."—*Monthly Film Bulletin*, May-79

"In its original release America was criticized as old-fashioned. The film was out of phase with other films of the time, but it works better today out of that context."—*Silent Film Sources-Reviews*

April Morning (Samuel Goldwyn, 1988)

Produced by Samuel Goldwyn, Jr. Directed by Delbert Mann. Story by James Lee Barrett, based on the novel by Howard Fast. Photography by Frank Tidy. Music by

April Morning (Samuel Goldwyn, 1988)—Adam Cooper (Chad Lowe) with his father Moses (Tommy Lee Jones).

April Morning—Preparing to meet the British at Lexington. Adam Cooper (Chad Lowe) and father Moses Cooper (Tommy Lee Jones) with patriot neighbor Joseph Simmons (Robert Urich, *right*).

Allyn Ferguson. Running time: 100 minutes.

Cast: *Moses Cooper* Tommy Lee Jones, *Adam Cooper* Chad Lowe, *Joseph Simmons* Robert Urich, *Sarah Cooper* Susan Blakely, *Solomon Chandler* Rip Torn, *Ruth Simmons* Meridith Salenger, *Granny Cooper* Joan Heney, *John Parker* Nicholas Kilbertus, *Samuel Hadley* Griffith Brewer, *Jonathan Harrington* Thor Bisophric, *The Reverend* Joel Miller, *Joash Smith* Brian Furlog, *Simon Casper* Anthony Ulc, *John Burkman* Philip Spensley and *Major John Pitcairn* Peter Colvey.

The Story: It's April 19, 1775, and 15-year-old Adam Cooper has difficulties getting along with his father Moses, who is stubborn and wants to guide Adam in everything. Information suggests that British troops are on their way to take over an ammunition store of the colonists.

The men in Lexington gather their weapons and go to persuade the British to leave town, but the British refuse to respond. Fighting is a fact and when the smoke clears several of the colonists have been killed, among them Moses Cooper. Adam leaves the battleground and runs for his life. During his escape he runs into some other colonials and joins them to defend what is rightfully theirs: their homeland.

Attack on Fort Boonesboro (American Mutoscope & Biograph Co., 1906)

Camera by G.W. Bitzer.

Documentary. Shot on location in Louisville, KY. "All of the persons comport themselves generally as if they were at a Picnic or public gathering." (*Motion Picture*, 1894–1912).

The Awakening Land (Bensen-Kuhn-Sagal Prods., Warner Bros. TV mini-series, 1978)

Produced by Robert E. Relay. Directed by Boris Segal. Screenplay by James Lee Barrett and Liam O'Brian. Based on a triology of novels by Conrad Richter. Photography by Michael Hugo. Music by Fred Karlin. Running time: 300 minutes.

Cast: *Sayward Luckett Wheeler* Elizabeth Montgomery, *Portius Wheeler "The Solitary"* Hal Holbrook, *Genny Luckett* Jayne Seymour, *Jake Tench* Steven Keats, *Huldah as an Adult* Devon Ericson, *Mistress*

Above, left: The Awakening Land (Warner Bros. TV, 1978)—Frontier sisters—Sayward Luckett Wheeler (Elizabeth Montgomery) and Genny Luckett (Jane Seymour). *Right:* Portius Wheeler "The Solitary" (Hal Holbrook) with wife Sayward Luckett Wheeler (Elizabeth Montgomery).

Bartram Dorrie Kavanaugh, *Jary Luckett* Louise Latham, *Will Beagle* William H. Macy, *Granny McWhirter* Jeanette Nolan, *Isac Barker* Bert Remsen and *Reverend Hutchins* Charles Tyber.

The story: The story in **The Awakening Land** covers a period from 1790 to 1817 in the life of a strong-willed, courageous woman, Sayward Luckett Wheeler, who settles on the Ohio frontier. Through hardships and setbacks we will follow her and her husband, a poetic Massachusetts lawyer known as "The Solitary" during the founding of a new society in the wilderness.

Notes: The script in this mini-series is built on 1951 Pulitzer Prize–winner Conrad Richter's novel trilogy: *The Trees* (1940), *The Fields* (1946) and *The Town* (1950).

Emmy nominations went to Montgomery, Holbrook, and Nolan for acting, Michael Hugo for cinematography, Fred Karlin for the music score and Bernard J. Small for editing.

Another of Richter's works which found its way to the movies was **The Light in the Forest** (Disney, 1958).

Battles of Chief Pontiac (Jack Broder Prod./Realart, 1952)

Produced by Irving Starr. Directed by Felix Feist. Screenplay by Jack DeWitt. Photography by Charles VanEnger. Music by Elmer Bernstein. Running time: 72 minutes.

Cast: *Kent McIntire* Lex Barker, *Winifred Lancester* Helen Westcott, *Chief Pontiac* Lon Chaney, Jr., *Col. Von Weber* Berry Kroeger, *Major Gladwin* Roy Roberts, *Hawkbill* Larry Chance, *Chia* Katherine Warren, *Gen. Amherst* Ramsey Hill, *Von Weber's Aide* Guy Teague, *Sentry* James Fairfax and *Doctor* Abner George.

The story: In 1763, General Amherst sends Lt. Kent McIntyre to Fort Detroit, which is under siege by Ottawa Chief Pontiac's Indians, with a message that Hessian Colonel Von Weber is coming to reinforce the fort. McIntyre doesn't like Amherst's choice of Von Weber as commander because he is known as a brutal Indian hater.

On his way, when trying to help some women captured by Indians, one of whom is Winifred Lancaster, Kent is captured himself. In Pontiac's village, Kent convinces Pontiac that he cannot expect help from the French because the war is over. Pontiac agrees to send Kent to Fort Detroit to suggest peace negotiations. Winifred has to stay as hostage in the village when Kent leaves for Detroit.

The fact that the garrison of the fort is suffering from a smallpox epidemic gives Von Weber an idea; he sends contaminated blankets as gifts to the Indians.

During the peace negotiations, Von Weber insults Pontiac while the Indians leave. Von Weber announces his intent to attack the Indian village as soon as the disease weakens the warriors.

Kent leaves to warn Pontiac. When he arrives at the village he finds out that the epidemic has broken out. Winifred is helping in nursing the diseased. When Pontiac hears about Von Weber's treachery he assembles his warriors for an ambush. The Indians beat Von Weber's force. At the Indian village, Von Weber is bound to a pole and wrapped in contaminated blankets. Later he dies a victim of his own medicine.

With the death of Von Weber peace is restored between the whites and the Indians and Kent and Winifred can unite as a couple.

"...the results are of dubious historical and boxoffice value ... its entertainment merits are very mediocre and the insertion of an obvious sexploitation angle mitigates any recommendation for the kiddie action fan."—*Variety*

"Whites did, in fact, introduce both the smallpox and the practice of scalping to the Indians of North America, but despite that basis in unsavory history this is a "B" meller with "Z" acting."—Brian Garfield *Western Films: A Complete Guide*

"...An almost irrelevant footnote to the earliest film on the history of the West is The Battles of Chief Pontiac ... notable only in that it is set a hundred years earlier than any number of otherwise identical quickies."—Kim Newman *Wild West Movies*

Big Jack (MGM, 1949)

Directed by Richard Thorpe. Screenplay by Gene Fowler, Marvin Borowsky and Otto Van Eyss. Photography by Robert Surtees. Music by Herbert Stothart. Running time: 85 minutes.

Cast: *Big Jack* Wallace Beery, *Kate* Marjorie Main, *Dr. Meath* Richard Conte, with Edward Arnold, Vanessa Brown, Clinton Sundberg, Charles Dingle and Clem Bevans.

The story: In the backwoods of Maryland and Virginia in 1802, a time when science was still a crime and a crime not yet a science, Big Jack and Kate are vagabond thieves.

Black Robe (Alliance Entertainment Samson Productions, 1991)

Produced by Robert Lantos, Stephanie Reichel and Sue Milliken. Directed by Bruce Beresford. Screenplay by Brian Moore, based on the novel *Black Robe* by Moore. Photographed by Peter James. Music by George Delerue. Running time: 100 minutes.

Cast: *Father Laforgue* Lothaire Bluteau, *Daniel* Aden Young, *Annuka* Sandrine Holt, *Chromina* August Schellenberg, *Chromina's Wife* Tantoo Cardinal, *Ougebmat* Billy Two Rivers, *Neehatin* Lawrence Bayne, *Awondoie* Harrison Liu, *Oujita* Wesley Cote, *Father Jerome* Frank Wilson,

Opposite, top: Battles of Chief Pontiac (Jack Broder Productions/Realart, 1952)—Winifred Lancaster (Helen Westcott) is nursing one of the smallpox victims. *Bottom:* Colonel Von Weber trapped by Pontiac's warriors.

Big Jack (MGM, 1949)—Dr. Meath (Richard Conte), Big Jack (Wallace Beery), and Kate (Marjorie Main).

Father Bourque Francois Tasse, *Champlain* Jean Brousseau, *Mestigoit* Yvan Labelle, *Kiotseaton* Raoul Trujillo, *Ondeson* James Bobbish, *Taratande* Denis Lacroix, *Older Workman* Gilles Planta, *Old Aenons* Gordon Tootoosis, *Laforgue's Mother* Marthe Tungeon, *Old Priest* Claude Prefontaine, *Mercier* Deano Clavet, *Workmen* Paul Stewart, Jean-Raymond Chales, Jean-Jacques Blanchet, *Montagnais* Marco Bacon, Patrick Tenasco, *Iroquois Leader* George Pachanos, *1st Iroquois* Minor Mustain, *Iroquois Guard* Don Brisebois, *Iroquois Elder* Jean-Baptiste Raphael, *Old Iroquois Member* Guy Provencher, *Tall Painted Iroquois* Joe DeLaronde, *She Manitou* Linlyn Lue, *Domergue* Bonfield Marcoux, *Pregnant Woman* Wanda Obomsawin, *Tallevant* Jean-Pierre Perusse, *Masse*

Gerard. Soler, *Iroquois Torture Women* Alison Reid, Brenda Adams, *Musicians* Denis Plante, Daniel Thonon, *Mile La Fontaine* Cordelia Beresford, *Algonquin Tribe Members* Annie Bearskin, Joseph Campean, Mirya Obomsawin, Rodrigue Boivin, Valerie DeContie, Roger Wylde, Helen Atkinson, Jonathon Blacksmith, Doreen Stevens, Eric Johnston, Zoe Hopkins, Waylon Hare, Walter Jacobs, John Tenasco, Earl Danyluk and Arnold Eyah-Saulteux.

The story: Father Laforgue, called the "Black Robe" by the Indians, is sent by Champlain, governor of Quebeck, north to a frontier Jesuit mission to assist in the conversion of the Huron tribe to Catholicism in 1634. As guides a party of Algonquin Indians, led by Chromina, accompanies Laforgue.

Black Robe (Alliance Entertainment Samson Productions, 1992)—Father Laforgue (Lothaire Bluteau, center) is escorted up-river by a group of Algonquin Indians. Tribe leader Chromina (August Shellenberg) is in front and his daughter Annuka (Sandrine Holt) is behind Laforgue.

Problems arise between Laforgue and Chromina's braves during the journey. When a holy man warns Chromina to continue the journey, and his daughter, Annuka, starts a love affair with Daniel, an accompanying young French interpreter, he abandons Laforgue. Chromina, however, fearing Champlain's vengeance, returns to retrieve Laforgue.

Iroquois attack the party. Chromina's

Black Robe—A Huron Indian and director Bruce Beresford on a production set.

braves are killed and the survivors are brought to the Iroquois camp. The Iroquois torture Chromina and the two white men. Annuka manages to arrange for their escape by seducing and subduing one of the guards.

At the end of their journey, Chromina dies and with his blessing Annuka and Daniel leave Laforgue. Arriving at the Huron settlement, Laforgue finds it wracked by disease and dissent. He decides to stay, however, and continue his predecessor's work in converting the Hurons.

Notes: Irish writer Brian Moore wrote the script for **Black Robe** based on his book with the same title. There were problems finding an American studio that was willing to do the film because of its religious content. Moore and Director Bruce Beresford therefore went to Canada to do the film. This proved to be a lucky move and **Black Robe** stands as one of Canada's biggest-grossing films. It won six Canadian

Academy Awards, including Best Picture, Director, Adopted Screenplay and Supporting Actor (August Schellenberg as *Chromina*).

Moore intended to show the Indians in the movie differently from what they are in most movies. One of the religious issues in the story deals with the torturing to death of enemies by Indians to capture their souls.

"...**Black Robe** tries to distinguish itself by pretending to a basic, at times brutal, 'honesty' in its depiction of native culture..."—*TVgen*

"...**Black Robe** has brutally lyrical dream moments ... evoking religious feeling ... without sentimentality. The final stretches, as the Jesuit demonstrates his true strength under torture and in the face of despair, are truly shattering, delivering an unforgettably powerful intellectual and emotional punch."—Kim Newman in *Empire*

"...Left to stand without comments is the hand the Indians had in their own demise, through constant intertribal warfare.... **Black**

Robe refuses to get beyond that point, instead repeating its theme over and over at the distinct risk of numbing the viewer."—*The Motion Picture Guide*

Not everyone appreciated the way the Indians were treated in the film. Native Americans accused the film of being racist.

"...**Black Robe** is a film in which the viewer's eyes are removed just as certainly, preventing them from seeing an accurate picture of natives in Canadian history.... Also presented without honor are the Iroquois. We see them as mindlessly violent..."—Joch Steckley in *Arch Notes Newsletter* published by the Ontario Archeological Society Inc.

Mostly, however, **Black Robe** was regarded as an enlightened picture by the critics:

"Amazing! **Black Robe** is one adventure film that is intelligent, as it is enthralling ... has everything that was missing from **Dances with Wolves**..."—*US Magazine*

"...Packs twice the intellectual punch of **Dances with Wolves**. Transcends its storyline in a way **"Wolves"** never did..."—*Newsday*

"...A TRIUMPH. The best film making Bruce Beresford has ever done ... **Black Robe** is an adventure story in the truest sense..."—*New Yorker*

"...a small epic of endurance. The production has an austere beauty and thoughtful approach. Bluteau gives a moving performance in the central role, and Schellenberg is particularly notable in the friendly Chromina."—*Variety Movie Guide*

Blauvogel (Blue Bird) (DEFA, 1979)

Produced by Hans-Eric-Busch. Directed by Ulrich Weiss. Screenplay by Ulrich Weiss, based on the novel by Anna Jurgen. Photography by Otto Hanisch and Bauten Hans Poppe. Music by Peter Rabenalt. Length: 96 minutes.

Cast: Robin Jaeger, Gabriele Osecinc, Jutta Hoffmann, Kurt Böwe and Jan Spitzer.

The story: During the French and Indian War, George is a young son of a white settler family on the frontiers. Iroquois attack the settlement and George is captured. To replace Blue Bird, an Indian boy who has been killed by the whites, the tribe adopts George. His new father, Kleinbär ("Small Bear") and mother Mittagssonne ("Noon Sun") take good care of him and make him adjust to the Indian way of living.

Seven years later after a peace treaty between the whites and the Indians, all captured and adopted whites must be released. George returns to his real parents. His previous Indian life complicates his adjustment to the white man's world, and he has a hard time understanding the white oppression of the Indians. He therefore decides to return to his Iroquois family.

Notes: This is one of 12 Indian movies produced between 1966 and 1983 by DEFA, an East German production company.

The movie was made for children and the story is based on a book by Ann Jurgen. It is free from standard action clichés seen in many Indian movies and shows respect for ethnographic and historical accuracy.

The story in **Blauvogel** is very similar to the story in Disney's **The Light in the Forest**, in which a white boy, captured and adopted by Indians, is returned to his white parents after the peace treaty at Fort Stanwix in 1764.

Brave Warrior (Columbia, 1952)

Produced by Sam Katzman. Directed by Spencer G. Bennet. Screenplay by Robert E. Kent. Photography in Technicolor by William V. Skall. Music by Mischa Bakaleinikoff. Running time: 73 minutes.

Cast: *Steve Ruddell* Jon Hall, *Laura Macgregor* Christine Larsen, *Chief Tecumseh* Jay Silverheels, *The Prophet* Michael Ansara, *Shayne Macgregor* Harry Cording, *Governor Harrison* James Seay, *Barney Demming* George Eldrege, *General Proctor* Leslie Denison, *Barker* Rory Mallinson, *Standish* Rusty Wescott, *Gilbert* Bert Davidson, *Chief Little Cloud* William P.

TEN THOUSAND SHAWNEE TOMAHAWKS TERRORIZE THE PLAINS!

COLUMBIA PICTURES presents

BRAVE WARRIOR

All the fierce fury and fire of America's greatest Indian war!

COLOR BY **TECHNICOLOR**

Troubleshooter

Chief

Prophet   Renegade   Spy

starring **JON HALL** with Christine Larson · Jay Silverheels · Michael Ansara

Written for the Screen by ROBERT E. KENT · Produced by SAM KATZMAN · Directed by SPENCER G. BENNET

00-Line Ad Mat No. 501—5 Cols. x 120 Lines. *See page 6 for 4-column size of this ad.*

Brave Warrior (Columbia, 1952)—From the pressbook.

Wilkerson, and *English Lieutenant* Gilbert V. Perkins.

The story: In the year 1811, war looms between England and the United States. The British are busily stirring up trouble in Indiana Territory, preparing the way for the conflict which is to come.

Steve Ruddell, a government agent in Vincennes, capital of the Indiana Territory, is sent out to uncover and smash the British plot, and to win friendship of the Shawnee Indian nation. Ruddell discovers that the fur trader Shayne Macgregor is helping the British provoke the Shawnees. Macgregor's daughter Laura falls in love with Ruddell.

Ruddell receives invaluable support of the great Shawnee chieftain Tecumseh, whose dream is to establish peace between his people and the white man, but Tecumseh's brother, the Prophet, challenges Tecumseh's leadership. Losing his bid for power in a terrifying tomahawk fight, the embittered Prophet abandons the Shawnee tribe. The British use the Prophet and his followers to strike terror through the plains. Time and again the Prophet sounds the cry which sends thousands of Shawnee braves on the war path, looting, killing and burning. With the British covertly backing him, the Prophet and his men attack the American militia at Tippecanoe. Although defeated in a desperate battle, the Prophet and his men burn the village at their retreat.

Brave Warrior—Tecumseh (Jay Silverheels) is about to win the fight with his brother, the Prophet (Michael Ansara).

Tecumseh bids a sorrowful farewell to Ruddell and Laura.

Notes: "...this one tries to be fair to the Indian (Shawnee) point of view, but what with the inadequacies of the 'B' script, the tedious direction and Hall's thespic inability, it's abysmal."—Brian Garfield in *Western Films A Complete Guide*

"A lackluster Indian Western from veteran quickie producer Katzman, one of the last independent producers to desert Westerns. Set just prior to the War of 1812, Kent's script features Hall as the government agent trying to find out who is turning the Indians' thoughts to rebellion. Silverheels (soon to become Tonto) is the good Indian and Ansara the villain of the piece."—Phil Hardy in *The Western-A Complete Film Reference*

The Broken Chain (Turner Pictures, 1993)

Directed by Lamont Johnson. Screenplay by Earl W. Wallace. Music by Charles Fox. From Ted Turner's Native Americans series. Running time: 93 minutes.

Cast: *Sir William Johnson* Pierce Brosnan, *Joseph Brandt* Eric Schweig, *Seth's wife* Buffy Sainte-Marie, *Peace Maker* Graham Green, *Seth* Wes Studi, with Elaine Bilstad, Kim Snyder, J.C. White Shirt, Floyd Red Crow Westerman and Nathan Chasing His Horse.

The story: Young Mohawk warrior Thayendunega and his friend Lahaheo fight on the British side against the French in the French and Indian War. Together with his

The Broken Chain (Turner Pictures, 1993)—*Top:* Sir William Johnson (Pierce Brosnan) and Joseph Brandt (Eric Schweig) fight the French at Fort Carillon. *Bottom:* Sir William Johnson (Pierce Brosnan) takes over British command after the death of General Prideaux during the attack on Fort Niagara.

brother-in-law, Sir William Johnson, he participates in the taking of Fort Niagara in 1759.

After the war Sir William sends him to school where he learns to become fluent in the English language. He also adapts an English name: Joseph Brandt.

During Ottawa Chief Pontiac's uprising against the whites in 1763, most of the nations of the Iroquois Confederacy fight against Pontiac due to their loyalty to Sir William. However, the Seneca join with Pontiac, and this is the beginning of the breakup of the Confederacy.

At the outbreak of the American Revolution, Joseph Brandt tries to keep the Six Nations united and neutral in the war. But the Oneida turn their back on him and fight with the Americans. When Brandt's life-long friend Lahaheo is killed, Brandt actively sides with the British in the war as an officer in the British Army. In spite of the destruction of the Six Nations Confederacy the Mohawk keep Brandt as their leader.

After the war, Brandt brings his people to the land awarded them in Canada as payment for their loyalty to England.

The Buccaneer (Paramount, 1938)

Produced and directed by Cecil B. DeMille. Screenplay by Edwin Justus Mayer, Harold Lamb, and C. Gardner Sullivan, based on an adaption by Jeanie Macpherson of *Lafitte the Pirate* by Lyle Saxon. Photography by Victor Milner. Music by George Antheil. Running time: 124 minutes.

Cast: *Jean Lafitte* Fredric March, *Gretchen* Francisca Gaal, *Dominique You* Akim Tamiroff, *Anette de Remy* Margot Grahame, *Ezra Peavey* Walter Brennan, *Crawford* Ian Keith, *Dolly Madison* Spring Byington, *Governor Claiborne* Douglas Dumbrille, *Capt. Brown* Robert Barrat, *Andrew Jackson* Hugh Sothern, *Aunt Charlotte* Beulah Bondi, *Beluche* Anthony Quinn, *Marie de Remy* Louis Campbell, *Adm. Cockburn* Montagu Love, *Gen. Ross* Eric Stanley, *Gramby* Fred Kohler, *Capt. Locker* Gilbert Emery, *Capt. McWilliams*

Holmes Herbert, *Madeleine* Evelyn Keyes, *Camden Blount* Francis McDonald, *Lt. Shreve* Frank Melton, *Collector of Port* Stanley Andrews, *Charles* Jack Hubbard and *Capt. Reid* Richard Denning.

The story: Lafitte and his pirates hold a territory of bayous, called Barataria, on the coastland of New Orleans. Lafitte has a strong loyalty to America and he refuses to attack and rob American ships. Lafitte loves the wealthy Anette de Remy.

In 1814, when the British advance to strike against New Orleans, Lafitte and his men join with General Andrew Jackson and beat off the attack. Because of the American gratitude for his support, Lafitte is going to be decorated, but the ceremony is interrupted when news comes in that Lafitte's pirates have captured and burned a ship, and also killed Anette's sister who happened to be onboard. With his honor now destroyed, Lafitte has to leave New Orleans, and he returns to the bayou country and takes up with the adoring Gretchen, an adventurous girl who loves him.

Notes: The film was shot on locations in New Iberia, LA, where the Mississippi bayous were recreated. The original Battle of New Orleans was fought at the Chalmette Fields, east of the city on January 8, 1815. Having similarities in landscape pictures, Balwin Oaks was selected for staging of the battle.

Paramount used an extensive budget to do the movie and to make it an epic. Two square-rigged warships and three gunboats from the period of 1814 were chartered for authenticity. The cast and crew totaled almost 10,000, and 63 functional iron cannons were specially built by Paramount's property shop for the movie.

The film did not become the epic the studio intended it to be but it had favorable production values and it has the large-scale romantic adventurous DeMille touch. The best moments in the film are those of battle mass action.

"...Numerous contemporary reviews applauded Tamiroff's comic performance as superior to that of March."—*American Film Institute Catalogue*

The Buccaneer (Paramount, 1958)

Produced by Henry Wilcoxon. Directed by Anthony Quinn. Supervised by Cecil B. DeMille. Screenplay by Jesse L. Lasky, Jr., and Bernice Mosk, from a screenplay by Harold Lamb, Edwin Justus Mayer and C. Gardner Sullivan; based on an adaptation by Jeannie Macpherson of *Lafitte the Pirate* by Lyle Saxon. Photography by Loyal Griggs in VistaVision/Technicolor. Music by Elmer Bernstein. Running time: 121 minutes.

Cast: *Jean Lafitte* Yul Brynner, *Andrew Jackson* Charlton Heston, *Bonnie Brown* Clair Bloom, *Dominique Yoy* Charles Boyer, *Annette Claiborne* Inger Stevens, *Ezra Peavey* Henry Hull, *Gov. Claiborne* E.G. Marshall, *Mercier* Lorne Greene, *Capt. Rumbo* Ted de Corsia, *Collector of Port* Douglas Dumbrille, *Capt. Brown* Robert F. Simon, *Scipio* Sir Lancelot, *Cariba* Fran Jeffries, *Deacon* John Dierkes, *Sentry* Ken Miller, *Pyke* George Mattews, *Capt. McWilliams* Leslie E. Bradley, *Gramby* Bruce Gordon, *Commandore Patterson* Barry Kelley, *Capt. Lockyer* Robert Warwick, *Beluche* Steven Marlo, *Whipple* James Todd, *Miggs* Jerry Hartleben, *Customs Inspector* Onslow Stevens, *Marie Claiborne* Theodora Davitte, *Tripes* Reginald Sheffield, *Lt. Shreve* Wally Richard, *Wench* Iris Adrian, *Creole Officer* James Seay and *Col. Butler* Stephen Chase.

The story: In 1814, Washington has fallen and the British are planning on attacking New Orleans. In the preparation of the defense, General Andrew Jackson real-

The Buccaneer (Paramount, 1958)—Lafitte (Yul Brynner, *right*) is "challenging" one of his pirates.

The Buccaneer—Andrew Jackson (Charlton Heston) behind the cannon fights the British at New Orleans with the help of his aide, backwoodsman Ezra Peavey (Henry Hull).

izes that he needs to be able to control the water routes to the city. The pirate Lafitte and his men control Barataria, a territory of bayous which separate the ocean from New Orleans.

When learning that the Americans try to secure gold by sending it overseas to Spain on the ship *Corinthian*, some of the pirates break Lafitte's rule of not attacking American ships, and board and sink the ship. The governor's daughter, Marie Claiborne, who is on board the ship, is killed.

The British try to win over Lafitte against the Americans, but Lafitte, who is trying to win the heart of Governor Claiborne's other daughter, Annette, decides to support the American side.

For control of the approaches to New Orleans, the Americans attack Barataria. This raises doubts with Lafitte about his choice of supporting Andrew Jackson. Lafitte meets with Jackson and negotiates an agreement in which he and his men, captured during the American attack on the pirate town, are released in exchange for arms and their support against the British attack. The British attack New Orleans but with Lafitte's help the Americans defeat them.

Lafitte is blamed for the capture of the *Corinthian* and the death of Marie Claiborne, and is threatened with hanging. He is, however, saved by Andrew Jackson, but he has to depart New Orleans. Leaving Annette behind, he takes off on the sea together with pirate girl Bonnie Brown, who is in love with him.

Notes: Paramount produced its first version of **The Buccaneer** in 1938 with

Cecil DeMille as director. When the company remade the story 20 years later DeMille was used as adviser to producer Henry Wilcoxon during the making of the movie. This would be DeMille's last involvement in film production.

"The Buccaneer is still a handsome, Technicolored spectacle full of sound but little fury, replete with picturesque vignettes..."
They all indicate that the age of Jackson was colorful and crowded, if not precisely the greatest show on earth."—A.H. Weiler in *The New York Times*

"Lackluster remake of the 1938 film ... Brynner is vary dashing and powerful as the pirate Lafitte and Heston very strong as the simple, yet forceful Andrew Jackson.... A climactic battle scene is excitingly well-handled, but ... direction is sluggish and the narrative a bit sloppy."—*The Motion Picture Guide*

Buying Manhattan (Edison, 1909)

Length: 400 feet.

Captain John Smith and Pocahontas (Eclipsa/UA, 1953)

Directed by Lew Landers. Screenplay by Aubrey Wisberg and Jack Pollexsen. Running time: 74 minutes.

Cast: *John Smith* Anthony Dexter, *Pocahontas* Jody Lawrence, *Rolfe* Robert Clark, *Wingfield* James Seay, *Powhatan* Douglas Dumbrille, *Kemp* Eric Colmar, *Macklin* William Cottrell, *King James* Anthony Eustrel, *Fleming* Alan Hale, Jr., *Nantaquas* Stephen Menken, *Opechanco* Stuart Randall and *Turnbull* Henry Rowland.

The story: In 1607 Captain John Smith is made governor of the new English settlement, Jamestown. One of his first undertakings is to negotiate a peace treaty with Chief Powhatan. His first meeting with Powhatan's daughter Pocahontas comes when he surprises her taking a bath in a lake. The two start a love affair.

Later a conflict develops between the whites and the Indians, which leads to war. Smith and some of his men are captured by the Indians and brought before Powhatan.

When threatened with death, Pocahontas saves Smith and later also marries him. Powhatan agrees to stop the hostilities against the settlers as long as the whites leave the Indians alone. The harmony is, however, disturbed by Wingfield, whom Smith is supposed to replace as leader. He attempts to find gold on Indian land, initiating troubles with them again. Wingfield is killed and Smith is wounded. Smith has to leave the colony on a ship back to England. Before leaving he asks his friend Rolfe to take over the leadership of the colony. In England, Smith later learns that Pocahontas, who has believed him to be dead, has married Rolfe.

Notes: This low-budget film was also released under the title **Burning Arrows**.

"This 1953 filmatization of the story is a bit too earthbound for its subject matter.... One of the few saving graces ... is that it doesn't bend over backward striving for political correctness, as did the recent Disney animated feature"—*All-Media Guide*

"Not bad, just nothing in particular to recommend it."—*TVgen*

The Capture of Fort Ticonderoga (Edison, 1911)

Directed by J. Searle Dawley. Length: 1,000 feet.

Cast: James Gordon, Guy Coombs, Rolinda Bainbridge, Herbert Prior and Robert Bower.

Cardigan (American Releasing Corp., 1922)

Produced by Messmore Kendell. Directed by John W. Noble. Based on Robert William Chambers's *Cardigan* (A.L. Burt, 1901). Adopted for the screen by Robert W. Chambers. Photography by John S. Stumar, Ned Van Buren and Max Schneider.

Cast: *Michael Cardigan* William Collier, Jr., *Silver Heels* Betty Carpenter, *Sir William Johnson* Thomas Cummings, *Captain Butler* William Pike, *Lord Dunmore*

Cardigan (American Releasing Corp., 1922)—Young Michael Cardigan (William Collier, Jr.) meets and falls in love with Silver Heels (Betty Carpenter).

Charles Graham, *Marie Hamilton* Madeleine Lubbety, *Lady Shelton* Hattie Delore, *Sir John Johnson* Louis Dean, *The Weazel* Colin Campbell, *Jack Mount* Jere Austin, *Chief Logan* Frank Montgomery, *Dulcina* Eleanor Griffith, *Quider* Dick Lee, *Colonel Cresap* Jack Johnston, *Molly Brant* Florence Short, *Patrick Henry* George Loeffler, *John Hancock* William Willis, and *Paul Revere* Austin Hume.

The story: In Johnstown, New York, two years before the American Revolution, young Michael Cardigan, an unwilling subject of King George III, falls in love with the English governor's ward, who is known as Silver Heels. At the outbreak of hostilities between the Colonists and the Indians, Michael is sent by Sir William Johnson to carry a peace message to the Cayugas but is intercepted by the British. He is saved from being burned at the stake by an Indian runner. In Lexington, Cardigan is admitted to the secret councils of the Minutemen, where he meets Patrick Henry, John Hancock and Paul Revere and joins in the cause for liberty. Following the famous ride of Paul Revere, the battles of Lexington and Concord prefigure the retreat of the Redcoats; Cardigan rescues his sweetheart from the advances of Captain Butler, then promises to return to her at the end of the war.

Notes: "In settings and costumes the picture seems authentic.... But it is not smooth in continuity, it is excessively wordy and it has little pictorial expressiveness. The acting, when not inadequate is only moderately good."—*The New York Times*

Cardigan—Michael Cardigan (William Collier, Jr.) is threatened with burning at the stake by British Captain Butler (William Pike) and the Cayugas.

Chingachgook—Die Grosse Schlange (DEFA, 1967)

Produced by Dorothea Hildebrandt. Directed by Richard Groschopp. Screenplay by Wolfgand Ebeling and Richard Groschopp, based on James Fenimore Cooper's *The Deerslayer*. Photography by Otto Hanisch. Music by Wilhelm Neel. Length: 91 minutes.

Cast: Gojke Mitic, Rolf Römer, Helmut Screiber, Jurgen Frohriep and Iilo Grahn.

The Story: Chingachgook's bride Wahtawah is captured and taken away by Hurons. Chingachgook and his friend Deerslayer go after the war party to free Wahtawah. On their track they obtain information that the English are trying to anger the Hurons against the Delawares to gain assurance of their own victory.

At Lake Otsega, Deerslayer and Chingachgook meet with trapper Tom Hutter, who lives a peaceful life there with his daughter. The British and the French are paying good prize money for Indian scalps. Greed for money causes Tom Hutter to join another trapper, Hurry Harry, to start raiding and murdering Indians.

British troops march to attack the Huron village, but the tribes unite and fight together against the white intruders and the attack is repulsed. Wahtawah is free and Chingachgook can marry her.

Notes: Between 1966 and 1983, twelve East German Indian films were produced by the DEFA movie company. Three of the movies dealt with subjects from the Colonial period of American history; **Chingachgook—Die Grosse Schlange**, 1967, (**Chin-**

gachgook, the Great Snake), Tecumseh (1972) and **Blauvogel (Blue Bird)** 1983.

The films were co-produced with studios in Yugoslavia, Romania, the Soviet Union, Bulgaria and Cuba. Most of the exterior filming was done in the mountains of Yugoslavia.

In general all the films in the series were part of the Communist propaganda against United States at the time. Native Americans were portrayed as proud heroes, being mishandled and pursued by greedy, power-hungry white Americans, the common enemy. Usually the films were co-produced by Hans-Joachim Wallstein, who together with a selected production crew kept watchful eyes on the political message in the movies.

The audience generally appreciated the movies and they also served the purpose of calming the frustrated East German citizens and satisfying their desire for Western entertainment. The impact on children served the filmmakers' purposes; when playing nobody wanted to be a "bad cowboy," all wanted to be the "good Indian."

In contrast to the West German Karl May's westerns, produced during the same time, Eastern movies tried to be historically correct. East German filmmakers performed extensive research to describe the historical events as truly as possible.

Chingachgook—Die Grosse Schlange in some instances pays more attention to historic details than to entertainment.

Chronicle of 1812 (Emmeritus Productions Inc.)

Produced by Michael MacLaverty. Written and directed by Allen Levine. Photography by Naomiko Kurita. Music by Paul Zaza. Cast: Craig Williams, Simon Henri, Alexandra Brown, Mark Lyle, Jon Austin, Tom Nursalt, Kevin May, Geoff Smither, Peter Hurley and Gregory Westland.

The Story: Canadian TV feature about espionage during General Dearborn's campaign against Kingston and Montreal during the War of 1812.

The Conspiracy of Pontiac (or At Fort Detroit in 1763) (Kalem, 1910)

Directed by Sidney Olcott. Length: 975 feet.

Notes: The story in this picture was based on *History of the Conspiracy of Pontiac* by Francis Parkman.

Courageous Mr. Penn (Esquire Films, Hoffberg/BN, 1941)

Produced by Richard Vernon. Directed by Lance Comfort. Screenplay by Anatole de Grunwald, based on the book *William Penn* by C.E. Vulliamy. Produced in England with the title **Penn of Pennsylvania**. Running time: 78 minutes.

Cast: *William Penn* Clifford Ewans, *Gugliema* Deborah Kerr, *Charles II* Dennis Arundell, *Chaplain* Aubrey Mallalieu, *Lord Arlington* D.J. Williams, *Lord Cecil* O.B. Clarence, *Fox* James Harcourt, *Adm. Penn* Charles Carson, *Samuel Pepys* Henry Oscar, *Elton* Max Adrian, *Bindle* John Stuart, *Cook* Marie O'Neill, *Bushell* Edward Rigby, *Lord Mayor* Joss Ambler, *Ford* J.H. Roberts, *Captain* Edmund Willard, *Holme* Percy Marmont, *Indian Chief* Gibb McLaughlin, *Cockle* Herbert Lomas and *Mate* Gus McNaughton.

The story: In London in 1667, William Penn, the son of an admiral to whom the King owes money, allies himself with Quakers and starts talking about religious freedom. This causes his father to repudiate him. On his missions to seek adherents, he meets with Lord William Pennington's daughter Gugliema, who develops an interest in him and his ideas. In his crusade for religious freedom, with speeches on the equality of man and freedom of thought, he and other Quakers are arrested and brought to trial in the Old Bailey in 1670.

After serving a sentence in jail he catches up with Gugliema and their love results in marriage. She suggests that he leave the country to develop his free spirit. Penn looks up the King (George II), and asks him to give him land in America in exchange for the money the king owed his deceased father.

Leaving his wife behind, Penn and other persecuted Quakers leave England for America in 1682 and start a colony, which they name Pennsylvania. In contrast to many other colonists, Penn and his ardent followers treat the Indians well, and he signs a peace treaty with the Algonquin Indians.

To secure the new colony, Penn returns to the mother country. He arrives in England just in time to learn of the death of his diseased wife. With the broken hope of bringing his wife to the New World, Penn returns to Pennsylvania.

Notes: "...Anatole De Grundwald, has not drawn this subject true to life, nor has he revealed anything more about the man than one may find in the most inadequate of elementary school histories.

"...*Courageous Mr. Penn* definitely is not one of England's better film efforts."—T.M.P. in *The New York Times*

The Courtship of Miles Standish
(Charles Ray Productions, 1923)

Directed by Frederick Sullivan. Screenplay by Al Ray. Photography by George Rizard. Length: nine reels.

Cast: *John Alden* Charles Ray, *Priscilla Mullens* Enid Bennett, *Miles Standish* E. Alyn Warren, *John Carver* Sam De Grasse, *William Bradford* Norval Mac Gregor, *Edward Winslow* Thomas Holding, *Isac Allerton* Frank Farrington, *John Howland* William Sullivan, with Tom Wilson, Norval McGregor, Hector Dion, James McElhern, Raymond Haller, Max Asher, Sidney Bracy, Marion Dixon, Charlotte Pierce, Gertrud Pedler, Adamae Vaughn, Robert Korton, Al Richmond and Ted Stewards.

The story: In 1620, a pilgrim sailing ship, *Mayflower*, leaves Southampton on a journey across the Atlantic for the New World. An adventurer, John Alden, is leader of the expedition. The sea journey proves to be rough with Alden's friend John

Howland being swept overboard during a storm.

Landing at what is now Plymouth, Massachusetts, on the new continent, the pilgrims face all kinds of hardships including attacks by Indians. But peace is restored with the Natives and a peace pipe is smoked during the first Thanksgiving.

A romance evolves between John Alden and Puritan maiden Priscilla, when actually he is proposing for her hand on behalf of his soldier friend Miles Standish. Priscilla, mute with amazement and sorrow, asks him to speak for himself.

Notes: This historical drama is based on Henry Wadsworth Longfellow's poem. Charles Ray, in the lead role as John Adams, also produced the film. The film turned out to be a fiasco and Charles Ray ended up bankrupted by the adventure.

"Oodles of money were spent on this costumer, but seemingly no effort was exerted to make the story interesting and involving."—*All-Media-Guide*

At the time of its release *The New York Times* was favorable in its criticism:

"There are numerous scenes in this beautiful production that call forth the undying lines of this glorious epic."

Daniel Boone (Chronicles of America, 1923)

Directed by Claude H. Mitchell. Screenplay by Esther Williard Bates, based on *The Pioneers of the Old Southwest* by Constance Lindsay Skinner.

Presented by Yale University Press.

Daniel Boone (RKO, 1936)

Produced by George A. Hirliman. Directed by David Howard. Screenplay by Daniel Jarret, based on a story by Edgecumb Pinchon. Photography by Frank Good. Music by Abe Meyer. Running time: 77 minutes.

Cast: *Daniel Boone* George O'Brien, *Virginia Randolph* Heather Angel, *Simon Girty* John Carradine, *Captain Marlow* Ralph Forbes, *Pompey* Clarence Muse,

Daniel Boone (RKO, 1936)—Daniel Boone (George O'Brien) is overlooking the tending to the wounded during the siege of Fort Boonesborough.

Black Eagle George Regas, *Derrick* Dickie Jones, and *Sir John Randolph* Huntley Gordon.

The story: In 1775, Simon Girty, a white renegade and Indian leader, terrorizes settlements on the Western frontier. In Yadkin, North Carolina, 30 colonists with their families decide to move west into the wilderness with Daniel Boone as their guide to Kentucky.

After some hostile encounters with Indians, the colonists reach Kentucky where they decide to build a fort and settle down. The fort is named Boonesborough after Daniel. A romance develops between Daniel and Virginia Randolph, daughter of Sir John.

Simon Girty unites five tribes and incites them to attack the new fort built by the settlers. The attack lasts for nine days,

and with the settlers' water and ammunition running low and the fort set on fire, the situation looks bad. Suddenly, however, it starts to rain, which puts out the fire, and the Indians scatter. In a final fight that ends in a river, Daniel defeats Girty.

A group of treacherous Virginian aristocrats usurp the settlers' land after it has been cleared and made livable. The colonists, led by Daniel, decide to move farther west to find a new place to settle down.

Notes: Daniel Boone is perhaps the best-known frontiersman in American history. He was borne in Exeter Township, near present day Reading, Pennsylvania, on October 22, 1734. In 1750 the family left Pennsylvania for the Western country, and settled in Rowan County, North Carolina, where Boone took up hunting as his business.

Daniel Boone—Lobby card: Daniel (George O'Brien) captured by hostile Indians.

During the French and Indian War, Boone fought with the British and participated in General Braddock's disastrous defeat in his campaign to strike against French-held Fort Duquesne.

In 1756 he married Rebecca Bryan and settled in Rowan County. With Rebecca he eventually had 10 children. In 1761, Daniel participated in a campaign against the Cherokees. In 1769, on a hunting trip, Shawnees captured him. After two years with the Indians in Kentucky, he returned home.

Later in 1773 he led a party of settlers to Kentucky, but was turned back by an Indian attack at the Cumberland Gap. Working for the Transylvania Company he, however, returned to Kentucky in 1775 and founded Boonesborough, and later the same year brought his family to the area. During his stay in Kentucky, Boone con-

tinuously ran into problems with the natives and was once more captured by the Shawnees, but managed to escape.

In 1779 he led a large party of emigrants to Kentucky and settled Boone's Station, north of the Kentucky River. Later Boone relocated his family to Limestone, on the Ohio River, and took up tavern keeping, surveying and land speculating. This would make him a wealthy person for a period. He owned 100,000 acres of land, but lost it in a series of lawsuits.

The area Boone once settled became too crowded for him, and in 1799 he moved to Missouri. He died on September 26, 1820.

Perhaps the best film about the frontier legend was done by RKO in the 1936 version of **Daniel Boone**. The story in the movie deals only with an episode of Boone's adventurous life when he led settlers from North Carolina across the Cumberland Mountains to the wilds of Kentucky.

Before appearing as the lead role in **Daniel Boone**, George O'Brien had made a series of westerns for Fox. By 1935, Fox, however, wanted to get out of the sagebrush business, and former Fox producer Sol Lessler, now working for RKO brought over O'Brien to do a series of RKO westerns, of which **Daniel Boone** was one.

"...George lost no time in making a deal with RKO which brought him aboard under Lesser. Their collaboration resulted in what remains as the best historical documentation of Daniel Boone's life ... the entire film enjoyed restrained performances..."—K. Lahue in *Riders of the Range*

The New York Times also praised the actors' performances in the movie:

"...George O'Brien manages to project Daniel Boone as a shy, unassuming adventurer, which is presumably what the man was. John Carradine plays Simon Girthy with all the malice he can command, and sets a new high in facial contortions."

The film was made on a surprisingly large scale, with a fair amount of comedy included in the story. George O'Brien did a noticeable performance in the movie and the O'Brien westerns for RKO took a distinct upswing for the genre for the company.

John Carradine did a masterful appearance in the film in his role as villain Simon Girty, who incites the Indians against the white settlers. He would later have a similar role appearance as a Tory leader arousing Iroquois against settlers in the Mohawk Valley in John Ford's **Drums Along the Mohawk**.

Not going too deep into documentary history, producer George Hirliman wanted the film to concentrate more on action. *Variety was* in favor of this:

"...It's Indian opera à la mode.... George O'Brien, Heather Angel, John Carradine, George Regas and Clarence Muse ... all play their roles as the story was written-phoney, with loads of action. But the kids won't know the diff."

Daniel Boone (Walt Disney TV Show, 1960-61)

Produced by Walt Disney and Bill Anderson. Directed by Lewis R. Foster. Story and teleplay by David Victor, based on the book *Daniel Boone* by John Bakeless. 4 episodes @ 52 minutes.

Cast: *Daniel Boone* Dewey Martin, *Rebecca Boone* Mala Powers, Terry Thompson, Richard Banke, and Kevin Corcoran.

Episode 1: "A Warrior's Path"

Daniel Boone meets a wandering trader who tells him about an unknown Indian trail over the mountains, which leads to the rich country of Kentucky. This stimulates Daniel's interest, and he assembles a scouting party to go and find out. Along the way they run into a Shawnee war party.

Episode 2: "And Chase the Buffalo"

In Virginia the ruling British are raising taxes, which causes violence and rebellion among the colonists. To pay his taxes Daniel is forced to sell his farm and he decides to leave for Kentucky with or without his wife.

Episode 3: "The Wilderness Road"

Episode 4: "The Promised Land"

Notes: With **Daniel Boone** on ABC's *Walt Disney Presents* show, the studio hoped to ride on their previous success with **Davy Crockett**. Actually, when Disney was in the planning process of doing **Crockett**, it also had **Daniel Boone** as an alternative on the script board. Going for **Crockett** proved to be a smart choice.

Disney's **Daniel Boone** was a reasonably well-produced series, even if it did not reached the heights of **Crockett**. Four one-hour episodes were produced in color, with the first episode airing on December 4, 1960. Later, 20th Century–Fox would do the "real" **Daniel Boone** hit series by bringing in **Crockett** hero Fess Parker to play Boone. The Fess Parker **Daniel Boone** series ran for six seasons in 165 episodes.

Daniel Boone (Arcola-Fesspar-Fox/ TV, 1964–70)

165 episodes @ 52 minutes each.

First season (1964-65)

Regular cast: *Daniel Boone* Fess Parker, *Rebecca Boone* Patricia Blair, *Jemima Boone* Veronica Cartwright, *Israel Boone* Darby Hinton, *Mingo* Ed Ames, *Yadkin* Albert Salmi, and *Cincinnatus* Dallas McKennon.

Episode 1: "Ken-Tuck-E" (Pilot Episode)

Written by Borden Chase. Directed by George Marshall. Produced by Aaron Rosenberg.

Guest players: Bobby Horan, Robert Simon and Arch Johnson.

George Washington sends Daniel and Yadkin into the hunting grounds of four Indian nations to find a site for a fort.

Episode 2: "Tekawitha McLeod"

Written by Paul King. Directed by Thomas Carr. Produced by Vincent M. Fennely.

Guest players: *Tekawitha* Lynn Loring, with Edna Skinner and Cris Alcaide.

Irony reigns supreme as the settlers refuse to pay the ransom for an Indian princess.

Episode 3: "My Brother's Keeper"

Written by Paul King. Directed by John English. Produced by Vincent M. Fennely.

Guest players: Ford Rainey, Peter Coe and Adam Williams.

Yadkin insists that Mingo led a band of Creeks who wounded him and killed an unarmed Cherokee.

Episode 4: "The Family Fluellen"

Written by Herman Miller. Directed by Byron Paul. Produced by Vincent F. Fennely.

Guest players: Bethel Leslie, Donald Loseley and Harold J. Stone.

Daniel tries to discourage a widowed Welshwoman bent on settling in hostile Indian Territory with her three children.

Episode 5: "The Choosing"

Written by Paul King. Directed by Thomas Carr. Produced by Vincent M. Fennely.

Guest players: David Brian, Richard Devon and Larry Chance.

A trip into the wilderness takes a nightmarish turn for Daniel and Jemima. Daniel wounds himself with an axe and Indians kidnap Jemima.

Episode 6: "Lac Duquesne"

Written by Paul Savage. Directed by Thomas Carr. Produced by Vincent M. Fennely.

Guest players: *Lac Duquesne* Emile Genest, with James Griffith and Barry Kelley.

Daniel, Yadkin and Mingo pursue river pirate Lac Duquesne, who stole a shipment of rifles from Boonesborough settlers.

Episode 7: "The Sound of Wings"

Written by John Hawkins. Directed By Harry Harris. Produced by Vincent M. Fennely.

Guest players: Michael Rennie, Frank de Kova and Michael Pate.

A British officer persuades the Indians to back up the British.

Episode 8: "A Short Walk to Salem"

Written by Paul King. Directed by Thomas Carr and Harry Harris. Produced by Vincent M. Fennely.

Guest players: *Simon Girty* James Waterfield, with Charles Briggs and Dean Stanton.

Simon Girty and his three sons set their greedy sites on the Boonesborough settlers' furs.

Episode 9: "The Sisters O'Hannrahan"

Written by David Duncan. Directed by John English. Produced by Vincent M. Fennely.

Guest players: Fay Spain, Nina Shipman and Don Megowan.

Yadkin gets involved with an auctioneer and ends up owning two indentured servant girls.

Episode 10: "Pompey"

Written by David Duncan. Directed by Joseph H. Lewis. Produced by Vincent M. Fennely.

Guest players: *Pompey* Brock Peters, with Peter Whitney and Joe Perry.

Daniel suspects a runaway slave, Pompey, of theft.

Episode 11: "Mountain of the Dead"

Written by David Duncan. Directed by Byron Paul. Produced by Vincent M. Fennely.

Guest players: Leslie Nelson, Kelley Thorsden and Charles Barne.

A man Boone believed dead and some British arrive, all wanting to be led to site of an Indian massacre.

Episode 12: "Not in Our Stars"

Written by John Hawkins. Directed by John English. Produced by Paul King.

Guest players: *Lord Dunsmore* Walter Pidgeon, with John Vivyan and Albert Sofaer.

The British General, Lord Dunsmore, orders the settlers of Boonesborough out of Kentucky within 30 days, claiming he owns the right of the territory.

Episode 13: "The Hostages"

Written by Carey Wilber. Directed by George Sherman. Produced by Paul King.

Guest players: Madlyn Rhue, Rhodes Reason and Ellen Corby.

A Loyalist officer is leading a band of Seneca who kidnap Rebecca and burn the Boone cabin.

Episode 14: "The Returning"

Written by Don Ingalls. Directed by John English. Produced by Paul King.

Guest players: *Will Carey* Pat Hingle, with George Lewis and Robert G. Anderson.

Delight turns to dismay when Will Carey arrives laden with furs, which he has obtained by killing three Cherokees.

Episode 15: "The Prophet"

Written by Carey Wilber. Directed by Robert Webb. Produced by Jules Schermer.

Guest players: John Russell, Kevin Hagen and Patrica Huston.

"The Prophet," an Indian holy man, has a plan to drive the settlers out of Kentucky.

Episode 16: "The First Stone"

Written by Theodore Apstein. Directed by Harry Harris. Produced by Paul King.

Guest players: Geraldine Brooks, Kurt Russell and Gene Evans.

Daniel gives shelter to a woman and her son. The woman might be a witch.

Episode 17: "A Place of 1,000 Spirits"

Written by David Humphreys Miller. Directed by George Sherman. Produced by Paul King.

Guest players: Macdonald Carey, Claude Akins and Ted White.

Daniel goes after Shawnees who abducted and terrified a British officer at a Salem tavern.

Episode 18: "The Sound of Fear"

Written by Dick Nelson. Directed by Harry Harris. Produced by Paul King.

Guest players: *Simon Perigore* Dan Duryea, with Peter Duryea and Jack Elam.

Simon Perigore and his murderous brood imprison Daniel. He wants Daniel's help to start an Indian War.

Episode 19: "The Price of Friendship"

Written by Frank Chase. Directed by John English. Produced by Paul King.

Guest players: Kurt Russell, Lloyd Nolan and Myrna Fahey.

Daniel meets some river pirates. They steal all they can, but they do not hurt anyone.

Episode 20: "The Quietists"

Written by Herman Groves. Directed by George Sherman. Produced by Paul King.

Guest players: Alexander Scourby, Eve McVeagh and Mary Jayne Saunders.

An unarmed Quaker family moves to a farm in dangerous Cherokee country.

Episode 21: "The Devil's Four"

Written by Herman Groves. Directed by David Butler. Produced by Paul King.

Guest players: Sean McClory, James Best and Charles Horvath.

Yadkin hires four manacled felons to drive wagons through the bandit-infested Cumberland Gap.

Episode 22: "The Reunion"

Written by Rita Lakin. Directed by George Marshall. Produced by George Sherman.

Guest players: John McIntire, Marvin Bradley and Hank Patterson.

After years of searching, Rebecca Boone, married to Daniel, is found by her father. Rebecca will not have anything to do with her itinerant peddler father.

Episode 23: "The Ben Franklin Encounter"

Written by David Duncan. Directed by Nathan Juran. Produced by George Sherman.

Guest players: Edward Mulhare, Anna Lee and James Forrest.

After a trip to Virginia, Daniel tells his family how he and Mingo almost got themselves shipped off to England after having met with the famous colonial insurgent.

Episode 24: "Four-Leaf Clover"

Written by Preston Wood. Directed by John English. Produced by George Sherman.

Guest players: George Gobel, Frank de Kova and Dick Wessel.

A new inept schoolteacher appears at Boonesborough.

Episode 25: "Cain's Birthday (Part One)"

Written by Carey Wilber. Directed by Paul Landres. Produced by George Sherman.

Guest players: *Colonel Michelet* Cesare Danova, with Ted De Corsia and Connie Gilchrist.

Daniel and his men surrender to an Indian war party when working at a salt-making camp. Only women and children are available to defend the fort.

Episode 26: "Cain's Birthday (Part Two)"

Written by Carey Wilber. Directed by Paul Landres. Produced by George Sherman.

Guest players: *Colonel Michelet* Cesare Donova, Ted De Corsia, and Connie Gilchrist.

With water running low and with no help in sight, the besieged defenders at Boonesbourgh see little possibility to defend the fort, especially when French colonel Michelet blows up the fort's powder magazine.

Episode 27: "Daughter of the Devil"

Written by Stephen Lorad. Directed by Joseph Sargent. Produced by George Sherman.

Guest players: Orville Sherman, Pearl Sherman and Norman Levitt.

Superstition breeds hysteria when the people of Boonesborough suspect that a beautiful wanderer is a witch.

Episode 28: "Doll of Sorrow"

Written by Herman Miller. Directed by Paul Landres. Produced by George Sherman.

Guest players: Eddie Little Sky, Adrienne Hayes and Edward Binns.

A tradesman causes problems for Daniel, who feels responsible for the peddler's loss of all his merchandise.

Episode 29: "The Courtship of Jericho Jones"

Written and directed by Nathan Juran. Produced by George Sherman.

Guest players: Robert Logan, Anne Helm and Joe Canutt.

The courtship of Jericho Jones threatens to disturb the Indian-white relationship when Jericho elopes with a Creek princess.

Season 2 (1965-1966)

Regular cast: *Daniel Boone* Fess Parker, *Rebecca Boone* Patricia Blair, *Jemima Boone* Veronica Cartwright, *Israel Boone* Darby Hinton, *Mingo* Ed Ames, *Cincinnatus* Dallas McKennon and J*ericho Jones* Robert Logan.

Episode 30: "Empire of the Lost"

Written by Herman Groves. Directed by Nathan Juran. Produced by George Sherman.

Guest players: *Colonel Worthing* Edward Mulhare, with George Backman and Tom Browne Henry.

British Colonel Marcus Worthing evacuates Fort Boonesborough, claiming he is battling a rebellion. Daniel arrives from one of his journeys to face the situation that Worthing wants him to turn over the fort.

Episode 31: "The Tortoise and the Hare"

Written by D.D. Beauchamp. Directed by George Sherman. Produced by George Sherman.

Guest players: Orville Sherman, Laurie Mann and James Griffith.

Settlers have bet on Daniel in an annual foot race contest with the Indians. He, however, sprains an ankle.

Episode 32: "The Mound Builders"

Written by Clyde Ware. Directed by Nathan Juran. Produced by George Sherman.

Guest players: Henry Silvia and Simon Oakland.

A stranger dressed as an Aztec chieftain is pursued by a party of Shawnees. Daniel and Mingo help the stranger.

Episode 33: "My Name Is Rawls"

Written by William Putman and D.D. Beauchamp. Directed by George Sherman. Produced by George Sherman.

Guest players: Rafer Johnson, Lawrence Montaigne and Harold Goodwin.

Daniel goes after a runaway slave who has been exposed as a fur thief.

Episode 34: "The Old Man and the Cave"

Written by Walter Black. Directed by George Marshall. Produced by George Sherman.

Guest players: Cyril Delvanti, Val Avery and Hal Jon Norman.

Israel Boone is rescuing an old starving Indian from a sacred burial cave. This arouses the wrath of an old Indian medicine man—an old enemy of Boone's.

Episode 35: "The Trek"

Written by Clair Huffaker. Directed by George Sherman. Produced by George Sherman.

Guest players: *John Brenton* Aldo Ray, with John Lupton and Charlie Horvath.

John Brenton, a renegade, sells defective weapons to the Indians. Daniel goes after him when he burns the Indians' camp when they refuse to pay him.

Episode 36: "The Aaron Burr Story"

Written by Raphael Hayes. Directed by Maurice Geraghty. Produced by George Sherman.

Guest players: *Aaron Burr* Leif Erickson, with Michael St. Clair, and Michael Ragan.

Former Vice President Aaron Burr arrives in Boonesborough to hire a guide who can take him to the Cumberland River. Burr hires impressionable young Jericho Jones when Daniel turns him down for the mission.

Episode 37: "The Cry of Gold"

Written by Dick Nelson, M. Finley and D.D. Beauchamp. Directed by Nathan Juran. Produced by George Sherman.

Guest players: *Thomas Crowell* Maxwell Reed, with William O'Connell and Kenneth MacDonald.

Two land surveyors are hindered by Boone in their efforts to buy Boonesborough property. In their frustration they hire English champion boxer Thomas Cromwell to dispose of Daniel.

Episode 38: "The Peace Treaty"

Written by John and Ward Williams. Directed by George Sherman. Produced by George Sherman.

Guest players: Larry Domasin, Peter Oliophant and Liam Redmond.

A Scottish clan builds a settlement on Cherokee hunting ground, against the advice of Daniel. When the Indians threaten to attack, the Highlanders refuse to evacuate their new home.

Episode 39: "The Thanksgiving Story"

Written by Ralph Hayes, Melvin Levy, and D.D. Beauchamp. Directed by George Marshall. Produced by George Sherman.

Guest players: *Chief Gabriel* Rodolfo Acosta, with John McIntire and Abraham Sofaer.

After a hunting trip, Daniel and Jericho return to Boonesborough to celebrate Thanksgiving. The holiday is threatened when a messenger brings news that the Choctaw Chief Gabriel is on the warpath.

Episode 40: "A Rope for Mingo"

Written by Raphael Hayes. Directed by John Florea. Produced by George Sherman.

Guest players: Peter Coe, George Kennedy and Gloria Mannon.

Near a burning wagon Jerico discovers a murdered family. Mingo's knife is buried in one of the victims.

Episode 41: "The First Beau"

Written by Barry Trivers and Raphael Hayes. Directed by John Florea. Produced by George Sherman.

Guest players: *David Ellis* Fabian Forte, with Sam Jaffe and Myron Healey.

Jemima Boone falls in love with young David Ellis when he arrives at Boonesborough, apparently looking for a job. In reality he is casing the fort for his partner in crime.

Episode 42: "Perilous Journey"

Written by Melvin Levey and D.D. Beauchamp. Directed by John Florea. Produced by George Sherman.

Guest players: Alan Napir, Steve Ihnat and Stacy Harris.

Daniel and Rebecca are away on a long-delayed honeymoon. The honeymoon is interrupted by a Continental Army officer who is shot by British agents and Daniel is forced to deliver the officer's presidential message to New Orleans.

Episode 43: "The Christmas Story"

Written by Stephen Lord. Directed by Maurice Geraghty. Produced by George Sherman.

Guest players: Alizia Gur, Valentin de Vargas and Morgan Woodward.

Daniel tries to persuade settlers to shelter an Indian brave and his pregnant wife caught in a blizzard.

Episode 44: "The Tamarack Massacre Affair"

Written By David Duncan and Tom Blackburn. Directed by James B. Clark. Produced by George Sherman.

Guest players: *Madeline Lorne* Dina Merrill, with Robert Lansing and Charles Bateman.

Daniel is negotiating a peace treaty with the Iroquois Indians. Madeline Lorne's claim that the Iroquois are guilty of a massacre of which she is the only survivor obstructs his plans.

Episode 45: "Gabriel"

Written by David Duncan. Directed by Gerd Oswald. Produced by George Sherman.

Guest players: *Captain Francisco* Carlos Romero, with Cesar Romero and Jacqueline Beer.

On a trading journey, Spanish Captain Francisco captures Daniel and Mingo. The Spanish Captain believes that Daniel is Gabrial Lajeune, a French revolutionary wanted by the Spaniards.

Episode 46: "Seminole Territory"

Written by Stephen Lord. Directed by John Florea. Produced by George Sherman.

Guest players: Channing Pollock, Diane Ladd and Leonard Nimoy.

Bounty hunter Simon Hartman is tracking two army deserters. When he finds one of them together with Daniel he believes that Daniel is the other deserter.

Episode 48: "Crisis of Fire"

Written by Lee Loeb and David Duncan. Directed by Bruce Humberstone. Produced by George Sherman.

Guest players: Rhodes Reason, John Crawford and Barbara Knudson.

A Continental ex-officer tries to use the threat of a smallpox epidemic for his own ambition.

Episode 49: "The Gun"

Written by Raphael Hayes. Directed by Robert Totten. Produced by George Sherman.

Guest players: Ted White, Robert Middleton and Warren Vanders.

Daniel Boone (Arcola-Fesspar-Fox/TV, 1964–70)—From episode 45: "Gabriel." Spanish Captain Francisco (Cesar Romero, *right*), Daniel (Fess Parker, *left*) and actor Simon Oakland.

Daniel and Mingo are on a scouting tour in Florida. By mistake they are trespassing on a forbidden Seminole territory. Here they encounter an itinerant magician who dazzles the Indians with his tricks.

Episode 47: "The Deserter"

Written by Robert Bloomfield and D.D. Beauchamp. Directed by Nathan Juran. Produced by George Sherman.

Guest players: *Simon Hartman* Slim Pickens, with Dick Sargent, and Henry Brandon.

Boone has a new rifle made for him in Pennsylvania. Two renegades are trying to force him to guide them through Indian Territory.

Episode 50: "The Prisoner"

Written by Robert Bloomfield. Directed by John Florea. Produced by George Sherman.

Guest players: *Matthew and Edward Eliot* Warren Stevens, *Colonel Richard Calloway* Gregory Morton and Kelton Garwood.

Edward Elliot, a convicted traitor, kidnaps Boone's children. With his hostages Elliot is trying to obtain Daniel's help to murder of Colonel Calloway, who commanded the firing squad in the execution of his brother.

Episode 51: "The Fifth Man"

Written by Jack Guess. Directed by George Sherman. Produced by George Sherman.

Guest players: Cameron Mitchell, John Hoyt and John McLiam.

Daniel is trying to obtain a safe passage through hostile Tuscarora country to carry out an important military mission for Governor Patrick Henry.

Episode 52: "Gun-Barrel Highway"

Written by Tom Blackburn. Directed by John Florea. Produced by George Sherman.

Guest players: John Kellogg, Arthur Space and Dennis Cross.

Daniel is trying to intercede between Shawnee and some road builders who have violated tribal grounds. The mission seems impossible when one of the whites kills an Indian boy.

Episode 53: "The Search"

Written by David Duncan. Directed by Harmon Jones. Produced by George Sherman.

Guest players: Michael Ansara, Douglas V. Fowley and Nita Talbot.

In New Orleans, Daniel is ambushed and robbed. When he is tracing his attackers he gets involved in a search for pirate gold.

Episode 54: "Fifty Rifles"

Written by Raphael Hayes. Directed by John Florea. Produced by George Sherman.

Guest players: Henry Wilcoxon, Tom Fadden and Barbara Pepper.

A renegade former British officer steals rifles and is planning to trade them to Shawnee Indians in exchange for land.

Episode 55: "The Trap"

Written by D.D. Beauchamp. Directed by Gerd Oswald. Produced by George Sherman.

Guest players: Lloyd Bochner, Jack Lambert and Marc Cavell.

Daniel is tracking a renegade who has terrorized his settlement and left Mingo helpless, caught in a bear trap.

Episode 56: "The Accused"

Written by David Duncan. Directed by John Florea. Produced by George Sherman.

Guest players: Joanna Moore, Jerome Thor and L.E. "Buck" Young.

Daniel is unjustly accused of a murder.

Episode 57: "Cibola"

Written by Raphael Hayes. Directed by Gerd Oswald. Produced by George Sherman.

Guest players: *Matty Brenner* Royal Dano, Jose Hector Galindo and Alejandro Rey.

Almost starved to death, old Matty Brenner arrives at Daniel's and Mingo's camp with a boy who is said to live in Cibola, one of the legendary seven cities of gold.

Episode 58: "The High Cumberland (Part I)"

Written by D.D. Beauchamp and Jack Guss. Directed by George Sherman. Produced by George Sherman.

Guest players: *Jim Santee* Armando Silvestre, with Ted White, Jack Williams and Charles Horvath.

In a flashback on Daniel's early life, he meets bondwomen Rebecca Brian on a wagon train on its way to Kentucky. A stranger, Jim Santee, whose life Boone saves, decides to go along with the wagon train after meeting Rebecca.

Episode 59: "The High Cumberland (Part II)"

Written by D.D. Beauchamp and Jack Guss. Directed by George Sherman. Produced by George Sherman.

Guest players: Jack Williams, Robert Terhune and Roy Jenson.

In a narrow canyon, renegades attack Boone's wagon train for supplies.

Season 3 (1966-67)

Regular cast: *Daniel Boone* Fess Parker, *Rebecca Boone* Patricia Blair, *Israel Boone* Darby Hinton, *Mingo* Ed Ames, and *Cincinnatus* Dallas McKennon.

Episode 60: "Dan'l Boone Shot a B'ar"

Written by D.D. Beauchamp. Directed by Alex Nicol. Produced by George Sherman.

Guest players: *Cletus Mott* Slim Pickens, with Claude Hall, and Chick Chandler.

A bear kills Cletus Mott's father and brother. Mott confronts Daniel when he tries to prevent him from killing the bear.

Episode 61: "The Allegiances"

Written by David Duncan. Directed by Earl Bellamy. Produced by George Sherman.

Guest players: Michael Pate, Walter Kray and Pat Hogan.

Cherokees are joining the British to drive Boone's family and other settlers out of the country.

Episode 62: "Goliath"

Written by D.D. Beauchamp. Directed by Barry Shear. Produced by George Sherman.

Guest players: *Otis Cobb* Jack Oakie, with Jerome Cowan, Orville Fisher and Shug Fisher.

Horse trader Otis Cobb is forced by renegades to buy a slave with settler's money. The problem starts when he has to repay them.

Episode 63: "Grizzly"

Written by Raphael Hayes. Directed by William Wiard. Produced by George Sherman.

Guest players: *Big Zack* Jeff York, Harold Goodwin and Percy Helton.

Big Zack is wrongly accused of murder. He meets with Israel during trouble with a bear. Afterward Israel manages to free him of the accusation.

Episode 64: "First in War, First in Peace"

Written by D.D. Beauchamp. Directed by Barry Shear. Produced by George Sherman.

Guest players: *President Washington* Ivor Barry, with Michael Rennie and John Hoyt.

George Washington is going to be murdered in a plot after being invited to Kentucky on a ruse.

Episode 65: "Run a Crooked Mile"

Written by D.D. Beauchamp. Directed by Tony Leader. Produced by George Sherman.

Guest players: Doodles Weaver, Myron Healey and Arthur Hunnicutt.

Israel is taken hostage by a group of renegade whites, and Daniel has to collect a ransom for him.

Episode 66: "The Matchmaker"

Written by D.D. Beauchamp. Directed by Earl Bellamy. Produced by George Sherman.

Guest players: Laurie Main, James J. Griffith and Brenda Benet.

To prevent war between Shawnee and Creek Indians, Daniel and Mingo go on a mission to bring a Creek princess to wed a Shawnee chief's son.

Episode 67: "Onatha"

Written by David Duncan. Directed by Earl Bellamy. Produced by George Sherman.

Guest players: Lila Perry, Alan Baxter and Rayford Barnes.

Onatha, a slave girl, is saved from drowning by Daniel. Daniel and Mingo have to battle two slave hunters who claim ownership of the girl.

Episode 68: "The Losers' Race"

Written by Judith Barrows and D.D. Beauchamp. Directed by William Wiard. Produced by George Sherman.

Guest players: Cameron Mitchell, Richard Devon and Brendan Dillon.

The settlers are facing a problem when an aide to the governor is forcing them to pay a doubtful tax. He is giving them two weeks to pay or they will lose their land.

Episode 69: "The Enchanted Gun"

Written by David Duncan, William L. Stuart and Charles O'Neal. Directed by Bud Springsteen. Produced by George Sherman.

Guest players: *Red Sky* Michael Ansara, with William Tannen, and Robert Wilke.

Daniel is giving his rifle to a Shawnee warrior, Red Sky. He also, however, has to prove that the weapon is not enchanted.

Episode 70: "Requirement for Craw Green"

Written by Sid Harris and William Driskill. Directed by George Sherman. Produced by George Sherman.

Guest players: *Roark Logan* Jeffrey Hunter, with Sabina Scarf, and Maltcolm Atterbury.

Mingo, disguised as a white trapper, goes to Logan's Fort, a place where no Indians are allowed. In the fort he learns that landowner Roark Logan is planning on driving away all the Indians of the country to gain more property.

Episode 71: "The Lost Colony"

Written by Ken Pettus and D.D. Beauchamp. Directed by Alex Nicol. Produced by George Sherman.

Guest players: Joseph Hoover, Buck Taylor and Kathryn Walsh.

In a hidden valley, Daniel and Mingo meet with settlers who claim they are descendants of the people who once colonized Roanoke Island.

Episode 72: "River Passage"

Written by D.D. Beauchamp. Directed by William Witney. Produced by George Sherman.

Guest players: James McCallion, Leif Erickson and Jim Davis.

Daniel is facing an adventurous journey when he is supposed to deliver gunpowder to Boonesborough.

Episode 73: "When a King Is a Pawn"

Written by David Duncan and Willard S. Davis, Jr. Directed by Lesley Selander. Produced by George Sherman.

Guest players: *Prince Charles* Morgan Mason, with Cesare Danova, Hagen Smith, and Lilyan Chauvan.

French Prince Charles is captured to be returned to France and a certain death. He is, however, saved by Daniel and Israel.

Episode 74: "The Symbol"

Written by W.J. Voorhees and David Duncan. Directed by R.G. Springsteen. Produced by George Sherman.

Guest players: Richard Montalban, Jeff Morrow and Carole Cook.

Daniel and Mingo set out to recapture the stolen Liberty Bell.

Episode 75: "The Williamsburg Cannon (Part I)"

Written by D.D. Beauchamp and Raphael Hayes. Directed by William Witney. Produced by George Sherman.

Guest players: Warren Stevens, Booth Colman and Jack Lambert.

Daniel and Mingo are recruiting three backwoodsmen to help an artillery officer transport a heavy cannon through enemy land.

Episode 76: "The Williamsburg Cannon (Part II)"

Written by D.D. Beauchamp and Raphael Hayes. Directed by William Witney. Produced by George Sherman.

Guest players: Tony Epper, George Backman and Richard X. Slattery.

The British are setting up an ambush for Daniel when he and his group are on their way with the heavy cannon to reinforce the Continentals on the frontiers.

Episode 77: "The Wolf Man"

Written by William Driskell. Directed by Earl Bellamy. Produced by George Sherman.

Guest players: R. G. Armstrong, Kenneth Tobey and Don Haggerty.

The question of slavery is brought up in Boonesborough. To decide on the issue, Boone gets involved with a councilman and a frontier man with a pet wolf.

Episode 78: "The Jasper Ledbedder Story"

Written by Martha Wilkerson and Helen McAvity. Directed by William Wiard. Produced by George Herman.

Guest players: *Jasper Ledbedder* Sidney Blackmer, with William Tannen and Abel Fernandez.

Old Jasper Ledbedder tells a story about how Shawnee have captured his family. Daniel and Mingo decide to follow him into hostile country to help. Ledbedder's story is, however, unveiled as a cover for the real reason for his search.

Episode 79: "When I Became a Man, I Put Away Childish Things"

Written by Jack Guss. Directed by Earl Bellamy. Produced by George Sherman.

Guest players: Richard Sargent, Mala Powers, and Harold Goodwin.

While growing up, Israel keeps a deer as a pet. To his sorrow he must see his pet put to death when the animal destroys the crop of a neighbor.

Episode 80: "The Long Way Home"

Written by D.D. Beauchamp. Directed by Earl Bellamy. Produced by George Sherman.

Guest players: *Birch Kendall* William Marshall, with Joel Ashley and Robert Shaw.

An old friend of Daniel, Birch Kendall, is wanted for murder of an Indian chief. Daniel pursues him because there is a risk of an Indian war.

Episode 81: "The Young Ones"

Written by D.D. Beauchamp and Sid Harris. Directed by Gerd Oswald. Produced by George Sherman.

Guest players: Kurt Russell, Clair Wilcox and Frankie Kabott.

Three young survivors of an Indian raid declare to the settlers that Daniel is their father.

Episode 82: "Delo Jones"

Written by Clyde Ware. Directed by Bud Springsteen. Produced by George Sherman.

Guest players: *Delo Jones* Jimmy Dean, with Lyle Bettger, and Eddie Little Sky.

Woodsman Delo Jones is in flight from a murder charge. Knowing that the pursuing officer committed the murder, he asks Daniel for help.

Episode 83: "The Necklace"

Written by David Duncan. Directed by Earl Bellamy. Produced by George Sherman.

Guest players: Philip Carey, Laurie Main and James J. Griffith.

Daniel sets out from New Orleans with a necklace that will free a man who has been wrongly convicted. Three renegades make the journey complicated for Daniel when they want to steal the jewelry.

Episode 84: "Fort West Point"

Written by D.D. Beauchamp. Directed by Gerd Oswald. Produced by George Sherman.

Guest players: *General Hugh Scott* Kent Smith, with Bill Fletcher and Robert Miller Driscoll.

General Scott, commander of West Point, is a traitor and is planning on turning over the fort to the British. His plan is, however, exposed by Daniel.

Episode 85: "Bitter Mission"

Written by James Byrnes. Directed by Bud Springsteen. Produced by George Sherman.

Guest players: William Tannen, Simon Oakland and Arnold Moss.

Although wounded, Daniel is escorting a prisoner on a dangerous journey to prevent a war. The traitor has a plan to overtake Boonesborough by stirring up Virginia against Kentucky.

Episode 86: "Take the Southbound Stage"

Written by D.D. Beauchamp. Directed by Gerd Oswald. Produced by George Sherman.

Guest players: *President John Adams* Torin Thatcher, with Mabel Albertson and Arnold Moss.

Daniel is undertaking a secret mission to free kidnapped President Adams for a sum of ransom money.

Episode 87: "The Fallow Land"

Written by D.D. Beauchamp. Directed by William Witney. Produced by George Sherman.

Guest players: John Ireland, Ralph Maurer and John Lodge.

Three trappers are intruding in Cherokee country. When this may end in an Indian war Daniel sets out to negotiate.

Season 4 (1967-68)

Regular cast: *Daniel Boone* Fess Parker, *Rebecca Boone* Patricia Blair, *Israel Boone* Darby Hinton, *Mingo* Ed Ames, and *Cincinnatus* Dallas McKennon.

Episode 88: "The Ballad of Sidewinder and Cherokee"

Written by Melvin Levey. Directed by Gerd Oswald. Produced by Barney Rosenzweig.

Guest players: Forrest Tucker, Victor Buono and Richard Hoyt.

Daniel and Mingo are trying to recover furs that have been stolen from them by a band of pirates. Mingo, played by Ed Ames, who sang with the Ames Brothers, sings a ballad in this one.

Episode 89: "The Ordeal of Israel Boone"

Written by Paul Playdon. Directed by James B. Clark. Produced by Barney Rosenzweig.

Guest players: Jim Davis, Teddy Eccles and Rory O'Brian.

Wild animals and enemy Indians complicate the task for Israel when he is trying to obtain help for Daniel, who has been snake bitten.

Episode 90: "The Renegade"

Written by Merwin Gerard, Melvin Levy and Rich Husky. Directed by William Wiard. Produced by Barney Rosenzweig.

Guest players: Ric Natoli, Gregory Walcott and Phyllis Avery.

A renegade is trying to retake his child from his adoptive parents. Daniel and Mingo intervene.

Episode 91: "Tanner"

Written by Raphael Hayes. Directed by John Newland. Produced by Barney Rosenzweig.

Guest players: Neville Brand, James Dobson and James Anderson.

Israel has to live through a night of terror due to a frightened outcast.

Episode 92: "Beaumarchais"

Written by Richard Collins and Merwin Gerard. Directed by Arthur Nadel. Produced by Barney Rosenzweig.

Guest players: *Beaumarchais* Maurice Evans, with Robert Wolders and Hugh "Slim" Langtry.

A traveling theater group headed by Shakespearean actor Beaumarchais is smuggling gold through British lines.

Episode 93: "The King's Shilling"

Written by Joel Oliansky. Directed by Ida Lupino. Produced by Barney Rosenzweig.

Guest players: Barbara Hersey, Robie Porter and Jeff Pomerantz.

Open warfare is threatening in the colony. Daniel intervenes to prevent two planned executions, which are the cause of the unrest.

Episode 94: "The Inheritance"

Written by David Duncan. Directed by Nathan Juran. Produced by Barney Rosenzweig.

Guest players: Peter Crowcroft, Edwin Mills and Royal Dano.

Rebecca inherits an old mansion that causes unpleasant surprises.

Episode 95: "The Traitor"

Written by Jack Sowards. Directed by Bill Wiard. Produced by Barney Rosenzweig.

Guest players: Patrick O'Moore, Lyn Peters and Joe Jennkes.

Shawnee Indians capture a British colonel's daughter. To escape execution as a traitor, Daniel volunteers to guide British soldiers to rescue her.

Episode 96: "The Value of a King"

Written by Judith and Robert Guy Barrows. Directed by John Newland. Produced by Barney Rosenzweig.

Guest players: James Gregory, Ken Gampu and Dort Clark.

Israel is held hostage by a group of runaway slaves. Daniel fights hostile Indians and a slaver to rescue Israel and free the slaves.

Episode 97: "The Desperate Raid"

Written by Harold Medford. Directed by Nathan Juran. Produced by Barney Rosenzweig.

Guest players: Lester Matthews, Hampton Fancher and William Beckley.

With the help of escaped convicts, Daniel assists an inexperienced lieutenant's efforts to bring supplies to a besieged fort.

Episode 98: "The Spanish Horse"

Written by Tom Blackburn and D.D. Beauchamp. Directed by William Wiard. Produced by Barney Rosenzweig.

Guest players: *Carl Trevor* Michael Burns, with Henry Jones and Jimmy Murphy.

Daniel helps Carl Trevor with a lame thoroughbred that has been left with him by his dying father.

Episode 99: "Chief Mingo"

Written by James Byrnes. Directed by Gerd Oswald. Produced by Barney Rosenzweig.

Guest players: John Larch, Hal Jon Norman and Michael Forest.

A Cherokee chief has been murdered. Daniel and Mingo argue about whether the perpetrator should be convicted by the Indians or by the whites.

Episode 100: "The Secret Code"

Written by Joel Oliansky. Directed by William Wiard. Produced by Barney Rosenzweig.

Guest players: Edward Mulhare, David Opatoshu and Lloyd Bochner.

Daniel is sent on a mission to recapture the Patriot army's top code expert. If he cannot rescue him, he has orders to kill him before the British-allied Indians can make him talk.

Episode 101: "A Matter of Blood"

Written by Judith and Robert Guy Barrows. Directed by Nathan Juran. Produced by Barney Rosenzweig.

Guest players: William Smith, Adrienne Hayes and Walter Coy.

An Indian princess is trying to prove herself to become Queen of the Delaware.

Episode 102: "The Scrimshaw Ivory Chart"

Written by Melvin Levey. Directed by George Marshall. Produced by Barney Rosenzweig.

Guest players: Jim Backus, Percy Helton and Ted Cassidy.

Pirate Scatway draws Boone into a treasure hunt.

Episode 103: "The Imposter"

Written by Merwin Gerard. Directed by Bill Wiard. Produced by Barney Rosenzweig.

Guest players: *Jeremiah* Jimmy Dean, with Lloyd Bochner, Roy Dean and Bryan Grant.

To prevent the British from gaining access to a new powerful rifle, backwoodsman Jeremiah acts as a British orderly.

Episode 104: "The Witness"

Written by Rick Husky. Directed by William Wiard. Produced by Barney Rosenzweig.

Guest players: John Carradine, Virginia Gregg and Harry Basch.

Israel and two of his friends become witnesses to a murder. No one, except the killer, believes them!

Episode 105: "The Flaming Rocks"

Written by Lee Karson and David Duncan. Directed by Nathan Juran. Produced by Barney Rosenzweig.

Guest players: Jimmy Dean, R.G. Armstrong and Dorothy Green.

A hardheaded Welshman intrudes on Tuscarora land for coal mining. Daniel, Mingo and Jeremiah intercede to prevent Indian actions.

Episode 106: "Then Who Will They Hang from the Yardarm if Willy Gets Away?"

Written by Martha Wilkerson. Directed by Fess Parker. Produced by Barney Rosenzweig.

Guest players: *George Perkins* Wilfrid Hyde-White, with Jack Bannon and Martin Horsey.

Old crafty George Perkins blackmails a young sailor, sought for mutiny.

Episode 107: "The Spanish Fort"

Written by Raphael Hayes. Directed by William Wiard. Produced by Barney Rosenzweig.

Guest players: Richard Angarola, Henry Brandt and Gary Conway.

Daniel is sent on a mission to sabotage a Spanish fort, which has been built on American land. His cover is jeopardized by an informer.

Episode 108: "Hero's Welcome"

Written by Joel Oliansky. Directed by Nathan Juran. Produced by Barney Rosenzweig.

Guest players: Charles Drake, Sarah Marshall and Ronnie Masterfield.

A friend of Daniel and Mingo is accused of being a coward. Daniel and Mingo prove he is not.

Episode 109: "Orlando, the Prophet"

Written by Melvin Levy. Directed by William Wiard. Produced by Barney Rosenzweig.

Guest players: Hans Conried, Anthony Alda and Harold Goodwin.

Mingo helps a young Gypsy bondservant gain his freedom from his master.

Episode 110: "The Far Side of Fury"

Written by Judith Barrows. Directed by William Wiard. Produced by Barney Rosenzweig.

Guest players: *Gideon* Don Pedro Colley, *Little Dan'l* Ezekial Williams and Med Flory.

Indians kidnap Gideon's son Little Dan'l while he is in care of Daniel. For revenge Gideon threatens to kill Israel.

Episode 111: "Nightmare"

Written by Paul Playdon. Directed by George Marshall. Produced by Barney Rosenzweig.

Guest players: Hans Wedemeyer, Charles Picerni and Fred Carson.

Daniel and Israel are trying to escape Shawnee Indians on the warpath.

Episode 112: "Thirty Pieces of Silver"

Written by D.D. Beauchamp and James Byrnes. Directed by Nathan Juran. Produced by Barney Rosenzweig.

Guest players: Andrew Prine, Herbert Anderson and Virginia Christine.

Gunrunners are trying to obtain weapons that Daniel and Mingo are delivering to the settlement in a secret mission.

Episode 113: "Faith's Way"

Written by Martha Wilkerson. Directed by Joel Oliansky. Produced by Barney Rosenzweig.

Guest players: *Faith* Julie Harris, with Jeff Morrow and Claude Woolman.

Schoolteacher Faith is believed by the Indians to be a witch because she has an uncommon ability to communicate with animals. This endangers her life.

Season 5 (1968-69)

General cast: *Daniel Boone* Fess Parker, *Rebecca Boone* Patricia Blair, *Israel Boone* Darby Hinton, *Cincinnatus* Dallas McKennon, *Josh Clements* Jimmy Dean, and *Gideon* Don Pedro Colley.

Episode 114: "Be Thankful for the Fickleness of Woman"

Written by Don Balluck. Directed by William Wiard. Produced by Barney Rosenzweig.

Guest players: Brooke Bundy, Sean McClory and James Davidson.

Josh Clements is facing a problem. By mistake he has bought a pretty bondservant. He either has to find her a husband or marry her himself.

Episode 115: "The Blackbirder"

Written by D.D. Beauchamp. Directed by William Wiard. Produced by Barney Rosenzweig.

Guest players: *Mason Pruitt* Jim McMullan, with Timothy Carey.

Daniel's friend Gideon is captured by a bounty hunter, who mistakes him for a runaway slave. Matters do not improve when Seaman Mason Pruitt falsely identifies Gideon as being the slave.

Episode 116: "The Dandy"

Written by Merwin Gerard. Directed by William Wiard. Produced by Barney Rosenzweig.

Guest players: David Watson, Johnny Cardos and Saundra Gayle.

Daniel has a hard time when he takes on the responsibility to teach a young dandy the woodsman's life.

Episode 117: "The Fleeing Nuns"

Written by Irve Tunick. Directed by William Wiard. Produced by Barney Rosenzweig.

Guest players: Kathleen Freeman, Brioni Farell and Maurice Marsac.

A French royal and her maid are trying to escape revolutionaries, and are helped by Daniel.

Episode 118: "The Plague That Came to Ford's Run"

Written by Harold Medford. Directed by Fess Parker. Produced by Barney Rosenzweig.

Guest players: Charles Drake, Gail Kobe and Ted White.

Episode 119: "The Bait"

Guest players: Skip Ward, Lois Nettleton and James Daris.

Episode 120: "Big, Black and Out There"

Written by Harry Basch. Directed by William Wiard. Produced by Barney Rosenzweig.

Guest players: Ezekial Williams, Yaphet Kotto and Harry Basch.

A runaway slave, dressed as an Indian, steals from the settlers. A loyalty conflict arises between Gideon and Daniel when dealing with the matter.

Episode 121: "A Flag of Truce"

Written by Irvine Tunick. Directed by William Wiard. Produced by Barney Rosenzweig.

Guest players: *General Grosscup* Mort Mills, with William Smith and H.M. Wynant.

Daniel is involved in treaty negotiations between Wyandot and the Army. A problem arises when General Grosscup plans on arresting a Wyandot chief.

Episode 122: "The Valley of the Sun"

Written by David Duncan. Directed by Nathan Juran. Produced by Barney Rosenzweig.

Guest players: Mariette Hartley and Severn Darden.

On a deer hunt, Josh runs into problems when a mad Englishman, who is protecting his hoard of Aztec gold, captures him.

Episode 123: "The Patriot"

Written by Melvin Levey. Directed by Fess Parker. Produced by Barney Rosenzweig.

Guest players: Ford Rainey, Teddy Eccles and Tom Lowell.

A former British loyalist arrives at Boonesborough. His son, who has been fighting against the British, questions his right to live in the community.

Episode 124: "The Return of Sidewinder"

Written by Melvin Levey. Directed by Nathan Juran. Produced by Barney Rosenzweig.

Guest players: *Joe Snag* Forrest Tucker, with Rex Holman and Charles Dierkop.

An old friend of Daniel, pirate Joe Snag, has taken to robbery. Daniel tries to prevent his friend's criminal behavior without revealing him to the British.

Episode 125: "Minnow for a Shark"

Written by Nathan Juran. Directed by Nathan Juran. Produced by Barney Rosenzweig.

Guest players: Henry Jones, Ivor Barry and George Keymas.

Israel becomes involved in stealing the king's dispatch box.

Episode 126: "To Slay a Giant"

Written by Arthur Browne, Jr. Directed by Nathan Juran. Produced by Barney Rosenzweig.

Guest players: Torin Thatcher, Lee Jay Lambert and Hy Chase.

Daniel clears Gideon of a murder charge, before he is subjected to a lynch mob.

Episode 127: "A Tale of Prater Breasley"

Written by Melvin Levey. Directed by George Marshall. Produced by Barney Rosenszweig.

Guest players: Burl Ives, Rory Stevens and Lyle Bettger.

A story teller brings self-reliance to a young crippled boy.

Episode 128: "Cooperhead Izzy"

Written by David Duncan. Directed by William Wiard. Produced by Barney Rosenzweig.

Guest players: Vincent Price, Elena Verdugo and J. Pat O'Malley.

During a visit to Williamsburg, Israel meets a group of orphans, who steal for their living.

Episode 129: "Three Score and Ten"

Written by Raphael Hayes. Directed by George Marshall. Produced by Barney Rosenzweig.

Guest players: Burgess Meredith, James Wainwright and Paul Fix.

To himself and his friends an old gunsmith must prove that he still is an able and productive man.

Episode 130: "Jonah"

Written by D.D. Beauchamp. Directed by William Wiard. Produced by Barney Rosenzweig.

Guest players: Yaphet Kotto, Booth Colman and Sean McClory.

Josh inherits a peace of land near Boonesborough from his uncle. There is, however, a passage in the will which claims that Josh has to give up his carefree life. With the inheritance comes an educated slave, who is supposed to make a respectable landowner out of his new owner.

Episode 131: "Bickford's Bridge"

Written by Al Ramrus, John Shaner and D.D. Beauchamp. Directed by Nathan Juran. Produced by Barney Rosenzweig.

Guest players: *James Bickford* Simon Oakland, with Kurt Russell and Peter Jason.

The Continental Army sends Daniel on a mission to destroy all bridges to prevent the advancement of the British Army. He runs into a problem when James Bickford and his son refuse to destroy their newly built bridge.

Episode 132: "A Touch of Charity"

Written by Judith Barrows. Directed by William Wiard. Produced by Barney Rosenzweig.

Guest players: *Jimmy McGill* John Davidson, with Shelley Fabares and Donald Barry.

To win the hand of a woman he loves, Jimmy McGill seeks the help of Daniel.

Episode 133: "For Want of a Hero"

Written by George F. Slavin and Stanley Adams. Directed by Lee Philips. Produced by Barney Rosenzweig.

Episode 135: "The Allies"

Written by D.D. Beauchamp. Directed by George Marshall. Produced by Barney Rosenzweig.

Guest players: *Mason Pruitt* Jim McMullan, *Cully* James Wainwright, with Ben Archibek.

Daniel, Cully and Mason prevent the British from bringing guns to their Indian allies by destroying a bridge on the gun transport route.

Episode 136: "A Man Before His Time"

Written by Dan Bullock. Directed by William Wiard. Produced by Barney Rosenzweig.

Guest players: *Luke* Michael Dante, with Warren Vanders and James Wainwright.

Ben goes after Sutter, a man who is accused of stealing and who has committed murder. In self-defense he is forced to kill Sutter. When Sutter's son Luke seeks Ben for revenge, Daniel and Cully come to Ben's assistance.

Episode 137: "For a Few Rifles"

Written by Judith Barrows. Directed by John Newland. Produced by Barney Rosenzweig.

Guest players: Michael Dante, Donald Losby and Ted De Corsia.

Indians capture Israel to use him in their efforts to obtain guns.

Episode 138: "Sweet Molly Malone"

Written by Patricia Falkenhagen and Jack Guss. Directed by William Wiard. Produced by Barney Rosenzweig.

Guest players: *Molly Malone* Barbara

Daniel Boone—Daniel (Fess Parker) and actor Jimmy Dean.

Guest players: Richard Anderson and Arch Johnson.

The Boones get involved with a party of soldiers, survivors of an Indian attack, who are planning to steal the army payroll.

Episode 134: "Love and Equity"

Written by Melvin Levy. Directed by William Wiard. Produced by Barney Rosenzweig.

Guest players: *Prater Breasely* Burl Ives, with Med Flory and Victor French.

When Prater Breasely goes to Boonesborough to help prevent the outbreak of an epidemic caused by ground squirrels, he is accused of witchcraft.

Bel Geddes, with Jack Kruschan and Jack Garner.

A retired Army sergeant, Molly Malone, involves Daniel and Rebecca as matchmakers.

Episode 139: "A Pinch of Salt"

Written by Merwin Gerard. Directed by William Wiard. Produced by Barney Rosenzweig.

Guest players: David Watson, Joan Hackett and Donna Baccala.

Daniel and a young artist are drawn into a love quarrel between a possessive woman and her proud domineering man.

Season 6 (1969-70)

General cast: *Daniel Boone* Fess Parker, *Rebecca Boone* Patricia Blair, *Israel Boone* Darby Hinton, *Cincinnatus* Dallas McKennon, *Josh Clements* Jimmy Dean, and *Gabe Cooper* Roosevelt Grier.

Episode 140: "A Very Small Rifle"

Written by Melvin Levy and Thomas P. Levy. Directed by Nathan Juran. Produced by Barney Rosenzweig.

Guest players: *Johnny Appleseed* Roger Miller, with Eddie Little Sky and Johnny Jensen.

A Cherokee uprising is threatening when a young Cherokee is shot accidentally by one of the settlers. Johnny Appleseed, who is planting apple seeds in the Boonesborough area, prevents the outbreak of hostilities.

Episode 141: "The Road to Freedom"

Written by Frank Moss and Virginia Brooks. Directed by William Wiard. Produced by Barney Rosenzweig.

Guest players: Floyd Patterson, George Spell and Warren Vanders.

Israel is once more involved in helping a runaway slave escape his owners.

Episode 142: "Benvenuto ... Who?"

Written by Walter Black. Directed by William Wiard. Produced by Barney Rosenzweig.

Guest players: Marj Dusay, Leon Askin and Richard Kiel.

To prevent her crime partners from finding a stolen diamond, a beautiful French woman hides it inside Josh's guitar.

Episode 143: "The Man"

Written by Jack Guss. Directed by Nathan Juran. Produced by Barney Rosenzweig.

Guest players: George Backman, Gene Evans and Kevin O'Neal.

Daniel enlists former slave Gabe Cooper and Tuscarora Chief Canawahchaquaoo to prevent a British cannon transport.

Episode 144: "The Printing Press"

Written by Lionel E. Siegel. Directed by William Wiard. Produced by Barney Rosenzweig.

Guest players: *Benjamin Franklin* Fred Wayne, with Peter Bromilow and Kilmethe Laurie.

In Philadelphia, Daniel's friend Benjamin Franklin counterfeits British pound notes to help Daniel obtain much-needed supplies for his settlements.

Episode 145: "The Traitor"

Written by David Duncan. Directed by Nathan Juran. Produced by Barney Rosenzweig.

Guest players: Jill Ireland, Ed Flanders and Richard Devon.

Daniel is guiding a woman to a rendezvous with her husband, who is commander at Fort Detroit and who is claiming that he will surrender the fort to the Americans.

Episode 146: "The Grand Alliance"

Written by Judith Barrows. Directed by Nathan Juran. Produced by Barney Rosenzweig.

Guest players: Armando Silvestre, Carlos Rivas and Hugo Fargo.

Josh and Gabe are informed by a Spanish pirate about a Spanish plan for an invasion of United States territory.

Episode 147: "Target Boone"

Written by N. Bernard Fox and D.D. Beauchamp. Directed by William Wiard. Produced by Barney Rosenzweig.

Guest players: *Adam Jarrett* Will Geer, with Kurt Russell and Ron Soble.

Revengeful Adam Jarrett and his son are going after Daniel for the death of Adam's wife in a boat accident.

Episode 148: "A Bearskin for Jamie Blue"

Written by Frank Chase. Directed by William Wiard. Produced by Barney Rosenzweig.

Guest players: *Jamie Blue* Christopher Connelly, with Charles Dierkop and Johanna Cameron.

The Boones are helping young Jamie Blue, a servant born in prison, adjust to life.

Episode 149: "The Cache"

Written by Irvine Tunick. Directed by Nathan Juran. Produced by Barney Rosenzweig.

Guest players: James Doohan, Alex Carras and Vaughan Taylor.

A trapper is found killed near Josh's camp. This results in Josh being accused of murder.

Episode 150: "The Terrible Tarbots"

Written by Harold Nedford. Directed by Nathan Juran. Directed by Barney Rosenzweig.

Guest players: Strother Martin, Anthony Costello and Zalman King.

Israel is taken as hostage by the Tarbot brothers when they steal army gold from a transport.

Episode 151: "Hannah Comes Home"

Written by Harry Basch. Directed by Fess Parker. Produced by Barney Rosenzweig.

Guest players: Mark Fickett, Ford Rainey and Teddy Eccles.

After 15 years in captivity by Indians a white woman and her half–Indian son return to her husband in Boonesborough. Her son has a hard time adjusting to the white way of living.

Episode 152: "An Angel Cried"

Written by Martha Wilkerson. Directed by Fess Parker. Produced by Barney Rosenzweig.

Guest players: *Sister Cecilia* Mariette Hartley, with Carlos Rivas.

Josh is helping Sister Cecilia, a Catholic nun, to escape hostile Indians.

Episode 153: "Perilous Passage"

Written by Lee Karson. Directed by Nathan Juran. Produced by Barney Rosenzweig.

Guest players: John Davidson, Liam Sullivan and Gloria Grahame.

The British track Daniel and Gabe after they have been scouting behind British lines. Someone must have carried information about their retreat route.

Episode 154: "The Sunshine Patriots"

Written by Jack Guss and Ricky Husky. Directed by William Wiard. Produced by Barney Rosenzweig.

Guest players: Gail Kobe, Ian Ireland and Laurie Main.

General Washington sends Gabe and Josh on a mission.

Episode 155: "Mama Cooper"

Written by Lionel E. Siegel. Directed by William Wiard. Produced by Barney Rosenzweig.

Guest players: Ethel Waters, Tyler McVey and Jean Howell.

Gabe is going to find his mother and buy her freedom. Information reveals that she still lives.

Episode 156: "Before the Tall Man"

Written by Albert Beich and William Wright. Directed by George Marshall. Produced by Barney Rosenzweig.

Guest players: *Nancy Hanks* Marianna Hill, *Tom Lincoln* Burr DeBenning, with Harlen Warde.

Nancy Hanks wants to marry Tom Lincoln. Tom wants nothing to do with her.

Episode 157: "Run for the Money"

Written by Walter Black. Directed by Chris Nyby. Produced by Barney Rosenzweig.

Guest players: *Linus Hunter* Ji-Tu Cumbuka, with Jack Albertson and Peter Mamakos.

There is an annual footrace between the settlers and the Indians. A slave, Lucas Hunter, is running for the whites. Cincinnatus is sure that Lucas will win the race. However, it turns out that Lucas's brother Linus will participate in the race on the side of the Indians.

Episode 158: "A Matter of Vengeance"

Written by Irve Tunick. Directed by Nathan Juran. Produced by Barney Rosenzweig.

Guest players: *Mason Pruitt* James McMullan, with Lina Marsh and David McLean.

Mason Pruitt's parents have been killed. Mason faces trouble when he accuses a visitor to Boonesborough of the killing.

Episode 159: "The Landlords"

Written by Melvin Levey. Directed by William Wiard. Produced by Barney Rosenzweig.

Guest players: *Ess* Victor Bochner, *Bingen* Med Flory, with Lloyd Bochner.

A man who convinces them that he has the ownership of Boonesborough swindles Ess and Bingen.

Episode 160: "Readin, Ritin', and Revolt"

Written by Lee Karson. Directed by William Wiard. Produced by Barney Rosenzweig.

Guest players: *Pickering* William O'Connell, with Tony Davis and Arthur Batanides.

Contrary to the liking of the schoolmaster and their parents, the schoolchildren want to learn about Indian culture.

Episode 161: "Noblesse Oblige"

Written by David Duncan. Directed by Nathan Juran. Produced by Barney Rosenzweig.

Guest players: Philip Proctor, Virginia Christine and Murray MacLeod.

To escape too much attention during a visit to Boonesborough, the exiled Prince of France changes identity with his chef.

Episode 162: "The Homecoming"

Written by Melvin Levey. Directed by Nathan Juran. Produced by Barney Rosenzweig.

Guest players: *Tamenund* David Opatoshu, with Sidney Clute and Bart Burns.

Tamenund, the last survivor of the Piqua tribe, raids white settlers in revenge for the extermination of his people.

Episode 163: "Bringing Up Josh"

Written by Jack Guss. Directed by William Wiard. Produced by Barney Rosenzweig.

Guest players: Jodie Foster, Ty Wilson and Lori Saunders.

Josh adopts two orphaned children. This gives widow Spoon an excuse for trying to get Josh to marry her, insisting that he cannot raise the children without a wife.

Episode 164: "How to Become a Goddess"

Written by Melvin Levy and Dan Bullock. Directed by William Wiard. Produced by Barney Rosenzweig.

Guest players: Paul Mantee, Ruth Warrick and Victor French.

The Onondaga mistake Rebecca for a goddess.

Episode 165: "Israel and Love"

Written by Melvin Levy. Directed by Nathan Juran. Produced by Barney Rosenzweig.

Guest players: *Brae* Robin Mattson, with Tim O'Connor and Len Wayland.

Israel is in love with Brae, the daughter of a woodcarver who has turned to drinking.

Notes: One of the most successful western television series was **Daniel Boone**. The series was produced by Arcola-Fespar Productions in association with 20th Century–Fox, and it ran for six seasons between 1964 and 1970, starting in black and white and later in color. At center in the series is the Boonesborough settlement where Daniel has his family and his friends. Together with his sidekick, a Cherokee named

Mingo, Daniel travels in and out of Boonesborough to carry out different adventurous missions. Cast as Boone was Fess Parker, famous as a frontier hero from his leading role in **Davy Crockett**. He also wears the famous coonskin cap from **Davy Crockett** in this series. Ed Ames appeared as Mingo. Ames came from the famous singing Ames Brothers.

This series has been criticized for its treatment of Native Americans. With the exception of Mingo, most other Indians were portrayed in a stereotypical way, spending most of their time trying to drive settlers out of Kentucky. This had a negative impact on the opinion of an otherwise good series held by many Native Americans. In 1971, the Boston Indian Council protested against a rerun of the series on the network, characterizing the program as "…little more than white racist indoctrination especially detrimental to Native American children."

The series added to the widespread fame of Fess Parker, and he has since been remembered as the coonskin-capped frontier hero.

Daniel Boone (or Pioneer Days in America) (Edison, 1907)

Directed by Wallace McCutcheon. Photography by Edwin S. Porter. Length: 1,000 feet.

Cast: Florence Lawrence, S. Willis, W. Carver and Mrs. Warver.

The story: Indians kidnap Boone's daughters, and then capture and torture him. Aided by a girl from the tribe, Boone escapes and saves the children.

Daniel Boone Thru the Wilderness (Sunset, 1926)

Directed by Robert North Bradbury. Photography by J.S. Brown.

Cast: *Daniel Boone* Roy Steward, *Hank Vaughan* Frank Rice, *Simon Girty* Jay Morley, *Otis Bryan* Tom Linghant, *Rebecca* Kathleen Colling, *Jim Bryan* Bob Bradbury, Jr., *Grey Eagle* James O'Neil and *Will Bryan* Edward Hearn.

The story: It starts in the valley of Yadkin, an area with few white settlers. Indians led by white renegade Simon Girty ambush Daniel Boone and his scout friend Hank Vaughan in a cabin. The offenders are defeated and Daniel captures Girty but lets him go.

Later in a small settlement, Indians, again lead by Girty, raid the Bryan family. Otis Bryan's daughter Rebecca is captured by the Indians but is saved by Boone, who happens to be nearby.

Daniel develops affection for Rebecca, which grows to love when he visits several times with the Bryans. During his visits Daniel tells them about the fertile and game-rich country of Kentucky in the West. A stranger arrives at the Yadkin settlement. At his arrival Daniel watches with what passion Rebecca receives him. Brokenhearted, he leaves with Hank for Kentucky without taking farewell of Rebecca.

Boone's stories about Kentucky have impressed the Bryans and they decide to leave and settle in the new country. At their arrival they stay with the Finleys, another pioneering family from Yadkin who had decided to break new ground.

The Cherokee Indians in the area live in peace with the whites. Simon Girty, who also has come there, shows desire for Chief Grey Eagle's daughter Nanna. At the reunion between Rebecca and Daniel it comes out that the stranger who caused Daniel to leave Yadkin in reality is not her lover, but her older brother Will, who had returned to his family.

In his attempt to obtain Nanna, against the warning of Grey Eagle, Girty kills Nanna's brother, who tries to protect her. Not to reveal himself, Girty carries the brother's body to Grey Eagle's village and claims that the white settlers committed the crime. This causes the Indians to go on the warpath against the whites.

The Indians attack the settlement. In

their exposed situation, Will goes to Daniel for help. The Indians capture Daniel when he is trying to save Rebecca. Girty leaves with the captured Rebecca, but her younger brother Jim saves her. In the Indian camp, Daniel is tied to a pole to be burned. He is, however, saved by Nanna, who arrives and reveals that it is Girty who has killed her brother. The Indians then burn Girty instead of Boone. The peace in the valley is restored between the whites and the Indians. Everyone is happy and Daniel and Rebecca become a couple.

Daniel Boone, Trail Blazer
(Republic, 1957)

Produced by Albert C. Gannaway. Directed by Albert C. Gannaway and Ismael Rodriguez. Screenplay by Tom Hubbard and John Patrick. Photography in Trucolor by Jack Draper. Music by Raul Lavista. Running time: 76 minutes.

Cast: *Daniel Boone* Bruce Bennet, *Blackfish* Lon Chaney, Jr., *Faron Callaway* Faron Young, *Simon Girty* Kem Dibbs, *Andy Callaways* Damian O'Flynn, *Rebecca Boone* Jacqueline Evans, *Susannah Boone* Nancy Rodman, *Israel Boone* Freddy Fernandez, *Jemima Boone* Carol Kelley, *Squire Boone* Eduardo Noriega, *Kenton* Fred Kohler, Jr., *John Holder* Gordon Mills, *James Boone* Claude Brook, *Gen. Hamilton* Joe Ainley and *Smitty* Lee Morgan.

The story: Daniel Boone and his band of settlers travel from Yadkin, North Carolina, to settle down in Boonesborough in Kentucky. Simon Girty, on the British side, is urging on the Shawnee Indians against the colonists.

The Indians are attacking the settlers and one of Boone's sons is killed. Daniel goes to the Shawnee village to convince the chief, Blackfish, that the settlers want nothing but peace. However, advised by Girty, Blackfish captures Daniel. Daniel proves his courage when he is forced to run a gauntlet, and Blackfish agrees to talk peace with the settlers.

A meeting place for peace talks is de-cided at the shadow of the "Thousand Falls." On their way to the meeting place British Redcoats attack a patrol of the Shawnees. During the attack, two of Blackfish's sons are shot. Girty blames the attack on the settlers, and Daniel must run away and manages to escape to Boonesborough.

The Indians attack the fort. Boone, however, convinces Blackfish that Girty is guilty of the killing of his sons. Blackfish kills Girty and peace is restored.

Notes: "This is a slightly better-than-average Western that has Daniel Boone (Bruce Bennet) not only pathfinding for settlers but fighting off what seems to be the entire population of native Americans. Good performances and lots of action save it from being mundane."—Mick Martin and Marsha Porter *Video Movie Guide*

"Generally well-acted low-budget version of the life of the famous frontier explorer and his skirmishes with Indians. Filmed in Mexico."—Leonard Maltin's *Movie and Video Guide*

Daniel Boone's Bravery (Kalem, 1911)

Length: 1,000 feet.

Davy Crockett (Selig Polyscope Co., 1910)

Length: 3,000 feet.

Cast: Hobart Bosworth and Tom Santschi.

Davy Crockett (Paramount, 1916)

Directed by William Desmond Taylor. Photography by Homer Scott.

Cast: *Davy Crockett* Dustin Farnum, with Winfred Kingston, Harry De Vere, Herbert Standing, Howard Davies, Page Peters, Lydia Yeamans Titus and Ida Darling.

Davy Crockett (Walt Disney TV series, 1988)

General cast: *Davy Crockett* Tim Dunigan; *George Russell* Gary Grubbs

Premiere Episode—"Rainbow in the Thunder"

Produced by Frank Fischer. Directed by David Hemmings. Written by William Blinn. Photography by Isidor Mankofsky.

Guest players: *Colonel Davy Crockett* Johnny Cash, *General Andrew Jackson* Matt Salinger, *President Andrew Jackson* David Hemmings, with Richard Tyson, Cheryl Abutt, Samantha Eggar, Brendan Chichlow, Jill Gambley, Jeff Irvine, Blu Mancumc, Freda Perry, Matt Walker, Terry Kelly, Lorraine Forman, and John "Bear" Curtis.

An older Davy Crockett is visiting President Andrew Jackson at his residence to discuss political matters. During the visit Crockett and Jackson come to talk about their time together during the Creek War of 1813.

In flashback, Davy and some Tennessee volunteers join with General Jackson's army to fight the Creek, who have been raiding settlements and murdering white settlers. In the army camp Davy meets with the braggart George Russel from Georgia, with whom he becomes friends after they have settled some arguments. Davy is signed in as a sergeant to represent the militia.

The army goal is to strike against one of the Creek villages. On a scouting mission, Davy and George save a young settler woman, Ory Palmer, from three approaching Indians when she is taking a bath in a river.

The next day at dawn, the army attacks the village. The brutality during the attack has a striking influence on one of the young volunteers, Lou, which results in his decision to desert the army. Lou later returns dressed as an Indian, and captures Ory to bring her to the Creek village as a peace offering.

Forward in time: At President Jackson's home we learn that Ory has been the wife of Jackson for several years. During a discussion between her and Davy, he tells her about his own life and that he married a young frontier woman, Polly, who has been dead for ten years.

Back to the Creek War: Davy pursues the deserter Lou and the captured Ory. He finds them in a deserted cabin in the woods, surrounded by Creeks. Lou is killed. To save Ory, Davy buries her alive, pretending she has been killed. He sets the cabin on fire, but escapes himself through a hidden retreat route. The Indians believe everyone is dead and leave. Later Davy returns to the burned cabin and digs up Ory, who is alive and well.

Episode 2: "A Letter to Polly"

Produced by Frank Fischer. Directed by Harry Falk. Written by Paul Savage.

Guest players: Aeryk Egan, Garry Chalk, Jeff Irvine, Eric Bryant Wells, Jerry Wasserman, Tod Schaffer, Robin Mossley, Sheelan Megill, Lalainia Lindberg, Terry Kelly, Lorraine Forman and Buffalo Child.

Davy and George are scouting the forests when Creek Indians attack them. George saves Davy from being fired upon by an Indian, when Davy suddenly does not react to the danger, being paralyzed by thoughts about the well-being of his wife Polly and their children.

Back in the army camp news comes in that a band of Creek joined by Cherokee has beaten General Coffee and his Tennessee militia. The plan is to strike against the Indian town in three days.

Food is required and Davy volunteers to go to Fort Pain with a message for supplies. At the same time he hopes to be able to send a letter to his family back home, but he needs to be back in time for the campaign in three days.

On his way, things complicate Davy's time schedule when he runs into a young boy who has survived an Indian attack in which his parents were killed. He also has to help an Indian squaw deliver her baby and help a pioneering family fix their broken wagon. He never makes it to Fort Pain to send his letter, but he returns in time to the army camp for the upcoming fighting.

Episode 3: "Guardian Spirit"

Directed by Harry Falk. Written by Robert Sonntag and Deborah Gilliland.

Guest players: Garry Chalk, Jeff Irvine, Henry Kingi and Evan Adams.

At the army camp, rumor says that there are Creek Indians all around in the woods for their annual Green Corn Dance. Jackson wants to strike and he sends Davy and George to scout.

In the woods Davy saves a young Creek boy from a wolf during his rites of manhood. The boy is brought to the army camp but is imprisoned by the soldiers. Davy, who cares for the boy, helps him escape.

A troop of soldiers is sent after them to recapture the boy. In the forest Indians attack them and Davy is wounded. He pretends that he is blinded by his wound so that he can return the Creek boy to his village and restore peace.

Episode 4: "A Natural Man"

Produced by Frank Fischer. Directed by Charles Braverman. Written by Steven Baum and Neil Alan Levy. Guest players: Barry Corbin, Molly Hagan, Jeff Irvine, Rodger Gibson, Charles André, Stephen Dimopoulos, Don S. Davis and R.G. Miller.

A grizzly bear attacks George, but Davy, to George's big surprise, manages to frighten the bear by shouting at him and saves George.

In the woods they run into an old trapper who proves to be Davy's old Uncle, Jimmy Crockett, who disappeared 20 years ago but who has since lived with the Creek.

In the army camp the soldiers are eager to learn about Jimmy Crockett's life among the Creek. His stories cause some of them to believe that the Indians have hidden gold. In trying to find out, some soldiers run into an ambush by Indians. One wounded soldier explains before he dies that he was shot by a blue-eyed Indian. Jimmy explains to Davy that this must have been Logan, a son from his Indian marriage.

For revenge the soldiers attack the Creek village. Logan manages to escape but he is tracked by George, who captures him. Davy interferes and saves Logan. He explains to him about their consanguinity. Logan has problems accepting the situation in his hate for the whites, and Davy lets him escape.

Episode 5: "Warrior's Farewell"

Directed by James J. Quinn. Written by William Blinn.

Guest players: Ken Swofford, Garry Chalk, Jeff Irvine, Sherri Stoner, Prudence Wright Holmes, Lloyd Berry and Clem Fox.

Settlers blame an earthquake on a Creek medicine man, as an invocation of wrath on the whites.

A Mr. Callahan arrives in the camp. He is said to have come for an important mission. Lt. North and Davy are assigned to work with Callahan on the mission. It turns out that it is about a new weapon—a Ferguson rifle, a modern weapon with improved properties.

To demonstrate his gun, Callahan leaves to kill the medicine man, but Davy hinders him. Davy goes to the Creek village to explain the situation and he breaks the new rifle to prove he is honest. The Indians accept this and a final lasting peace is restored with the Creek.

Notes: In 1988, The Disney Studio ran a series of children's programs in their production *The Magic World of Disney* on NBC. To balance cartoons and to introduce some live adventures the studio decided to once again breath new life in their old hit with **Davy Crockett** from the 1950s.

The idea behind the series was to have an older Crockett introduce stories, which would be flashbacked as adventures in which Tim Dunigan played Crockett. The role as "old" Crockett was offered to Fess Parker, but he turned it down and instead country music star Johnny Cash was selected for the role. The flashback idea only worked through the pilot episode, and in spite of being heavily promoted by NBC, the series did not made it through more than a few episodes.

Davy Crockett and the River Pirates (Walt Disney/Buena Vista, 1956)

Produced by Bill Walsh. Directed by Norman Foster. Screenplay by Tom Blackburn and Norman Foster. Photography in Technicolor by Bert Glennon. Music by George Bruns. Running time: 81 minutes.

Cast: *Davy Crockett* Fess Parker, *George Russel* Buddy Ebsen, with Jeff York, Kenneth Tobey, Clem Bevans, Irvin Ashkenazy, Mort Milles, Paul Newland, Frank Richards, Walter Catlett and Douglas Dumbrille.

Notes: Sequel feature to **Davy Crockett, King of the Wild Frontier**, cut from the two episodes of the *Frontierland* segment of the *Disneyland* TV series: "**Davy Crockett and the Keelboat Race**" and "**Davy Crockett and the River Pirates**." Songs: "Ballad of Davy Crockett," "King of the River," "Yaller, Yaller Gold" by George Bruns and Tom Blackburn.

"Davy" Crockett in Hearts United (Bison, 1909)

Directed by Fred J. Balshofer. Screenplay by Charles K. French. Alternate title: **Hearts United**. Filmed on location in Fort Lee, N.J. and Palisades, N.J. Length: 836 feet.

Cast: Charles K. French, Evelyn Graham, C. Baumann and Charles W. Travis.

Davy Crockett, King of the Wild Frontier (Buena Vista, 1955)

Produced by Bill Walsh. Directed by Norman Foster. Screenplay by Tom Blackburn. Photography in Technicolor by Charles P. Boyle. Music by George Bruns. Running time: 93 minutes.

Cast: *Davy Crockett* Fess Parker, *George Russel* Buddy Ebsen, *Andrew Jackson* Basil Raysdeal, *Thimblering* Hans Con-

ried, *Tobias Norton* William Bakewell, *Colonal Jim Bowie* Kenneth Tobey, *Chief Red Stick* Pat Hogan, *Polly Crockett* Helene Stanley, *Bustedluck* Nick Cravat, *Colonel Billy Travis* Don Megowen, *Bigfoot Mason* Mike Mazuraki, *Charles Two Shirts* Jeff Thompson, *Swaney* Henry Joyner and *Henderson* Benjamin Hornbuckle.

The story: Davy Crockett and his friend George Russel participate with General Andrew Jackson in the war against the Creek Indians in the early part of 1800.

During a scouting mission, the Indians capture Davy and George. Davy is challenged by Indian Chief Red Stick in combat. He wins the confidence of Red Stick when he saves his life after having conquered him in the battle.

General Jackson, who is running for president, encourages Davy to run for a seat in Congress. Davy is also elected, but when he and Jackson disagree over a bill

Davy Crockett, King of the Wild Frontier (Buena Vista, 1956)—Davy Crockett (Fess Parker).

Davy Crockett, King of the Wild Frontier—Chief Red Stick (Pat Hogan) and his Creek warriors attack Andrew Jackson's troops.

that would take land away from the Indians, he decides to leave Congress.

Davy and George then take off for Texas to join with Colonel Jim Bowie at the Alamo in his fight against the Mexicans. When arriving they find the place in a serious situation: Commander Jim Bowie is wounded and cannot leave his bed. He informs Davy that they are running out of food and ammunition. The Mexicans attack and break into the fort. In the violent combat that follows the men fight furiously but the superiority of the Mexicans is too great, and the Alamo's defenders are all killed.

Notes: "*Davy Crockett*" was first shown on TV on *Frontierland*, as a part of the Walt Disney's series *Disneyland*. The first episode, "*Davy Crockett Indian Fighter*" was aired on December 5, 1954, and was soon followed by two more episodes: "*Davy Crockett Goes to Washington*" and "*Davy Crockett at the Alamo*." The three episodes were edited together and released to the movie theaters as a feature film, **Davy Crockett, King of the Wild Frontier. Crockett** became a great success and caused a tremendous "*Davy Crockett*" fever, first in United States but soon also around the world. Aiding the success of **Crockett** was most certainly the theme song, "The Ballad of Davy Crockett." The song became a hit and was placed number one on the Hit-Parade list for 13 weeks. **Davy Crockett** made Fess Parker, in the lead role, an overnight star and he would later appear in several Disney productions. The industry picked up on the Crockett idea and soon toy and department stores were filled with Davy Crockett items. It's said that more than ten million Crockett-coonskin hats were sold.

In late 1955, two more Crockett episodes were aired on television: "**Davy Crockett's Keelboat Race**" and "**Davy Crockett and the River Pirates.**" These were also cut together to a feature-length film and released as **Davy Crockett and the River Pirates**. This film, however, never became as popular as the original Crockett film.

"Although filmed economically ... this colour production made ideal movie fodder after its TV exposure.... In the midst of the idealism and fantasy of this romantic interpretation of the old West, **Davy Crockett** managed to evoke something of the hardship suffered by the pioneers..."—James R. Parish and Michael R. Pitts in *The Great Western Pictures*

"...Parker's cheerful interpretation of the title role (originally intended for Ebsen who subsequently took the supporting role of the journalist who publicizes Crockett's exploits) is perfectly matched by Foster's energetic direction."—Phil Hardey *The Western—A Complete Film Reference*

"...an episodic but wellpaced entertainment. Special animation involving Davy Crockett's *Journal,* and a colorful relief map of the country, provide transitions between segments, accompanied by special lyrics to the Davy Crockett theme song...

...The film itself is fairly well made, although occasional economies are apparent..."—Leonard Maltin *The Disney Films*

The Deerslayer (Vitagraph, 1913)

Directed by Hal Reid and Larry Trimble. Screenplay by Eugene Mullin from the novel by James Fenimore Cooper. Length: 2,000 feet.

Cast: *Natty* Wallace Reid, with Hal Reid, Florence Turner, Harry T. Morey, Walter Long, Ethel Dunn, Ed Thomas and Evelyn Dominicus.

Deerslayer (Luna Film, Germany, 1920)

Directed by Arthur Wellin. Story based on James Fenimore Cooper's *Leatherstocking Tales*. Length: 5 reels.

Cast: *Chingachgook* Bela Lugosi; *Deerslayer* Emile Mamelok.

The story: In 1740, in upstate New York, Deerslayer is a hunter who as an orphaned boy was adopted and raised by the Delawares. His boyhood friend is Chingachgook, son of the chief.

Chief Rivenoak, head of a band of Iroquois Indians, has in secret made an alliance with the French army. The plan is to capture Fort William and drive out the British settlers.

Deerslayer is on his way to meet with Chingachgook to help him recapture his bride Watawah, who has been taken away by the Iroquois, when he meets with trapper Hurry Harry at Glimmerglass Lake. Hurry Harry tells him about his friend, old Tom Hutter, who with his two daughters, Judith and Hetty, lives on the lake and claims that the lake is his. According to Harry, Tom has adopted the two girls after their parents were killed in an Indian raid, and he has built a castle on the lake for their protection.

Indians attack Deerslayer and Harry, but they escape and join the Hutters on the lake. When Deerslayer and Judith meet, affection arises between the two. Judith, however, has another love interest, Lt. Warley, at the fort. Because of the threatening situation, Warley planns to get the girls and bring them to the safety of the fort.

Tom and Harry, who both hate the Indians, go to the Iroquois village for revenge. Deerslayer tries to stop them but is unsuccessful. Their mission fails and the Indians capture Tom and Harry.

General Montcalm, commander of the French troops, finds out about the weakness of Fort William and decides to strike. The fort is taken, and when the British are leaving the French-allied Indians attack them in an ambush.

At the castle, Deerslayer, now joined by Chingachgook, informs the others about the capture of Tom and Harry by the Iroquois. Hetty decides to go on her own to save her father. Hetty is considered by the Indians to be feebleminded and under watch of the Great Spirit. Therefore no harm is expected for her.

At the Indian camp, Tom and Harry have been bound to poles and are threatened with burning. Hetty arrives and preaches to Rivenoak that one should love everyone, including one's enemy. Unwilling to listen, Rivenoak orders her returned to the lake. The situation calls for strategy and a two-tailed beast "an ivory elephant," found in Hutter's sailor chest, is sent to the Indians as a gift in exchange for the captives.

In the forest General Munro, commander of Fort William, joins Lt. Warley on his route to rescue the Hutters. The two-tailed beast has worked its magic on the superstitions of Rivenoak, and the captives are released.

Deerslayer and Chingachgook set out to save Watawah. Watawah is saved, but the Indians capture Deerslayer and he is threatened with death. Rivenoak, however, releases Deerslayer on condition that he shall bring back Watawah. If she is not willing to come, he must return himself.

The Indians attack the castle and Tom is mortally wounded. Before he dies he tells the girls that he is not their real father. Judith, who wants to find out the truth about her parents, discovers the answer in a letter left by Tom in his chest. In the letter he explains that their real father is General Munro, who shamefully had abandoned their mother when they both were infants. Later, when Tom met with their mother, she was killed by Rivenoak's band the day he was to marry her.

To keep his word, Deerslayer returns to the Indian camp. In the last minute before being burned, he is saved when British soldiers attack. During the battle, Hetty dies. Munro, regretful, realizes that he is the father of the girls. In spite of her love for Deerslayer, Judith decides to marry Warley. Deerslayer takes his farewell and joins Chingachgook and Watawah.

Notes: The story in this version of Cooper's *Deerslayer* may seem confusing. It is confusing only because it is a mix of two films. In its original release this German-produced film was issued in two parts: **Der Wildtöter** (**The Deerslayer**) and **Der Letzte der Mohikaner** (**The Last of the Mohicans**). When released as **Deerslayer** in the United States, the film was trimmed from 12 to five reels.

The story accordingly mixes events, people and timing from that of the original work. The attack on Fort William (Fort William Henry) appears parallel in time with Deerslayer's and Chingachgook's involvement with the Hutters on Glimmerglass Lake. In Cooper's original stories, *Deerslayer* takes place circa ten years earlier than the story in *The Last of the Mohicans*.

An interesting touch to the story is that Munro is revealed as the father of Hutter's "daughters." In *The Last of the Mohicans*, Munro also had a complicated father-daughter relationship. Cora in the Mohicans appears to be a result of a love affair he had with a slave woman during his military services in the West Indies. The real Colonel Munro (Monro and Monroe are also used as accepted spellings of his name), who served as the model character in Cooper's work, had three Scottish-born children: two sons, George and Sackville, and a daughter, Jane.

The Deerslayer (Republic, 1943)

Produced by E. B. Derr. Directed by Law Landers. Screenplay by E.B. Derr and P.S. Harrison. Photography by Arthur Martinelli. Running time: 67 minutes.

Cast: Bruce Kellogg, Yvonne DeCarlo, Warren Ashe, Trevor Bardette, Clancy Cooper, William Edmund, Wanda McKay, Jean Parker, Larry Parks, Addison Richards, Philip Van Zandt and Robert Warwick.

Notes: An independent production released through Republic. A cult film.

The Deerslayer (20th Century–Fox, 1957)

Produced and directed by Kurt Neumann. Screenplay by Carrol Young and Kurt

Neumann, based on the novel by James Fenimore Cooper. Photography in Cinemascope and De Lux color by Karl Strauss. Music by Paul Sawtell and Bert Shefter. Running time: 78 minutes.

Cast: *Deerslayer* Lex Barker, *Hetty* Rita Moreno, *Harry March* Forrest Tucker, *Judith* Cathy O'Donnell, *Tom Hutter* Jay C. Flippen, *Chingachgook* Carlos Rivas, *Old Warrior* John Halloran and *Huron Chief* Joseph Vitale.

The story: In 1740–45, Deerslayer is a young man who has been raised by a Mohican Indian tribe, of which Chingachgook is the chief. In the wilderness, the two friends save Albany trader Harry March from a band of hostile Huron Indians. Harry tells them of old Tom Hutter and his two daughters, who are besieged by Hurons farther down the river. Upon reaching the trio, they find them upon a strange floating raft-citadel. Hutter makes it clear that he hates all Indians since his wife was tortured and murdered by them.

On a scouting mission, Deerslayer and Chingachgook are trapped by Indians, but then saved by Hutter and Harry, who kills one of the Indians. Old Tom scalps the dead Indian and Deerslayer realizes that the half-mad man is a bounty hunter interested only in scalps. The Indians want to retrieve the scalp of their dead so that his soul may rest

The Deerslayer (20th Century–Fox, 1957)—From the pressbook.

The Deerslayer—Deerslayer (Lex Barker, *left*), Hetty (Rita Moreno) and Judith (Cathy O'Donnell) are imprisoned by the Hurons.

in peace. They attack the citadel, and capture Tom who is brought to their camp.

Deerslayer finds out that Hetty is not the old man's daughter but an Indian girl whom he carried away as a companion for Judith. To ransom the old man, Deerslayer and Chingachgook go to their camp to return the scalp. Harry has, however, stolen the scalp and at the Indian camp, when the Hurons find out that they have been duped, they attack the two men. They also capture Hetty and Judith. Just as the Indians are about to put the two friends to death, Harry fires upon the Huron camp with a cannon he has brought from the citadel. All are saved except old Tom, who is killed. Judith and Harry are reconciled and leave for Albany together, while Hetty and Chingachgook, drawn close by their blood tie, leave for the Mohican camp with Deerslayer.

Notes: A low budget version of Cooper's story, therefore a hesitating reception by critics:

"Again the one about the young white man raised by Mohican Indians. Cheapie was filmed on indoor sets with stock rear-projection footage of scenery. It's marginally better than the ludicrous 1943 version but who cares?"—Brian Garfield *Western Films A Complete Guide*

"A quickie that has its origins somewhere in Fenimore Cooper's often filmed classic... Inept, but not as inept as Lew Landers's 1943 version of the novel."—Phil Hardy *The Western*

The Deerslayer (Schick Sunn Classics, 1978)

Produced by Bill Donford. Directed by Dick Friendenberg. Screenplay by S.S. Schweitzer, based on James Fenimore Cooper's novel. Photography by Paul Hipp. Running time: 98 minutes.

Cast: Steve Forrest, Ned Romero and John Anderson.

Notes: This TV-feature depicts further adventures of Steve Forrest as Hawkeye and his Indian companion Ned Romero as Chingachgook, first seen in **Last of the Mohicans.**

The Devil's Disciple (United Artists 1939)

Produced by Harold Hecht. Directed by Guy Hamilton. Screenplay by John Dighton and Roland Kibbee. Photography by Jack Hildyard. Music by Richard Rodney Bennett. Running time: 83 minutes.

Cast: *Rev. Anthony Anderson* Burt Lancaster, *Dick Dudgeon* Kirk Douglas, *Gen. John Burgoyne* Laurence Olivier, with Janette Scott, Eva LeGallienne and Harry Andrews.

The story: Rev. Anthony Anderson and rabble-rouser Dick Dudgeon get involved in a story in which General "Gentleman Johnny" Burgoyne loses the New England colonies because of a stupid mistake by the British War Office.

Notes: This is a film version of George Bernard Shaw's satire set during the American Revolution.

Drums Along the Mohawk (20th Century–Fox 1939)

Produced by Raymond Griffith and Darryl F. Zanuck. Directed by John Ford. Screenplay by Lamar Trotti and Sonya Levien, based on the novel by Walter D. Edmonds. Photography in Threecolor Technicolor by Bert Glennon and Ray Rennahan. Music by Alfred Newman. Running time: 103 minutes.

Cast: *Lana Borst Martin* Claudette Colbert, *Gilbert Martin* Henry Fonda, *Mrs. McKlennan* Edna May Oliver, *Christian Reall* Eddie Collins, *Caldwell* John Carradine, *Mary Reall* Dorris Bowdon, *Mrs. Weaver* Jessie Ralph, *Father Rosenkrantz* Arthur Shields, *John Weaver* Robert Lowery, *General Nicholas Herkimer* Roger Imof, *Joe Boleo* Francis Ford, *Adam Hartmann* Ward Bond, *Mrs. Demooth* Kay Linaker, *Dr. Petry* Russel Simpson, *Blue Back* Chief Big Tree, *Landlord* Spencer Charters, *George* Arthur Aysleworth,

Drums Along the Mohawk (20th Century–Fox, 1939)—Violence and death: Gil returns with reinforcements to save the fort.

Jacobs Si Jenks, *Amos* Jack Pennick, *Robert Johnson* Charles Tannen, *Captain Mark Demooth* Paul McVey, *Mrs. Reall* Elisabeth Jones, *General* Lionel Pape, *Paymaster* Clarence Wilson, *Pastor* Edwin Maxwell, *Mrs. Borst* Clara Blandick, *Daisy* Beulah Hall Jones, *Mr. Borst* Robert Greig.

The story: Just before the Revolutionary War, Gil Martin marries Lana, an Eastern girl, and brings her to his farm in the Mohawk Valley. The drastic changes in way of life make it difficult at the beginning for Lana to adjust. She becomes hysterically frightened at the sight of the Christian Indian Blue Back. However, Lana soon adjusts and helps her husband with the daily farm work. She also bears Gil a baby.

The English are mobilizing the Indians against the American patriots. They attack Gil's farm and burn it to the ground. During the assault Lana loses her baby. Winter is approaching, leaving the family without hope for the future. Old Mrs. McKlennan hires the Martins as help on her farm.

Gil goes to war and becomes seriously wounded. His wife finds him in the wilderness and brings him home, which saves his life. Lana becomes pregnant again and the birth of the new baby restores the family's happiness.

The Indians attack again, and the farm families ensconce themselves in the fort. The English agent Caldwell assembles 1,000 Indians to attack the fort. The first attack is beaten off. Under protection of darkness, Gil slips away and goes to the nearest fort for help. When he returns with reinforcements, the Indians have attacked again and managed to get inside the walls. In a violent fight the Indian intruders are beaten and Gil takes his wife and child into his arms. As a sign of victory the farmer hoists the new American flag over the fort.

Notes: The script in **Drums** was based on Walter Edmonds's novel from 1936. *Drums Along the Mohawk* was Edmonds's most successful novel, and sold almost 250,000 copies when it was published, a phenomenal amount for the time. After

being published it stayed on the best-seller list for two years.

When producer Zanuck first read the draft script by Lamar Trotti and Sonya Levren in 1938, he criticized it for focusing too much on historical events. Zanuck wanted the story to be more of a romantic saga, concentrating on the lead couple, Gil and Lana Martin's efforts to adjust to a life in the Mohawk Valley during the Revolutionary War. To make it more adaptable to film, the final script had a lot of the Revolutionary background of the book excised.

To do **Drums Along the Mohawk** and to make it an epic, the studio allocated one of the largest budgets in its history to assure the utmost in effectiveness. After doing a thorough search to find a place similar to what the Mohawk Valley would have looked like during the American Revolution, Cedar County in South Utah was chosen.

Director John Ford and a crew of 300 were sent there to do pre-production work. A few weeks later, after cutting roads through dense forests and marsh land, the crew had reproduced an authentic Mohawk Valley atmosphere with a fort, a church and some settler farms. When the filming was completed, the studio was obligated to dismantle all the sets. This inspired Ford to include the destruction of the fort in the manuscript. When the Indians and the Tories attack the fort at the end of the movie, the well-constructed building structure was dynamited. When Fox left, workers only had to carry away the debris.

To add to authenticity, Fox spent money to search for unique props for the production. To supplement 18th-century artifacts, flintlock muskets once used by Ethiopian soldiers against Mussolini's aggression in the 1930s were tracked down and used in the settings.

For the battle scenes, casting required extras, and Fox hired approximately 1,000 natives from the area. For additional verisimilitude, 300 native Indians belonging to the Iroquois Confederacy were desired. In answer to a call, only two true Iroquois Indians turned up, and one of these was too

Drums Along the Mohawk—Gilbert Martin (Henry Fonda, *center*) and Lana (Claudette Colbert) revere the American flag after the final battle.

short for picture specifications. Ultimately Indians from other tribes was brought in for the production.

Henry Fonda's role as Gil Martin was probably a good choice, since he had his family roots in the Mohawk Valley area. Fonda's family dates back to the 1600s in American history. Douw Fonda, one of the characters in Edmonds's novel, had one of Henry Fonda's ancestors for a model. Claudette Colbert, cast as Lana Borst Martin, played a convincing role as a sophisticated young Eastern woman of nobility who in all senses grew and adjusted to the rough life on the frontier.

Drums Along the Mohawk was director John Ford's first color feature, and it remains one of his most commercial entries. A strength in all Ford's productions was good casting in the supporting roles, as is true here. Perhaps most memorable is Edna May Oliver in her role as Mrs. McKlennan.

In her role she was cast as a frontier "aristocrat," decisive and independent, but at the same time a warm-hearted person who cared about her fellow frontiersmen and was always ready to give a helping hand during a crisis. One of the most impressive scenes in the movie occurs when drunken Indians come to burn down her house and she forces them to carry her out of the home, bed and all. Viewers liked this scene, and for the role Oliver was nominated for an Academy Award for Best Supporting Actress.

Drums Along the Mohawk is one of the most remembered and discussed films dealing with American colonial history. Critics at the time the movie was released as well as later have generally been positive:

"**Drums Along the Mohawk** ... is a singularly satisfying film. The adaptation of Walter D. Edmonds' novel ... is an honest and faithful script and it has been blessed with truly brilliant handling."—*New York Herald Tribune*

"Certain vivid impressions can be recalled: Chief Big Tree's wonderful performance as Blue Black ... Edna May Oliver brow-beating the Indians as they carry her out of the house ... the unforgettable race when Henry Fonda outlasts his Indian opponents in a dash across the Wilderness."—Ralph and Natasha Friar in *The Only Good Indian*

"**Drums Along the Mohawk**, a fringe Western ... never lacked for excitement and was one of the better pictures of the period, both artistically and commercially."—Les Adams and Buck Rainey in *Shoot-Em-Ups*

"There is no doubt or ambiguity in this film—the American dream is still very much intact. This is possibly the only Ford film that deals so explicitly with the American dream where everything comes together with no uncertain edges."—J.A. Place in *The Western Films of John Ford*

"**Drums Along the Mohawk** is a powerful and inspiring cultural history of the American colonial pioneers. It is one of the building blocks of John Ford's monumental chronicle of the frontiers."—William R. Meyer in *The Making of the Great Westerns*

The Far Horizons (Paramount, 1955)

Produced by William H. Pine and William C. Thomas. Directed by Rudolph Maté. Screenplay by Winston Miller and Edmund H. North, based on the novel *Sacajawea of the Shoshones* by Della Gould Emmons. Photography in VistaVision and Technicolor by Charles Lawton Jr. Music by Hans Salter. Running time: 108 minutes.

Cast: *Captain Meriwether Lewis* Fred MacMurray, *Lieutenant William Clark* Charlton Heston, *Sacajawea* Donna Reed,

The Far Horizons (Paramount, 1955)—Before leaving for the Northwest expedition, Captain Meriwether Lewis (Fred MacMurray, *left*) and Lieutenant William Clark (Charlton Heston) compete for the affection of Julia Hancock (Barbara Hale).

The Far Horizons—Love develops during the expedition between Sacajawea (Donna Reed) and William Clark (Charlton Heston).

jawea at their side, to present their report. Though she loves Clark, Sacajawea realizes that she could never adapt to civilization; she leaves Clark and returns to her tribe in the Far West.

Notes: "A surprisingly dull account ... this slow and unimaginative safari seldom suggests either history or life. In some respects it is absurd.... Rudolph Mate's direction could hardly be more fumbling and erratic."—H.H.T. in *The New York Times*

"Great liberties were taken with the true characters here but ... even so provides a great deal of entertainment and visual reward as director Mate, a former cinematographer, records a stunning panorama of the American West."—*The Picture Guide*

Julia Hancock Barbara Hale, *Sergeant Gass* William Demarest, *Charboneau* Alan Reed, *Cameahwait* Eduardo Noriega, *Wild Eagle* Larry Pennell and *President Jefferson* Herbert Heyes.

The story: The year is 1803. President Jefferson has bought the Louisiana Territory from the French and sends Captain Meriwether Lewis and Lieutenant William Clark to explore the new-bought territory and proceed farther West to find a way to the Pacific Ocean.

Lewis and Clark compete for the affections of Julia Hancock, with Clark winning before the journey into the unknown. The expedition sets off on its way west on a riverboat on the Missouri River. On their way they meet with Shoshone woman Sacajawea, who leads the intrepid explorers to their far destination. Captain Lewis becomes further vexed when his partner also receives the love of Sacajawea.

The journey is troubled by Indian attacks, river hazards and seemingly insurmountable mountains. Finally the expedition reaches the Pacific and the explorers can return to Washington, D.C., with Saca-

The Fighting Kentuckian
(Republic, 1949)

Produced by John Wayne. Directed by George Waggner. Screenplay by George Waggner. Photography by Lee Garmes. Music by George Antheil. Running time: 100 minutes.

Cast: *John Breen* John Wayne, *Fleurette De Marchand* Vera Ralston, *Col. George Geraud* Philip Dorn, *Willie Paine* Oliver Hardy, *Ann Logan* Marie Windsor, *Blake Randolph* John Howard, *Gen. Paul De Marchand* Hugo Haas, *George Hayden* Grant Withers, *Mme. De Marchand* Odette Myrtil, *Beau Merritt* Paul Fix, *Sister Hattie* Mae Marsh, *Capt. Dan Corall* Jack Pennick, *Jacques* Mickey Simpson, *Carter Ward* Fred Graham, *Marie* Mabelle Koenig, *Friends* Shy Waggner, *Friends* Crystal White, *Announcer of Wrestling Contest* Hank Worden, *Band Leader* Charles Cane, *Drivers* Cliff Lyons, and Chuck Robertson.

The story: In 1819, John Breen is a

The Fighting Kentuckian (Republic, 1949)—John Breen (John Wayne, *right*) meets with lovely Fleurette De Marchand (Vera Ralston) on his return from New Orleans with his friend Willie Paine (Oliver Hardy, *center*).

member of a Kentucky regiment returning from New Orleans where Andrew Jackson has beaten the British army. In Mobile, Alabama, he meets lovely Fleurette De Marchand and stays behind with his friend Willie Paine to court Fleurette. Fleurette is the daughter of a French general who has fought with Napoleon and has led an exile contingent of French to settle in Alabama. The De Marchand family and their fellow exiles are under the influence of the powerful Blake Randolph, who also is in love with Fleurette.

Breen and Willie Paine take jobs as surveyors and find out that Randolph and his villainous companion George Hayden, who is leader of the rivermen, are trying to appropriate land of the French settlers. The plot leads to a battle between the French

troops and Randolph with Hayden and his rivermen. Randolph, however, changes his mind because of his love for Fleurette, and tries to stop the conflict. For that, he is shot down in cold blood by Hayden.

In the last minute a force of Kentucky Riflemen arrives and rescues the French. Breen kills Hayden and the French settlers are saved. John Breen marries Fleurette and the Fighting Kentuckians continue on their way home.

Notes: "Republic saw fit to co-star Wayne with Vera Ralston (first billed as 'Vera Hruba Ralston'), a Czechoslovakian ex–figure skating champion. It required the immense 'pulling power' of John Wayne to aid Miss Ralston's career whenever feasible, for she was an inept actress."—Gene Fernett in *Starring John Wayne*

"...It was one of his [Wayne's] lesser pictures.... It is distinguished visually by Lee

The Fighting Kentuckian—John Breen (John Wayne, *right*) ready to help Fleurette's father General Paul De Marchand (Hugo Haas), who has fought with Napoleon and leads exiled French soldiers in Alabama, against Blake Randolph.

Garmes' deep focus photography but otherwise gives little cause to stick in the mind…"—Allen Eyles in *John Wayne and the Movies*

Fighting the Iroquois in Canada (Kalem, 1910)

Length: 795 feet.

Follow the River (Hallmark, 1995)

Produced by Tom Luse. Directed by Martin Davison. Based on the 1981 novel by James Alexander Thom. Running time: 93 minutes.

Cast: *Mary Ingles* Sheryl Lee, *Wildcat* Eric Schweig, *Gretel* Ellen Burstyn, *Will* Tim Guinee, *Bettie Draper* Renee O'Conner, *Tommy Ingles* Tyler Noyes, *Henry Lenard* Andy Stahl, *Johnny Draper* Gabriel Macht, *LaPlante* Tony Amendola, *Goulart* Sammy D. Miller, *Buchanan* Graeme Malcolm, *Deer Following* Judson Keith Linn, and *Snake Stick* Jimmie F. Skaggs.

The story: A settlement on the Virginia frontier is raided by a Shawnee war party. Wildcat, the war party leader, and his warriors capture Mary Ingles and some other pioneer women to take them to their village. Being captured, Mary fights back with the only weapons she has: courage and determination. This impresses Wildcat, and he decides to make Mary his mate. This leads Mary to try to escape the Shawnee village. Together with another captive woman, Gretel, she enters on a harrowing journey through the Virginia wilderness toward freedom and home.

Fort Ti (Columbia, 1953)—From the pressbook.

Fort Ti (Columbia, 1953)

Produced by Sam Katzman. Director: William Castle. Story and screenplay by Robert E. Kent. Photography in 3-D and Technicolor by Lester H. White. Music by Ross DiMaggio. Running time: 78 minutes.

Cast: *Capt. Jedediah Horn* George Montgomery, *Fortune Mallorey* Joan Vohs,

Fort Ti—Captain Jed Horn (George Montgomery) inspects the new recruits while Sergeant Monday Wash (Irving Bacon) is watching.

Sergeant Monday Wash Irving Bacon, *Mark Chesney* James Seay, *Francois Leroy* Ben Aster, *Running Otter* Phyllis Fowler, *Major Rogers* Howard Petrie, *Bess Chesney* Cicely Browns, *Lord Jeffrey Amherst* Lester Matthews, *Captain Delacroix* George Dee and *Raoul de Moreau* Louis Merrill.

The story: In 1759, during the French and Indian War, Captain Jed Horn is an aide to Major Robert Rogers. He organizes a band of Rangers to march north to protect the territory against raiding Indians. At the same time, the main British army under Lord Jeffrey Amherst gathers for an attack on the French-held Fort Ticonderoga and Quebec.

Captain Horn and his men press on through dense forests, beset by hostile Indians and French regulars. On their route, Jed rescues from Indians the beautiful For-tune Mallorey, an English girl escaped from Fort Ti, who tells Jed that his sister and two children are prisoners in the fort. The Rangers fight their way to the fort to rescue the captives. The mission is further complicated because Jed expects that at any moment he and his men may be betrayed by Fortune, with whom he has fallen in love, but whom he suspects may be a French spy. Fortune, however, proves her reliability when she helps Jed spirit out his sister and her children from Fort Ti. Amherst and the main English force arrive and help Jed and his Rangers capture the fort. Jed and Fortune are now free to pursue their love.

Notes: This Sam Katzman production was filmed in Technicolor and in 3-D. When the movie was released three dimensional movie pictures were a new, interesting marketing tool to bring audiences to the movie theaters at a time when television was gaining more and more market share. The reason 3-D movies failed was probably the inconvenience the audience experienced with the special spectacles which were required to view the movies. *Variety* commented:

"Boxoffice chances for this stock outdoor actioner have been bolstered by use of Natural Vision 3-D, but despite value of the gimmick, its overall prospects are not big.

...Chief annoyance of 3-D is cheap paper viewers that refuse to stay fixed over the eyes..."

In spite of the new 3-D technology, the main focus for Columbia Pictures when releasing the film was on traditional exciting adventures. This is what the studio suggested for a 15-second radio spot in its pressbook:

"Make way for Rogers' Rangers as they ride, fight, love ... see the spectacular siege of 'Fort Ti'! ... all coming your way in Columbia Pictures' 'Fort Ti,' in color by Technicolor at the ... Theater. Be sure to see the thrill picture of the year, 'Fort Ti!'"

Rogers and his Rangers have been associated with their green buckskin uniforms. When shooting the film there were some problems matching the color of the uniforms with the surroundings. Also according to the pressbook:

"However, the green of the location forest wasn't the right shade for the green buckskins. Instead of dyeing the suits, it was decided to dye the forest. A film painter with a 12-foot spray handle attached to a bucket pump, used 1,000 gallons of special prepared tartrazine vegetable dye to make the forest match the costumes. It was cheaper, and more efficient a process!"

Francis Marion, the Swamp Fox
(Kalem, 1914)
Length: three reels

Cast: *Marion* Guy Coombs, with Marguerite Courtot.

The story: Marion is fighting Cherokee Indians and English troops during the Revolutionary War.

The Frontiersman (MGM, 1927)
Directed by Reginald Baker. Scenarios by L.G. Rigby. Story by Ross B. Wills and Madeleine Ruthven. Photography by Clyde de Vinna. Length: five reels.

Cast: *John Dale* Tim McCoy, *Lucy* Claire Windsor, *Abner Hawkins* Tom O'Brian, *Andrew Jackson* Russel Simpson, *Mrs. Andrew Jackson* Lillian Leighton, *Athalie Burgoyne* Louise Lorraine, *Mandy* May Foster, *Grey Eagle* Chief Big Tree, *White Snake* Frank Hagney, and *Colonel Coffee* John Peters.

The Story: In 1813, Captain John Dale and Sergeant Abner Hawkins are aiding General Jackson in his campaign against the Creek Indians. Dale is assigned by Jackson to escort his niece Lucy to a frontier fort where she is supposed to meet with her father. Dale has just recently left a disappointing love affair and he has problems handling Lucy's flirting.

When they reach the fort they find it abandoned and the entire garrison massacred by Indians, so they return. Jackson is seeking a way to make peace with the Creeks, and he sends Dale and Hawkins to negotiate with Chief White Snake. White Snake, however, rejects the options. A conflict arises between Dale and Hawkins, which Dale settles in a duel.

Dale's feelings for Lucy change, and he starts to fall in love with her. During an Indian raid she is captured but Dale arrives and rescues her.

Notes: Tim McCoy appeared in a series of successful silent westerns for MGM

Opposite, top: The Frontiersman (MGM, 1927)—In between scenes shot. Lucy (Claire Windsor) is entertained by Native American actors. *Bottom:* Director Reginald Barker (*center*) surrounded by the main cast. *From left to right:* Lucy (Clair Windsor), Abner Hawkins (Tom O'Brien), cameraman Clyde Devina, John Dale (Tim McCoy), and Andrew Jackson (Russell Simpson).

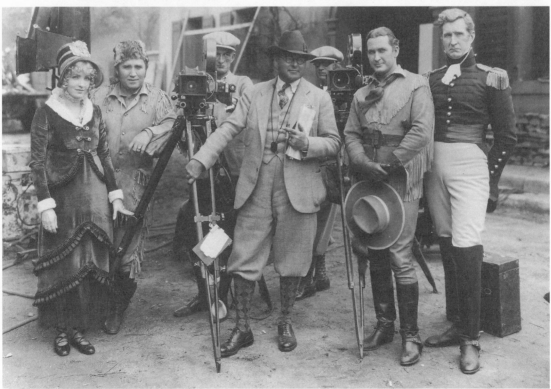

during the 1920s. **The Frontiersman** was one of these, even if it was not more of a western than was **Winners of the Wilderness**, released during the same year.

Variety considered the story too elaborate, with too much emphasis on flair and costumes rather than on action:

"For some reason the punch doesn't eventuate, possibly because the material is ineffective.... Fair enough program picture for the juvenile fans. Otherwise just a release."

A more recent review did not share this opinion:

"The action sequences as in **The Frontiersman** were quite brutal for their time, making one wonder if MGM was really gearing the Tim McCoy pictures for the 'kiddie matinee' trade..."—*All-Media Guide*

Gathering of the Council of the Six Nations (1911)

General Marion, the Swamp Fox
(Champion, 1911)
Length: 950 feet

The story: In 1781, General Marion and his guerrilla troops fight the British in South Carolina at Fort Warren and Eutaw Springs.

George Washington (MGM/UA TV mini-series, 1984)

Produced by Richard Fielder. Directed by Buzz Kulik. Story by Richard Fielder and Jon Boothe, based on the biography by James Thomas Flexner. Photography by Harry Stradling, Jr. Music by Laurence Rosenthal.

Cast: *George Washington* Barry Bostwick, *Martha Washington* Patty Duke Astin, *George William Fairfax* David Dukes, *Sally Fairfax* Jaclyn Smith, *Lieut. Gov. Robert Dinwiddie* Jose Ferrer, *John Adams* Hal Holbrook, *Lord Fairfax* Trevor Howard, *General Horatio Gates* Jeremy Kemp, *George Mason* Richard Kiley, *General Benedict Arnold* Stephen Macht, *General Edward Braddock* James Mason, *Mary Ball Washington* Rosemary Murphy, *Lord Loudoun* Clive Revill, *General John Stark* Robert Stack, *St. Pierre* Anthony Zerbe, *Dan* Jace Alexander, *General Gage* Michael Allinson, *Caleb Quinn* Lloyd Bridges, *Eban Krutch* Leo Burmester, *Billy Lee* Ron Canada, *Lafayette* Philip Casnoff, *John Laurens* Kevin Conroy, *Abigail Adams* Christine Estabrook, *Sam Adams* Richard Fancy, *Peggy Shippen* Megan Gallagher, *General Charles Lee* John Glover, *Lieutenant Stewart* Kelsey Grammer, *Patrick Henry* Harry Groener, *General Nathanael Greene* Scott Hylands, *Colonel Joseph Reed* Tom Mason, *Baron von Streuben* Kurt Knudson, *Loudoun* Clive Revill, *Alexander Hamilton* Robert Schenkkan and *General Artemus Ward* Brad Sullivan.

Part I
Running time: 150 minutes.

The story: Events begin in Virginia in 1743. During George Washington's childhood his father dies and wills his larger farms to two sons from a previous marriage. This leaves George, his mother and his younger brothers and sisters to live in near poverty. George finds a substitute father in his admired half brother Lawrence. Lawrence is living at the farm he has inherited and named Mount Vernon.

Lawrence marries one of the young ladies of Lord Fairfax's family. The Fairfaxes are one of the most powerful families in Virginia. Through Lawrence's marriage, George is introduced into the Virginia aristocracy and becomes good friends with Lawrence's wife's brother Will.

On a journey into the wilderness to explore the Ohio country, George and Will learn practical surveying and woodsmen's life. Back in Virginia, Lawrence and Will

Opposite: The Frontiersman—top: Production shot; *bottom:* Director Reginald Barker directs his "troops."

George Washington (Part I of the MGM/UA TV mini-series, 1984)—A young George Washington (Barry Bostwick, *left*) with his friend Will Fairfax (David Dukes).

Fairfax enter politics and are elected to the House of Burgesses. During a visit to Williamsburg, George meets Will's new wife Sally. For George, Sally will be his distant love for the rest of his life. Lawrence dies of tuberculosis to the great distress of George.

On the frontiers the French are advancing forces to secure land. On recommendations by Lawrence, Governor Dinwiddie sends George to the French Fort Le Boeuf to claim the land rights for the British. The mission is a failure and Washington returns and advises Dinwiddie to send a military force to drive off the French. Promoted to lieutenant colonel, Washington is sent out with a regiment to attack Fort Le Boeuf. On their journey Washington ambushes a French patrol and kills a French officer. This would be the first shot in what became a world war.

For protection Washington is erecting a small fortification named Fort Necessity. French and Indian allies attack the fort and Washington has to surrender to the French. Back in Virginia, Dinwiddie accuses Washington of surrendering the fort and starting a war. George decides to take up civil life and is allowed to lease the Mount Vernon property of the Fairfaxes.

To deal with the "French problem," the British are sending an army under command of General Edward Braddock to the colony. Braddock's army is advancing into the wilderness to capture Fort Duquesne at the junction of the Monongahela and Allegheny rivers. Washington is accompanying the campaign as a colonial officer. To support the troops, Braddock sends Washington to Williamsburg to bring back funds. On the journey, Sally nurses George, who falls sick with fever. Partly recovered,

George returns to the army. In a furious attack, French and Indians ambush Braddock's army. The British are defeated and the army retreats. Braddock is killed, and due to Washington's bravery during the retreat of the army, Dinwiddie later appoints him to colonel and commander of a Virginia regiment.

In 1757, George meets a wealthy widow, Martha Dandrige Curli, to whom he proposes and later marries.

Once again to bring the French to terms, the British send a new army under General John Forbes against Fort Duquesne. At its arrival, Washington camps with Forbes's army and finds out that the enemy had burned the fort and disappeared down the Ohio.

After the campaign Washington decides to leave military service and returns to Mount Vernon. His new-wedded wife and her children from her previous marriage are moving in.

A few years later in 1764 a growing dissatisfaction against the British stamp taxation brings Washington into politics.

Part II

Running time: 100 minutes.

In 1764, there is a growing dissatisfaction among the colonies with the British rule. George is elected to represent Fairfax County in the Virginia House of Burgesses. The forbidden love between him and Sally continues. George's stepdaughter, Patsy, is facing a serious problem with epilepsy.

George Washington—The retreat of Braddock's army. Caleb Quinn (Lloyd Bridges, *right*) pulls a cart through the river while George Washington (Barry Bostwick, *left*) attends the mortally wounded General Braddock. (Note the woman at the far right corner in striped shirt and the "cowboy" in the center—probably horse wranglers).

In the House of Burgesses, the new Stamp Act laid upon the colonies by the king becomes a source for lively discussions. Will takes the side of the British, which creates a tension between him and George. The progress of Patsy's illness results in her death.

A new source of dissatisfaction comes with the British enforcement of a tax on tea. An open rebellion first starts in Massachusetts. After the Boston Tea Party, the country is further divided. Will and Sally decide to leave their home and escape to England, which leaves George alienated from the woman he truly loves.

In 1774 the First Continental Congress is held in Philadelphia. John Adams from Massachusetts argues for military resistance against England. News arrives about firing on the king's troops at Lexington and Concord, and an open conflict is a fact.

John Adams wants George to be the military leader of the patriots, and in June 1775 Washington is appointed to general and commander of the American Army. In a meeting with his generals after the American defeat in Boston, Yankee General Stark expresses his doubts about the selection of a Virginian for commander.

During an inspection of the troops, Washington finds them demoralized and in bad condition. Realizing the need for supplies and training, he starts to raise funds for the army. Benedict Arnold arrives and offers his services for the American task, and Washington orders him to lead a Northern campaign to take Quebec. Arnold's campaign fails, however, and he is wounded. The route for a British invasion from the North is now open.

The Americans gain a symbolic victory when Captain Knox brings in cannons he has captured at Fort Ticonderoga on Lake Champlain. With the help of the cannons, the Americans recapture Boston when they bombard the British troops from Dorchester Heights.

In 1776 Washington moves his army to New York, which initiates an advance of the British toward the city. During the British landing on Long Beach, the Americans are there to meet them, which starts some violent fighting. At the Brooklyn Heights the Americans are beaten. Scottish Highlanders and British-allied Hessians force them to retreat.

To save the army Washington comes up with a plan, and during the night he evacuates all of the troops across the Hudson to Manhattan. The maneuver is successful and in the morning the British find out that the American Army is gone.

Part III
Running time: 148 minutes.

In December 1776, the morale is low in the American Army. The British have so overwhelmed it that the defeats have an astounding effect nationwide. Desperate measures are required in order for Washington to score a much-needed victory. Washington makes up a plan to strike the British in New Jersey. The plan is to cross the Delaware and surprise the enemy during New Year's time. The password for the operation is "Victory or death." The plan works, and the much-needed victory comes at Trenton, where Washington captures the Hessian army.

At Morristown, New Jersey, young Captain Alexander Hamilton arrives and offers his services to Washington. For the rest of the war he will be one of Washington's faithful military aides. Another young officer also joins Washington, the passionate Marquis de Lafayette from France.

Intelligence shows that British General Howe intends to take Philadelphia. This causes Washington to move his army from the area. Information about a major victory in New York, where General Gates has defeated Burgoyne's invading army, raises the spirit of the troops.

Washington moves his army to Valley Forge for the winter, where he faces a challenge of his leadership abilities and the possibility of the new war hero, Gage, succeeding him. With his wife Martha's arrival comes strength and support, and he regains his power. To raise spirits among the troops,

George Washington—After Yorktown, Washington (Barry Bostwick) bids an emotional farewell to his officers.

German Baron Von Streuben is brought in. In spite of his hard drilling of the men they like him.

British Commander Clinton intends to evacuate Philadelphia and move his army to New Jersey. On their route the Americans attack Clinton's wagon train at Monmouth. During the battle Washington's second in command, General Lee, fails in an attempt to strike against the British rear. This starts a dispute between Washington and Lee and an angry Washington relieves Lee of his command.

In 1778, the American Army is starving in Morristown. General Benedict Arnold, wounded in the Northern campaign, is appointed military commander of West Point. To the great distress of Washington, Arnold is revealed as a traitor.

With the French entering as allies to the Americans, the war moves to a close. At the Battle of Yorktown in 1781, Cornwallis surrenders to Washington. Washington bids an emotional farewell to his officers. He resigns from his military service and returns home to Mount Vernon, where a new life awaits him as a private citizen.

Notes: This massive eight-hour TV mini-series covers the life of Washington from age 11 to his farewell to the troops at Yorktown. A couple of years later a sequel was done, **George Washington: The Forging of a New Nation**, which deals with Washington's presidency.

The series was filmed entirely on location in Virginia and Pennsylvania, which gave it an authentic look. The battle scenes under the direction of Buzz Kulik are beautifully realized, particularly General Braddock's defeats at Duquesne, Monmouth and Yorktown.

Barry Bostwick makes a good performance in this film, and there are some convincing role appearances: Lloyd Bridges as a trapper in the French and Indian War episode, George Mason as General Brad-dock, Trevor Howard as Lord Fairfax, Hal Holbrook as John Adams and Stephen Macht as the traitorous Benedict Arnold.

Variety was positive in its review:

"...they have been able to make history from the Revolutionary Period not only palat-able but entertaining; any history teacher can envy that—and be thankful to the creators of the work."

George Washington: The Forging of a Nation (MGM/UA TV mini-series, 1986)

Produced by David Gerber. Directed by William A. Graham. Story by Richard Fielder, based on the biography by James Thomas Flexner. Photography by James Crabe. Music by Bruce Broughton. Run-ning time: 190 minutes.

Cast: *George Washington* Barry Bost-wick, *Martha Washington* Patty Duke Astin, *Thomas Jefferson* Jeffrey Jones, *John Adams* Paul Collins, *Monroe* Robert Kelly, *Edmund Randolph* Norman Snow, *Alexan-der Hamilton* Richard Bekins, with Penny Fuller, Guy Paul, Lise Hilboldt, Haviland Morris, Daniel Davis, Sam Tsoutsouvas, Farnham Scott, Leo Burmester, Nicholas Kepros, Richard Fancy, Clayton Prince, Erica Alexander, Timothy Landfield, Gre-gory Abels, Eve Bennett-Gordan, Christo-pher Goutman and Jonathan Farwell.

The Story: The story starts in 1788 at Virginia's Constitutional Ratification Con-vention. A president has to be elected and George Washington is an obvious choice. To support Washington, Thomas Jefferson is assigned as secretary of state affairs and Alexander Hamilton as secretary of treasury.

During his presidential period, Wash-ington has to handle opposed viewpoints on the politics by individualists such as Jefferson, Hamilton and Adams. Among matters he must deal with are such things as the Whisky Rebellion.

Back home at Mount Vernon, Martha Washington carries out the day-to-day ne-cessities on the estate, and gets involved with slaves who, with the forging of a new nation, are looking for new opportunities in seeking their freedom.

The story concludes with Washington's ending of his second presidential term.

Notes: As a follow-up to the 1984, eight-hour TV series **George Washington**, this mini-series was produced using some of the same actors. Barry Bostwick is back as Washington, as is Patty Duke Astin as Martha Washington. The film concerns it-self with the events of 1788 through 1797 during Washington's presidential adminis-tration. Historians were skeptical:

"All too often, it is a trivial, inaccurate, usually outmoded view of one of the most significant periods of the United States history. If teachers use it for classroom purposes, they should do so only with great caution."—Robert F. Jones in *Film and History*

The Great Meadow (MGM, 1931)

Directed by Charles Brabin. Screenplay by Edith Ellis and Charles Brabin, based on the 1930 novel by Elizabeth Madox Rob-ert. Photography by William Daniels and Clyde de Vinna. Running time: 80 minutes.

Cast: *Berk Jarvis* Johnny Mack Brown, *Diony Hall* Elenor Boardman, *Elvira Jarvis* Lucille La Verne, *Betty Hall* Anita Louise, *Evan Muir* Gavin Gordan, *Reuben Hall* Guinn Williams, *Thomas Hall* Russell Simpson, *Mistress Hall* Sahra Padden, *Sally Tolliver* Jerome Eddy, *James Harrod* James Marcus, *Joe Tandy*, Andy Shoford, with Jack Winn, Chief Whitespear and William Bakewell.

The story: Berk Jarvis and Diony Hall, a newly-married couple inspired by a speech by Daniel Boone, accompany a band of pioneers journeying from Virginia to Kentucky in 1777.

On their adventurous route, they cut their feet walking through the mountains and watch food and baggage sweep away in turbulent rivers. Finally they reach Fort Harrod and are welcomed by a little group of settlers who have preceded them there.

Diony's child is to be born soon. While

The Great Meadow (MGM, 1931)—Problems on the route to Kentucky: Indians attack at the Cumberland Gap.

she and Berk's mother are working in the fields, an Indian attacks them, and the older woman dies protecting the girl. The baby is born in Berk's newly-built cabin outside the fort while Berk is away on a long expedition to the salt deposits.

On his return Berk is off almost at once on another expedition to recover his mother's scalp, which swings at the belt of Black Fox. He is captured, turned over to the British, escapes and is captured again. Finally his death is reported, and Diony, helpless by herself in the wilderness, marries another man. After two years Berk returns, and Diony, according to the law of the wilderness, must make her choice between the two men.

Notes: The Great Meadow is a Daniel Boone story which recreates the struggle of Virginia colonials who, during the Revolu-

tionary War, move to settle the wilderness of Kentucky, called by the Indians "The Great Meadow."

A *New York Times* review was generally favorable:

"Somehow the film catches the warm personal quality and quiet rhythm of the author's prose.... Both Miss Boardman and Mr. Brown deliver sterling performances and the work of the entire cast is noteworthy."

Also a more recent review was positive:

"Naive and primitive but still compelling story of Virginians who undertake mountainous trek to settle new land in Kentucky, circa 1777. Fairly authentic drama gives a real sense of the hardship these pioneers endured."—Leonard Maltin's *Movie and Video Guide*

The film was reported to take one year to make. *Variety* had a hilarious sarcastic review for this:

The Great Meadow—A "cliff-hanger": Berk Jarvis (Johnny Mack Brown) is in trouble.

"How this got through its rushes, how it escaped from the Metro shelves or how it got in to the Capitol ("movie theatre") probably never will be explained."

Also, *The Motion Picture Guide* was hesitant:

"Ambitious but utterly abysmal ... Battling Indians, clearing forests, and foraging for food are minor annoyances in comparison to watching this monstrosity, which reportedly took a year to film. Leading lady Boardman retired a year after its release—not soon enough."

Director Charles Brabin tried to be correct on the colonial settings in the picture even if most of the outdoor filming was done within 50 miles of Los Angeles. Johnny Mack Brown cast as Berk Jarvis did his first western appearance in this movie. His western stardom would come later in 1935 when he did several independent westerns for Republic and Supreme.

Hannah Dustin: The Border Wars of New England (Kalem, 1908)

Directed by Sidney Olcott. Length: 825 feet.

Hawkeye and the Last of the Mohicans (CBC-Normandie Prods. TV series, 1956-57)

Produced by Sigmund Neufeld and Sam Newfield. 39 episodes @ 26 minutes.

Below are the premier and some of the other episodes.

General cast: *Hawkeye* John Hart; *Chingachgook* Lon Chaney, Jr.

"Hawkeye's Homecoming"

Directed by Sidney Salkow. Written by Richard Schayer. Produced by Irving Cummings, Jr.

Cast: *Ogano* Michael Ansara, *Captain West* Casey Adams, *Marian* Lili Fontaine, *Colonel Thorne* Leslie Denison, *Captain Bownell* Stacy Harris, *Mrs. Cutler* Don Garner, *Ottawa Chief* Frank De Kova and *General Montcalm* Gregory Gaye.

The time is 1757, on the Iroquois Trail in New York. British scout Nat Cutler, known as Hawkeye, has a younger brother Tommy who is in service of the British. He is sent from Fort William Henry to request military aid from General Johnson in Albany. Indian traitor Ogano kills Tommy in the woods when he is carrying a dispatch from Johnson, who refuses help.

French General Montcalm is planning an attack on Fort William Henry. Returning to the fort, Ogano falsely informs its occupants that help is to be expected from Albany. Hawkeye and his Mohican friend Chingachgook express their doubts about Ogano's information, which leads to their jailing. A Captain West, however, arrives and confirms that Ogano is a traitor who provokes the Indians against the British.

The French and the Indians attack the fort. Ogano captures Colonel Thorne's daughter Marian. Hawkeye and Captain West go after them. When approaching the escapees in the woods, they run into a party of Ottawa. Ogano claims Marian against Hawkeye's protests. According to Ottawa law, the chief decides that their arguments shall be settled in a combat. Hawkeye besieges Ogano and the white party is allowed to leave in peace.

Colonel Thorne suggests that Hawkeye stay in the service of the British, but Hawkeye turns down the offer because he and Chingachgook are heading north.

"The Way-Station"

Directed by Sidney Salkow. Written by Art Browne, Jr. Produced by Sidney Salkow.

Cast: *Tonkawa* Jim Droohaa, *Nacona* Rex Devlin, *Liza* Marjorie Purvey, *Odanna* Frank Perry, *Willow Whist* Joan Blackman, and *Zac* Paul Endersly.

Hawkeye and Chingachgook are attacked and captured by Mingos. Chief Nacona is peaceful but one of his young braves, Tonkawa, has a hostile attitude against the intruders.

Both Tonkawa and another young warrior, Odanna, have love interests in Chief Nacona's daughter Tankalo. To settle matters Nacona proclaims a contest between the two young opponents. The one who shoots the biggest deer will win Tankalo and also become the next chief, according to tribal rules.

On their hunting expedition in the forest, Tonkawa double-crosses his competitor and shoots him in the back. Hawkeye and Chingachgook find Odanna, who is only wounded.

In the Mingo camp, Tonkawa claims that Hawkeye has shot Odanna. The Mingos attack the trading station where Hawkeye has brought the wounded Odanna. The treachery of Tonkawa is disclosed. In a fight Hawkeye defeats Tonkawa, Odanna gets his bride and peace is restored.

"The Delaware Hoax"

Directed by Sam Newfield. Written by Louis Stevens. Produced by Sigmund Neufeld.

Cast: *Stanwell* W.M. Walker, *Johnson* Pawys Thomas, *Major Tilton* Earl Grey, *Black Fox* Alex Denaszody and *Blaisdell* Glynn Morris.

Trader Stanwell accuses the Delaware tribe of robbery of merchandise transports. Hawkeye and Chingachgook go to their village to settle things. Wrongly accused, Chief Black Fox wants to go on the warpath against the whites. To prevent war, Hawkeye and Chingachgook promise to find the real robbers.

Hawkeye discloses the plot when land speculator Johnson together with Stanwell and his men are undertaking an "Indian" raid. By laying the blame on the Delaware, Johnson hopes to obtain their land. With the help of British soldiers the renegades are caught and the Delaware are freed from suspicion.

"The Contest"

Written by Bob Bailey and Hugh King.

Cast: *Stark* Jim Barron, *Anoki* Don Garrard, *Wandam* Ed Holmes, *Negus* Lee Cramford, *Travis* Brendan Dillon, and *Medicine Man* Eric Clavering.

A masked trapper and his Indian companion are stealing furs from friendly Seneca Indians. Hawkeye and Chingachgook are blamed and a price is put on their heads. They leave for the Seneca camp. The real renegades, half-blood Stark and his Indian ally, arrive at the camp and accuse Hawkeye and Chingachgook. The chief's son Negus defends them.

To prove guilt according to "Indian rules," a contest between Hawkeye and Stark is going to take place. After three days of starvation and no sleep, the two antagonists meet in different combats. During a last shooting contest his Indian companion unveils Stark's guilt. Stark is killed.

"False Witness"

Written by Louis Stevens.

Cast: *Lt. Trelway* Rodney Bunker, *Col. Courtney* William Walsh, *Jim Foster* Donald Gerrard, *Sam Martin* Frederic Diehl, *Sally* Margaret Griffin, and *Brown* Sid Brown.

Two payroll messengers are found in the woods after having been ambushed by white men. At Fort McKenzie, Colonel Courtney finds out that one of the dead is his brother. He sends Hawkeye on a mission to seek information in an area where the renegades may be located. As a cover, Hawkeye is appointed as head of a trading post. Hawkeye meets with trader Jim Foster, who claims that land surveyor Sam Martin is the leader of the robbers. Martin in his turn accuses Jim Foster of the same crime.

A trap is set up by spreading false rumors about a new extensive money transport. The true renegade Martin and his gang fall into the trap and are caught when they are on their way to overtake the transport. Jim Foster is cleared of all suspicions.

"False Faces"

Written by Bob Bailey and Hugh King.

Cast: *Major Adams* William Walsh, *Captain McIntyre* Peter Humphreys, *Snowbird* Helene Gilbert, *Raven* Fred Evringer, *Chief Sanehu* Ed Holmes and *Kling* Jon Granik.

Persons wearing Mingo facemasks rob an army supply transport. Major Adams blames the Mingos. Hawkeye and Chingachgook are sent to Post Soya to help the post commander, Captain McIntyre, deal with the problem.

The "False Faces" rob an Indian, Raven, and his wife Snowbird of their pelts. To protect himself Raven tries to obtain a rifle. Trader Happy Sealy, who lies behind the "False Faces," gives him a rifle which was stolen from the army transport, with the purpose of directing suspicion at him. Raven is arrested for being leader of the "False Faces." Hawkeye and Chingachgook, however, unveil Sealy. With the help of Mingos, the real "False Faces" are captured.

"The Threat"

Written by Endre Bohem and Lois Vittes.

Cast: *Jack Flint* John Paris, *Rafe* Lloyd Chester, *Hiram Bass* George Barnes, *Sarah Bass* Elizabeth Cole and *Stark* Eric Heath.

Hurons attack Chingachgook and Hawkeye in the woods. In the area some English City folk have settled. The local trader Jack Flint is treating the settlers badly.

Tired of Flint's discrimination, settler Hiram Bass leaves with his family. On their way Hurons ambush them. Hawkeye and Chingachgook come to their relief. Hawkeye suggests Bass move north to the land of the Iroquois, which would be safer.

Hawkeye goes to Flint's trading post to reclaim pelts that have been stolen from some trappers. An exhausted Bass arrives to say that Flint has arranged the kidnapping of his family. Turning against Flint, Hawkeye and Chingachgook are caught and tied to a raft that is sent drifting downriver toward the Huron camp.

Flint and two Hurons follow in canoes. Hawkeye and Chingachgook manage to get loose, and take the pursuers by surprise. With Flint out of the way the English settlers can live in peace.

Notes: Based on James Fenimore Cooper's novels, this syndicated Canadian TV production ran for 39 episodes; the 30 minute episodes were action-packed. The series had the typical build-up of any western series on TV during the 50s. A quick plot, villains (white or Indians) are harassing nice people, heroes (Hawkeye and Chingachgook) come to the rescue and everyone is happy (except the villains).

Not to interfere with the plots, only rare moments were spent filling in viewers on Cooper's work and the history of the period. One exception might be the premiere episode, "Hawkeye's Homecoming," in which the heroes are involved in Montcalm's siege of Fort William Henry in accordance with Cooper's *Last of the Mohicans* story. Actually the episode is a short version of the 1950 movie, **The Iroquois Trail** (United Artists), and it contains stock footage from this movie as well as from the 1936 version of *The Last of the Mohicans*.

Throughout the episodes in this series, Hawkeye and Chingachgook try to keep peace on the Eastern frontiers. In the cast as Hawkeye, the tall, good looking John Hart had many stage performances under his belt before he entered the movie industry. Like that of many other actors of the period, his career was interrupted by World War II. After returning from the war, the **Hawkeye** series brought him some fame. As his sidekick Chingachgook, Lon Chaney, Jr., was selected. His father was known as "the man of thousand faces" because of his elaborate disguises in macabre roles, a tradition that was largely followed by Chaney Jr.

Four feature movies were edited from the series: **The Long Rifle and the Toma-**

hawk, **The Pathfinder and the Mohican, The Redmen and the Renegades** and **Along the Mohawk Trail.**

"This Canadian series is curious in making insistent reference to Cooper, yet actually having almost no real relation to his story."—Martin Barker and Roger Sabin in *The Lasting of the Mohicans*

"Hawkeye was one of TPA's strongest '57 properties, its 39 episodes drawing fans from all viewer age groups. All this proved, perhaps, that if you had a frontier hero, and an Indian companion, and a series that looked enough like a western to satisfy western happy viewers of the time, you had it made."—Hal Erickson in *Syndicated Television The First years 1947–1987.*

Hawkeye, the First Frontier (Stephen J. Cannell Productions Inc. TV series, 1994)

Produced by Stephen J. Cannell.

General cast: *Hawkeye* Lee Horsley, *Elizabeth Shields* Lynda Carter, *Chingachgook* Rodney A. Grant, *Captain Taylor Shields* Garwin Sanford, *McKinney* Lochlyn Munro, and *Peevey* Jed Rees. 22 episodes @ 50 minutes.

Episodes 1 and 2 (Pilot)

Written by Kim LeMasters. Directed by Brad Turner and James Cortner.

Guest players: *William Shields* Michael Berry, with Eric Keenley-Side and Richard Sali.

In 1755 the quiet land of the Hudson valley is enmeshed in the turmoil of the French and Indian War. William and Elizabeth Shields are on their way from Virginia to set up a trading post at Fort Bennington. On their route they are attacked by Hurons, but are saved by British scout Hawkeye and his Mohican friend Chingachgook. Arriving at the fort, Elizabeth is setting up the trade and hires young McKinney and Peevey. William Shields's brother Taylor is an officer in the fort, which is commanded by Colonel Munro.

In exchange for previously having bought Taylor his officer commission,

William requires Taylor to help him set up fur trading relations with neighboring Indian tribes. Taylor is double-crossing his brother by sending him into the forest guided by two renegade trappers. On a river Hurons attack them and William is captured.

Later Elizabeth sets out to rescue William, who is believed to be captured and brought to a French fort. Hawkeye follows. McKinney and Peevey also go on their own mission to save William. They are, however, caught in the woods by a French patrol.

Hawkeye and Elizabeth blow up an ammunition store of the French fort and relieve McKinney and Peevey. William is not to be found in the fort, and the hope of finding him is faint when rumors suggest that he has been taken away by Iroquois.

Episode 3: "The Bear"

Written by Tom McBeath. Directed by Richard Compton.

Guest players: Tom McBeath and Andrew Kavadas.

After Elizabeth's encounters with wild animals in the forest, she decides to take lessons from Hawkeye in wilderness survival skills. In exchange she will teach him how to read.

Some renegade traders steal ammunition, which they are supposed to deliver to the British at Fort Bennington, to trade with the French.

In the woods Hawkeye and Elizabeth find out about the treachery and when a French patrol is arriving to collect the ammunition from the renegades, they fool the French, by using explosive gunpowder, into believing that they are surrounded by English troops. In the last minute when the trick is about to be revealed, Captain Taylor arrives with a company of British soldiers and rescues Hawkeye and Elizabeth.

Episode 4: "The Furlough"

Written by Steve Feke. Directed by Christopher Leitch. Guest players: Gordon Tootoosis, Jill Teed, Eli Gabay, Kate Twa and Lorne Cardinal.

Hawkeye, the First Frontier (Stephen J. Cannell Productions Inc., 1994)—Hawkeye (Lee Horsley) and Elizabeth Shields (Lynda Carter).

Sara Prichard is helping a woman at the fort who has been offended by a soldier. A French trapper who is a British spy for Captain Taylor arrives at the fort with his Huron wife, North Wind.

During a journey in the woods the French trapper attacks and captures Sara, but Hawkeye kills the offender and saves her. Chief Revanok and his Hurons, seeking revenge for the killing of North Wind's husband, later capture Hawkeye. Hawkeye is bound to a pole and the warriors start throwing tomahawks at him. Most threatening is North Wind's brother. Sara is trying to get Taylor to send a relief party for Hawkeye but he refuses.

Chingachgook and Sara decide to rescue Hawkeye on their own. Sara tries to purchase Hawkeye's freedom, and explains that the reason for his killing the trapper was that he had offended her. Revanok accepts her explanation, but North Wind's brother wants to settle their argument in a man-to-man combat. The Huron falls, but Hawkeye spares his life, temporarily restoring peace so that Hawkeye and Sara can leave.

Episode 5: "The Siege"

Written by Steve Feke and David Levinson. Directed by Brad Turner. Guest players: Duncan Fraser, John Novak, Robert Lewis and Barry Greene.

The French attack Fort Bennington. Rumors have it that they are bringing an enormous 32-pound cannon from Fort Carillon to smash the fort. In a parley the French give the British commander 12 hours to surrender. The affection between Hawkeye and Elizabeth is growing during the crisis.

Hawkeye gets an idea to penetrate behind the enemy lines. Acting as a wounded French scout, he is brought by Elizabeth, playing a nurse, into the French camp. When the plot is unveiled, they have to escape into the woods. Pursued by Hurons, they are saved by Chingachgook.

At Fort Bennington the British prepare for capitulation. In the forest, Hawkeye and Chingachgook track the route of the French troops bringing the cannon and manage to put it out of action by pushing it over a mountain ridge. Just before the capitulation is signed, the heroes arrive and announce that the main threat to the fort has been eliminated.

Episode 6: "The Child"

Written by John Boorstin. Directed by Richard Compton. Guest players: Tamsin Kelsey, Chris Humphreyes and Byron Chief-Moon.

Beatrice and Henry Richards arrive at Fort Bennington with a baby niece. Beatrice is not that interested in the child but Elizabeth takes a motherly liking toward the infant.

A Huron warrior captures the child in the fort, intending to replace his own child, who has been killed by whites. Hawkeye is sent out into the woods to find out about the child. Henry Richard, on his own, is going after his niece, but he is ambushed and killed by the Hurons.

Elizabeth goes to the Huron camp to reclaim the baby. Hawkeye, having been raised by Indians, is confused about the sit-

uation, especially when Elizabeth tells him that a Christian child is not the same as a heathen Indian child. The women in the Huron camp have taken good care of the child.

A Redcoat Huron warrior, who has taken a liking to Elizabeth, attacks her, but Hawkeye and Chingachgook save her. Elizabeth starts to realize Hawkeye's native point of view about the child and she agrees to leave it with the Hurons. Elizabeth's understanding of the conditions of wilderness life is growing.

Episode 7: "The Vision"

Written by Vivienne Radkoff. Directed by Ken Girotti.

Guest players: Daniel Richter, Jesse Moss, and Sandra Ferens.

In the Delaware village, Chingachgook has a vision that hostile Indians will kill Hawkeye. The vision makes him ponder about the safety of his friend.

Elizabeth is going into the wilderness to help Mrs. Jackson at Bear Creek deliver her baby. The baby is delivered, but Hurons

Hawkeye, the First Frontier—Chingachgook (Rodney A. Grant), the Mohican tribesman.

inconveniently attack the Jackson cabin. Elizabeth and Jackson's young son are heroically defending against the attack. Chingachgook realizes that in his vision he has seen Hawkeye being killed by an arrow at the Bear Creek cabin, and he therefore leaves for Bear Creek intending to sacrifice himself for Hawkeye.

Chingachgook arrives just in time before the attackers besiege the place. In his defense against the assault, an arrow strikes Chingachgook, much as Hawkeye was struck in his vision.

Hawkeye arrives and beats off the Indian attack. By pulling out the arrow, Hawkeye saves the life of Chingachgook.

Episode 8: "Out of the Past"

Written by William Bentley. Directed by Neill Fearley.

Guest player: Ron Ely.

Hawkeye's old mentor arrives at Fort Bennington, not for a reunion but for revenge.

Episode 9: "The Warrior"

Written by David Levinson. Directed by Ken Girotti.

Guest players: Jonathan Scarfe, Duncan Fraser, and Gary Chalk.

Her nephew Andrew, from Virginia, visits Elizabeth. He plans to become an artist, but he also wants to be a soldier. On his way to Fort Bennington he is attacked by Hurons but is saved by Hawkeye and Chingachgook.

Sergeant Porter at the fort is a traitor and is giving away information to the French about British troop movements. Andrew, who finds out about his treachery, has drawn his portrait from memory, which causes Porter to order his execution by the French.

During military training, Andrew and two British troopers are attacked by Hurons in the woods. The soldiers are killed but Andrew manages to escape because he does not stand up against the enemy. His cowardice troubles him with guilt, and

Hawkeye steps in to train him to become a "real" soldier.

On the basis of Porter's information, the French attack the fort at its weakest position, the south bastion. During the attack Andrew proves himself in battle. Hawkeye reveals Sergeant Porter. Andrew realizes his limitations in wilderness warfare and decides to leave for Harvard to take up studies.

Episode 10: "The Quest"

Written by Linda Elstad. Directed by Jeff Woolnought.

Guest player: Lindsey Ginter.

Jack Sharp arrives at Fort Bennington with information that William Taylor, Elizabeth's husband, is kept as a prisoner at Fort Frontenac. For a ransom, Sharp is supposed to lead Elizabeth to her husband. Taylor and Hawkeye are suspicious about the serious intention of Sharp, and insist on going along.

In the woods the party is attacked by a group of white renegades, allied to Sharp, who are defeated. During the night Sharp leaves with his money but is captured by Hawkeye.

Taylor and Elizabeth run into a French patrol. Taylor is wounded but together with Elizabeth and Hawkeye he escapes. Hawkeye tracks and captures Sharp and forces him to take them to the place where William is supposed to be. It all turns out to be a trap but Hawkeye saves the situation.

Episode 11: "The Escape"

Written by Steve Feke and David Levinson. Directed by Michael Caffey.

Guest players: Steve Makaj, Yves Cameron and Andrew Johnston.

Two strangers enter Fort Bennington at night to steal ammunition and supplies. One soldier is killed. The crime is revealed but the older man manages to escape. The other man, his younger brother, is captured. Hawkeye takes a liking to the youth, who is sentenced to hang for his crime.

In revenge for the hanging of his younger brother, the older brother contacts the French to suggest a plan to capture Captain Taylor. The plan is to double-cross Taylor, knowing he has a future commercial plan to find an unexplored water route between New York and Montreal. Guided by the conspirator, Taylor and Elizabeth are captured by the French. At a fort the French are pressing Taylor for military information. Hawkeye, aided by Elizabeth, Peevey and McKinney, manages to free Taylor, and during a final battle, Hawkeye kills the renegade.

Episode 12: "Fly with Me"
Written by Ken Biller. Directed by Brad Turner.

Guest players: Robert Wisden, Roger R. Cross, Topaz Hasfal-Schou and Danny Virtue.

A Virginian, August Hale, is on his way to return two runaway slaves, Ngali and his wife. Chingachgook saves them in the woods and brings them to the Delaware village.

In accordance with British law, Hale, with the aid of the British military at Fort Bennington, reclaims the escapees. However, Ngali manages to escape but is once again caught and he and his wife are both brought to the fort. Elizabeth tries to purchase the freedom of the slaves but is turned down by Taylor. Ngali is whipped at the fort.

Hale departs with the two slaves for Virginia. Hawkeye and Chingachgook have a skirmish with a party of Hurons in the woods. In a deal with the Hurons they lead them to help free the two slaves in exchange for letting the Hurons have the whites.

Episode 13: "The Ally"
Written by Jon Boorstin. Directed by George Bloomfield.

Guest players: Eric Schweig and Marianne Jones.

A provoked attack on Captain Taylor by Delaware Claw, who tries to steal some supplies at the fort, prompts Taylor to ban the entire Delaware tribe from the fort. Hawkeye is sent to the Delaware village to bring Claw in for justice, but the latter refuses.

Elizabeth, fooled by a Delaware woman, enables Claw and the Delawares to take over the fort during a period when all troopers are outside for a military drill. Peevey and McKinney are captured in the fort. Hawkeye captures Husa, Claw's wife, as she is going to the French with information that the British fort can be taken easily.

Hawkeye tries to free Peevey and McKinney in the fort. In the meantime Chingachgook and Elizabeth deliver some hidden guns to the British so that they can recapture the fort. In a knife duel with Claw, Hawkeye defeats him but spares him his life. Claw, however, commits suicide. Captain Taylor wants to punish the Delawares but Hawkeye and Chingachgook persuade him to free them to prevent a major war.

Episode 14: "The Boxer"
Written by Steve Feke and David Levinson. Directed by Brad Turner.

Guest players: Edward Arnold and Garvin Cross.

Indians attack Hawkeye and a couple of British soldiers on a survey tour. One of the Indians proves to be a French soldier, coming from the South. Brought in as a prisoner at the fort, he explains that he is a freedom pilgrim.

Captain Taylor is planning an attack on Fort Carillon. To strengthen the morale of his soldiers, he agrees to have the captives participate in a boxing game arranged by Peevey and McKinney. In a fight with Sergeant Fallon, the Frenchman loses intentionally. This ploy gives him an opportunity to escape. During his escape he kills Fallon.

Hawkeye sets off after him and reveals that his real purpose has been to find out about the British plans to attack Carillon.

When the French traitor tries to escape, Hawkeye kills him.

Episode 15: "The Traitor"

Written by Jon Boorstin. Directed by Jesus Trevino.

Guest players: Hrothgar Mathews, Duncan Fraser, Scott McNeil and Jason Gray-Stanford.

The fort is under attack by the French. Scouting shows that the French have three cannons on the ridge, but only 40 troopers. The cannons must be eliminated and Taylor orders a frontal attack, against the advice of Hawkeye, who suggests they circle through the forest to attack from the rear. This conflict causes a heated argument between the two men.

The attack is successful, but Taylor is wounded by a bullet in his back. Taylor blames Hawkeye for the crime because he has been seen aiming his rifle in Taylor's direction. Hawkeye is tried for treason. Elizabeth advises Hawkeye to get legal assistance but his sense of honor hinders her efforts.

A rifle bullet with Hawkeye's mark has been collected from Taylor's map-holder and this settles the matter. Hawkeye is sentenced to death as a traitor, against his denial. During the night before his execution, Elizabeth tries to obtain information about what really happened on the battlefield. The soldiers, who are afraid of Captain Shields, have only told part of the story during the trial. The full story proves that Hawkeye has fought with great bravery and that he has actually saved the soldiers from a disaster. This causes remorse among the troopers and at dawn, when Hawkeye is put in front of the execution squad, the soldiers aim elsewhere when firing. Hawkeye is set free and he discloses the real criminal, who proves to be a colonial who had stolen rifle bullets from him.

Episode 16: "Amnesty"

Written by Kathryn Baker. Directed by Brad Turner.

Guest players: Anthony DeLongis and David MacNiven.

A trapper, Jack Munch, arrives at the fort. He has bullying manners and starts a quarrel with McKinney at the fort's tavern. Hawkeye interferes and prevents a fight. Munch has come to the fort to offer Captain Shields information that can lead to the capture of an important French general. In return Munch wants amnesty for an earlier crime he committed. A secret deal is closed between the two.

Munch continues his bullying manners against McKinney and he also sexually humiliates Elizabeth. Peevey decides to take revenge on Munch for harassing his friends, but his attempt fails. Peevey gets his revenge when he informs Hawkeye about the setup between Taylor and Munch to capture the French general.

Hawkeye spoils their plan and captures the general himself at his night camp on his journey between Fort Duquesne and Ticonderoga. Hawkeye delivers the general to Taylor, and the deal between Taylor and Munch is no longer valid. Humiliated, Munch has to leave the fort.

Episode 17: "The Visit"

Written by Leon Tokatyan. Directed by Jesus Trevino. Guest players: James Cromwell and Oliver Becker.

Hawkeye and Elizabeth are practicing archery in the woods when they become witnesses to an assault on a white man by Hurons. They save the man, who turns out to be Elizabeth's father. He has come to bring her home to Virginia.

Elizabeth hesitates to return to Virginia with her father. Taylor, who sees an opportunity in Elizabeth's leaving, conspires with a renegade trapper, Devlin, to implant proof of Elizabeth's husband's death, which would lower her motivation to stay in the area. The proof is a family ring that is supposed to be put on a deceased, unidentifiable scalping victim.

Trapper Devlin, as proof of William's death, brings a body with Shields's family ring to the fort. To Hawkeye, Elizabeth's father discloses that he is seriously ill and that the main reason why he wants Elizabeth back in Virginia is to have her stay with him during his last days. He dies of his disease in the fort. Hawkeye, who has been suspicious about the identity of the "false" corpse, unveils the plot about the ring; William is no longer dead, but a missing person.

Episode 18: "Vengeance Is Mine"

Written by Shelly Moore. Directed by Brenton Spencer.

Guest players: Michael Horse, Norman Browning, Renae Morriseau and Bill Croft.

Winema, wife of Huron Chief Gin-Daga, is captured by British soldiers and wounded when she is trying to escape. She is brought to the fort and nursed by Elizabeth.

With Winema as hostage, Taylor wants to negotiate with Gin-Daga for support against the French. A medallion is found with Winema, which used to belong to Hawkeye's mother, who was killed in an Indian raid years earlier. In grief and anger Hawkeye sets out after Gin-Daga. Chingachgook, worried over Hawkeye's incautiousness, tries to calm him down. In the Delaware camp the negotiations between Taylor and Gin-Daga are disturbed by a vengeful Hawkeye. Hawkeye's rage causes Gin-Daga to leave the negotiations and declare his revenge on white settlers.

When Gin-Daga finds out that Winema has died from her wound, he captures Elizabeth and ties her to a pole to be burned. Hawkeye and Chingachgook arrive and save her life. In a fight Chingachgook kills Gin-Daga.

Episode 19: "The Plague"

Written by Vivenne Radkoff. Directed by Michael Caffey.

Guest players: Larry Sellers and Andrew Wheeler.

A Delaware Chief, Tagua, blames Elizabeth for a smallpox epidemic that ravages his tribe shortly after her inadvertent violation of sacred ground. It turns out that contaminated blankets distributed to Indian tribes by a false reverend who is after their land spread the epidemic. Hawkeye proves the "reverend's" guilt in the Delaware camp, and the conspirator falls from an arrow shot by Tagua.

Episode 20: "Hester"

Written by Sarah Bird. Directed by Jeff Woolnough.

Guest players: Charlene Fernetz, Malcolm Stewart and Brent Stait.

Hawkeye captures a wanted Huron Chief, Black Eagle, when he is about to kill a woman in the woods. According to Black Eagle, the woman, Hester, is a demon.

Fort Bennington is wasted by a fever epidemic. A humiliated army surgeon, Chalmers, orders Hester out of the fort when she wants to treat the severely sick soldiers with an herb brew, contradictory to his own treatment. Elizabeth and Hawkeye convince Captain Taylor Shields that it might be worth trying Hester's recipe.

Supported by Chalmers, rumors are spread that Hester is a witch and that she is the one who is the cause of the epidemic. Black Eagle breaks out from prison. To prevent him from informing the French about the epidemic at the fort, Hawkeye and Chingachgook go after and capture him.

At the fort it proves that Hester's brew works, but the heated atmosphere calls for lynching of the "witch." To protect her, Elizabeth locks her in a secret room. Hawkeye arrives and disperses the mob. When Hawkeye and Elizabeth unlock Hester's hiding place, she has disappeared!

Episode 21: "The Bounty"

Written by Shelly Moore. Directed by Brenton Spencer.

Guest players: Sarah Sawatsky, Lori Ann Triolo, Tom Cavanaugh and Robert Lewis.

Hawkeye is on several occasions attacked by persons who obviously are out to kill him. A grown-up, self-confident frontier girl from Albany, Emma Sikes, whom

Hawkeye remembers from his past, arrives at the fort. She has come to search for her brother-in-law Charles, a British trooper.

It happens that the French have put a bounty on Hawkeye's head. Army intelligence says that Charles Sikes is held prisoner at the French post Vandreuil at Lake Champlain. To help Emma, Hawkeye, dressed as a French officer, and Chingachgook as a Huron, enter the French post. It turns out that it is all a trap to capture Hawkeye. Chingachgook frees Hawkeye and together they capture Emma, whose plan has been to collect the bounty for Hawkeye's capture. Emma is left alone in the forest.

Episode 22: "The Return"

Written by David Levinson. Directed by Brad Turner.

Guest players: Michael Berry and Yvan Labelle.

After a long time, Elizabeth's husband William returns to Fort Bennington. His past with the Indians makes it hard for him to adjust to white civilization. He also realizes that Taylor, who initially planned William's capture by Hurons, has betrayed him for control of family assets.

In an attempt to kill William, Taylor sets fire to his tent outside the fort at night. Mentally deranged by torture and harassment, William stabs Taylor for revenge and forces Elizabeth, against her will, to leave the fort with him. William has also understood Elizabeth's attraction to Hawkeye. Hawkeye is following the escapees. The episode ends with a fight between William and Hawkeye. Hawkeye is nearly killed, but Elizabeth shoots William and saves him.

Notes: To capitalize on the successful reception of Michael Mann's **The Last of the Mohicans** from 1992, a syndicated TV series on the same subject was produced in 1994, **Hawkeye: The First Frontier**. Emmy-winning writer and producer Stephen J. Cannell produced the series. Many have considered **Hawkeye** to be one of the best western series ever done, with careful attention to historical details.

For the production Cannell brought in a team of skillful historians, designers and craftsmen. A lot of attention was paid to authenticity when it came to historical details on props and other matters. Being filmed in Vancouver, British Columbia, gave the production the natural surroundings similar to those of the Hudson Valley in the mid–1700s.

In the center of the adventures is a British outpost, Fort Bennington, which was constructed in the middle of the wilderness in 30 days. To add to the authenticity, all Indian roles in the series were cast with Native Americans. In the role as Chingachgook, Rodney A. Grant was selected. He had won good appreciation for his previous roles in **Dances with Wolves** and **Son of the Morning Star**. Lee Horsley was cast as Hawkeye and Lynda Carter was chosen for the role as Elizabeth Shields, a woman from Virginia who sets up a trading business at Fort Bennington and gets involved in a love affair with Hawkeye.

Hiawatha (Charles Urban Trading Co., 1905)

Directed by Joe Rosenthal. Photography by Joe Rosenthal. Conceived by E. A. Armstrong. Length: 1,065 feet.

Based on the poem *The Song of Hiawatha* by Henry W. Longfellow. The first dramatic film shot in Canada. Filmed in Desbarats, Ontario.

Hiawatha (Independent Moving Picture Co., 1909)

Produced by Carl Laemmle. Directed by William V. Ranous. Edited by Jack Cohn. Length: 985 feet.

Cast: *Hiawatha* William Ranous; *Minnehaha* Gladys Hulette.

The story: Hiawatha, an Ojibway, overcomes many obstacles before he can marry Minnehaha, a member of the hostile Sioux tribe.

Notes: Producer Carl Laemmle started his own company to do the film: Independent Motion Picture Company (IMP). The production started Laemmle on his film production career, which led to the formation of Universal Pictures in 1912.

Filming was done along the shores of Lake Michigan. At the time **Hiawatha** was made, motion picture production and distribution was more or less controlled by the Motion Picture Patents Company.

"**Hiawatha** was enthusiastically booked by dozens of distributors, who had grown weary of unserious tactics of the Patents Company."—*All-Media-Guide*

Hiawatha (Monogram, 1952)

Produced by Walther Mirisch. Directed by Kurt Neuman. Screenplay by Arthur Strawn and Dan Ullman, from the poem of Henry Wadsworth Longfellow. Photography in Cinecolor by Harry Neuman. Music by Marlin Skiles. Running time: 79 minutes.

Cast: *Hiawatha* Vincent Edwards, *Minnehaha* Yvette Dugay, *Pau Puk Keewis* Keith Larsen, *Chibiabos* Gene Inglesias, *Kwasind* Armando Sylvestre, *Neyadji* Michael Tolan, *Megissagwon* Ian MacDonald, *Nokomis* Katherine Emery, *Igaoo* Morris Ankrum, *Lakku* Stephen Chase, *Mudjekeewis* Stuart Randall, *Chanung* Richard Bartlett, *Ajawac* Michael Granger, *Wabeek* Robert Bice, *Hikon* Gene Peterson and *Ottobang* Henry Corden.

The story: A conflict arises between Hiawatha, an Ojibwa brave, and one of his fellow tribesmen, Pau Puk Keewis, about the death of an Illinois Indian.

On a scouting mission, Hiawatha is attacked by a bear, but is saved by Lakku, a

Hiawatha (Monogram, 1952)—Hiawatha (Vincent Edwards, *fighting at right*) battles the traitor, Pau Puk Keewis (Keith Larsen).

Dakota Indian. Wounded, Hiawatha is brought to the Dakota village where Lakku's daughter, Minnehaha, nurses him.

A scouting party led by Pau Puk kills some Illinois Indian hunters, which causes the Illinois to go on the warpath. Hiawatha arrives just in time at the Ojibwa village to warn them of the attack by the Illinois.

Hiawatha announces to his tribal council that he wishes to marry Minnehaha. The council agrees to his marriage plan because it may strengthen the bond between the tribes.

During the winter the Ojibwa suffer from lack of food. Pau Puk leads a raiding party against the Dakotas for food supplies. Hiawatha finds out that Mudjekeewis, Chief of the Dakotas, in reality is his father. From talking to Mudjekkewis, Hiawatha realizes that Pau Puk is a traitor and in a combat he kills him. With all misunderstandings set aside the two tribes now can live in peace with each other.

Notes: "Anyone who would criticize *Hiawatha*, the Cinecolored holiday package which served to reopen the Bijou yesterday, deserves to suffer the slings and arrows of every moviegoer from the age of 4 to 14. There isn't a gunshot in the entire adventure to disturb older audiences."—A.W. in *The New York Times*

"An entertaining film for kids that masks its theme in a flurry of arrows and romance."—*The Motion Picture Guide*

"The family and juve trade in the general situations will find 'Hiawatha' moderately satisfactory ... a rather placid course in telling a story based on the Henry Wadsworth Longfellow poem and would have been better had more action and excitement been stirred up."—*Variety*

Hiawatha, the Indian Passion Play (State Rights, 1913)

Produced and directed by Frank E. Moore. Photography by Victor Milner. Length: four reels.

Cast: Minnehaha Soon-goot; Jesse Cornplanter and "his Indians."

The story: According to Manito, a prophet will appear to unite all Indians.

Wenonah and her husband Mudjekeewis give birth to a son, Hiawatha. Wenonah dies and her mother Nokomis claims that Hiawatha is the long-awaited prophet.

Iaganoo trains Hiawatha in wilderness skills. When visiting an arrow-maker across the lake, he meets his daughter Minnehaha, with whom he falls in love. They marry and start a happy family life. The village encounters bad times and Minnehaha dies by starvation.

By sea, white men in tall ships arrive. Hiawatha, after meeting with the newcomer's priest, a Black Robe, proclaims that the true prophet finally has arrived. When the Black Robe starts to preach Christianity, Hiawatha disappears into the sunset.

Notes: The story is based on Henry Wadsworth Longfellow's poem *The Song of Hiawatha* from 1855. It was filmed at locations in New York and near Lake Superior. A Native cast of 150 Indians from New York, Canada and the Dakotas were used in the picture. Prior to making the film, producer and director Frank E. Moore directed a theatrical version of the play at parks and private estates throughout the United States.

The Howards of Virginia (Columbia, 1940)

Produced by Frank Lloyd. Directed by Frank Lloyd. Screenplay by Sidney Buchman, based on the novel *The Liberty Tree* by Elizabeth Page. Photography by Bert Glennon. Music by Richard Hageman. Sound by William H. Wilmarth. Running time: 117 minutes.

Cast: *Matt Howard* Cary Grant, *Jane Peyton-Howard* Martha Scott, *Fleetwood Peyton* Sir Cedric Hardwicke, *Roger Peyton* Alan Marshal, *Thomas Jefferson* Richard Carlson, *Captain Jabez Allen* Paul Kelly, *Tom Norton* Irving Bacon, *Aunt Clarissa* Elizabeth Risdon, *Mrs. Norton* Ann Revere, *James Howard at 16* Richard Alden, *Mary Howard at 17* Rita Quigley, *Peyton Howard at 18* Phil Taylor, *Dicey* Libby Tay-

The Howards of Virginia (Columbia, 1940)—Matt Howard (Cary Grant) and his wife Jane Peyton-Howard (Martha Scott).

lor, *Patrick Henry* Richard Gaines and *George Washington* George Houston.

The story: Through the friendship of Thomas Jefferson, Matt Howard goes to work as a surveyor for the aristocratic Fleetwood Peyton. Matt meets Peyton's daughter Jane and they fall in love and marry. After the marriage they return to Matt's home in Pennsylvania.

Years pass, and through the encouragement of Jefferson, Matt enters Colonial politics. When the revolution occurs, Matt sides with the colonists and joins the army against Jane's wishes. His two sons join him in the hostilities, and one of them is wounded as the war ends.

The story is told against the background of the Boston Tea Party, the suffering of the Colonial Army at Valley Forge,

and other famous incidents of the War of Independence. The war ends with Cornwallis's surrender at Yorktown, and Matt Howard returns home to Jane.

Notes: The timing for doing films about the American Revolution has always turned out to be wrong. Whenever a film about America's rebellion against British rule is brought up, world politics have been too sensitive for the subject; so also with this production:

"A lobby display poster of Patrick Henry shouting for liberty or death in protest against foreign policy stupidities doesn't jibe with page-one news of united military hemisphere protection against Hitler."—*Variety*

"...this cavalcade of Colonial and Revolutionary America, while ambitious, expensive, and generally interesting, comes to life all too

The Howards of Virginia—Thomas Jefferson (Richard Carlson, *left*), Fleetwood Peyton (Sir Cedric Hardwicke) and actor Guy Bellis.

infrequently.... Obviously miscast, Cary Grant meets the exigencies of a difficult role with more gusto than persuasion."—*Newsweek*

"...defies anyone not to believe in the struggles of the colonists before and during the Revolution ... never once does Mr. Lloyd's film falter in its integrity to show the earnest fight for freedom that took place in this cradle of liberty."—Philip T. Hartug, *The Commonweal*

Hudson Frontier (Also titled *The Adventure of a Lady*) (HTV Ltd., TV mini-series, 1986)

Produced by Peter Graham Scott. Directed by Victor Vicas and Pierre Lary. Script by Pat Ferms from an adoption by Didier Decoin of a story by Pierre Nivolet and Jean-Claude Cameron. Music by Hagood Haedy.

Cast: Mel Martin, Matt Birman, Daniel Ceccaldi and Mathieu Carriere.

The story: It is 1743. A new conflict between France and England is threatening, and concerning rights to the part of the North American continent which today is Canada.

In France, Baron Griffard, an ex-officer, lives on his estate in poverty. One day he discovers an Iroquois Indian who has been caught in one of his traps. The Iroquois turns out to be a white man by the name of Fucillon, who has been brought as a captive from Louisbourg. As a child he was captured by the Indians and raised as one of their tribal members. He convinces Minister Maurepas that it is important to seek alliance with the Iroquois for the upcoming conflict.

At the same time there is a court process ongoing in England in which beautiful Lady Howard is sentenced to death for a crime of murder by poison, of which she claims she is innocent. In the last minute she is saved from the gallows in return for accepting assignment as a secret agent for the English. Together with Captain Richter she will sabotage all attempts by the French to win over the Iroquois in North America.

During their adventures in America the conspirators get involved with the British siege of the French-held fortress of Louisbourg.

Hudson's Bay (20th Century–Fox, 1940)

Produced by Darryl F. Zanuck and Kenneth MacGowan. Directed by Irving Pichel. Screenplay by Lamar Trotti. Photography by Peverell Marley and George Burnes. Music by Alfred Newman. Running time: 95 minutes.

Cast: *Pierre Esprit Radisson* Paul Muni, *Gooseberry* Laird Cregar, *Barbara Hall* Gene Tierney, *Lord Edward Crewe* John Sutton, *Nell Gwyn* Virginia Field, *King Charles* Vincent Price, *Prince Rupert* Nigel Bruce, *Gerald Hall* Morton Lowry, *Sir Robert* Robert Greig, *Orimha* Chief Thundercloud, *English Governor* Frederic Warlock, *Governor* Montague Love, *Mayor* Ian Wolf, *Chief* Chief Big Tree, *Germaine* Jody Gilbert, *Captain* Jean Del Val, *Sentries* Constant Franke, *Maid* Lilyan Irene, *Footman* Keith Hitchcock, *Girl* Dorothy Dearing, *Sailor* John Rogers, *Clerk* Reginald Sheffield, *Orderly* Robert Cory and *Concillors* Eric Wilton.

The story: In the 1660s, French Canadian Pierre Esprit Radisson and his zesty companion Gooseberry encounter Lord Edward Crewe, a British nobleman who has been sent to Canada as an exile for transgressions at court. The three decide to take up fur trading with the Indians.

When they equip their expedition in Quebec, the French governor becomes interested in their plans. At Hudson's Bay they come to an agreement with the Indians which results in good trade. Loaded with furs they return to Quebec where, however, the governor confiscates their furs, claiming they are French property.

Because of their lost furs, Lord Crew agrees to leave for England in spite of the personal risk. The decision is easier for him to take as he is looking forward to meeting his fiancée, Barbara. When Barbara's brother Prince Rupert learns about the British trade possibilities in Canada, he takes up the matter with the king, who agrees to support an expedition to Hudson's Bay.

On the journey back to Canada, Rupert accompanies the expedition. In Canada, however, Rupert does not show much interest in trading and he starts drinking. A serious problem arises when Rupert kills an Indian. In order to prevent an Indian uprising, Radisson is forced to execute Rupert.

Back in England, Radisson is sent to prison and is threatened with hanging. Radisson, however, reveals that he has come to an agreement with the Indians that if anything happens to him, they will turn over the monopoly of fur trading for the British Hudson's Bay Company to the French. At this threat, Charles II saves Radisson's life and Radisson and Gooseberry return to Canada.

Notes: "...there is little or no fast action in the film, no accumulation of suspense, no propulsion toward a crashing climax.

...any suggestion of the boldness, the hardship and peril that went into the founding of the Hudson's Bay Company is lacking in this film."—Bosley Crowther in *The New York Times*

"This sprawling film represents more distorted history from the aegis of studio mogul Darryl F. Zanuck. The ambitious frontier epic cost over eight hundred thousand dollars (a very tidy sum in the 1940s), but it failed to evolve as the splendid outdoor drama intended."—James R. Parish in *Vincent Price—Unmasked*

"...there is very little action, even though the cameras dwell on splendid scenery in the northern wilds of Idaho, where much of the on-location shooting was made. Muni, an independent and powerful actor, simply overwhelmed Pichel and ... overplayed his part lavishly..."—*The Motion Picture Guide*

Hudson's Bay (20th Century–Fox, 1940)—Loaded with furs, Pierre Esprit Radisson (Paul Muni, *left*) and Lord Crewe (John Sutton) return to Quebec.

Hudson's Bay (North Star TV series, 1959)

Produced by Sidney J. Furie. 39 episodes @ 25 minutes.

Cast: Barry Nelson and George Tobias.

Notes: Canadian produced northwood series. Adventures of fur trappers in the Hudson's Bay region.

The Huron Converts (Reliance, 1915)

Length: two reels.

Cast: Joseph Henabery, Bessie Buskirk, H. Moody and Dark Cloud.

In the Days of Daniel Boone (Universal, 1923)

Directed by Frank Messenger, William Kraft and Jay Marchant. Scenario by Jefferson Moffitt. Screenplay by Paul Bryan and Jefferson Moffitt.

Cast: *Daniel Boone* Jack Mower, with Ruth Royce, Charles Brinley, Duke R. Lee, Eileen Sedgwick, and Albert J. Smith.

The story: Boone fights his way through the French and Indian War in 15 episodes (2 reels each except no. 1 which is 3 reels): 1) "His Country's Need"; 2) "At Sword's Point"; 3) "Liberty or Death"; 4) "Foiling the Regulators"; 5) "Perilous Paths"; 6) "Trapped"; 7) "In the Hands of the Enemy"; 8) "Over the Cliff"; 9) "The Flaming Forest"; 10) "Running the Gauntlet"; 11) "The Wilderness Trail"; 12) "The Fort in the Forest"; 13) "The Boiling Springs"; 14) "Chief Blackfish Attacks"; 15) "Boone's Triumph."

In the Days of the Six Nations (Republic, 1911)

Length: two reels.

The story: A *Last of the Mohicans* plot. A treacherous Indian leads a lieutenant and two women into a trap. The hero rescues them. Later, warriors capture the same women. At the last moment the hero brings soldiers, who save the captives from being killed.

The Indian Uprising at Santa Fe (Kalem, 1912)

Length: 1,000 feet.

Cast: Carlyle Blackwell, C. Price, Arthur Travers, Knute Rahmn, Mona Knoll, Mae Marsh, W.H. West, George Armigo, Lorenzo and Emilio.

The story: Adventure about the Pueblo Revolution in 1680 against the Spanish Colonists in New Mexico.

The Iroquois Trail (United Artists, 1950)

Produced by Edward Small and Bernard Small. Directed by Phil Karlson. Screenplay by Richard Schayer, based on the *Leatherstocking Tales* by James Fenimore Cooper. Photography by Henry Freulich. Running time: 85 minutes.

Cast: *Hawkeye* George Montgomery, *Marion Thorne* Brenda Marshall, *Captain West* Glenn Langan, *Captain Brownell* Reginald Denny, *Ogano* Sheldon Leonard, *Sagamore* Monte Blue, *Colonel Thorne* Paul Cavanagh, *General Johnson* Holmes Herbert, *Lieutenant Blakely* Dan O'Herlihy, *Tom Cutler* Don Gerner, *General Montcalm* Marcel Gourmet, *Adjutant Dickson* Arthur Little Jr., *Ma Cutler* Esther Somers and *Sam Girty* John Doucette.

The story: In 1756, French General Montcalm prepares for a campaign against Crown Point. Huron Indian runner Ogano and Sam Girty, both French spies, are carrying false dispatches to confuse the British about the French war plans. British scout Hawkeye and his Delaware friend Sagamore go after the traitors, and Hawkeye traps and kills Girty.

Ogano is sent to guide Marion Thorne and Captain West through the wilderness en route to Fort William, where Marion's father is in command. On their way they are attacked by Hurons but are saved by Hawkeye and Sagamore. The party arrives safely in the fort.

Colonel Thorne sends out a company of colonial militia, with Ogano as scout to ambush Montcalm's troops. Betrayed by Ogano the colonials are ambushed themselves. On false grounds, Hawkeye is accused of treachery and is imprisoned by the British.

The Iroquois Trail (United Artists, 1950)—*Top:* Hawkeye (George Montgomery) with Delaware companion Sagamore (Monte Blue). *Bottom:* Captain West (Glenn Langan) protects Marion Thorne (Brenda Marshall) against attacking Hurons.

Montcalm's troops and the Hurons attack the fort. Ogano captures Marion and brings her to the Huron camp to become his wife. Hawkeye, who has fallen in love with Marion, breaks out of jail and with Sagamore and Captain West he goes after Marion. Hawkeye succeeds in freeing Marion, but Sagamore and West encounter the Hurons. Sagamore falls and West is wounded. Followed by the Hurons, Hawkeye and Marion escape into an Ottawa camp. Ogano appears in the camp and claims Marion as his squaw. The Ottawa chief decides on a combat to settle the difference of opinions, a combat in which Hawkeye defeats and kills Ogano.

Back behind British lines, Hawkeye is cleared of all accusations and when Marion assures him of her love, he decides to continue to serve as scout for the British.

Notes: George Montgomery, as a coonskinned-capped frontier scout for the British, appeared in three French and Indian War cheap productions in the early 1950s. **The Iroquois Trail** was one of these; the others were **The Pathfinder** (1952) and **Fort Ti** (1953). The story in **The Iroquois Trail** is loosely based on Cooper's *The Last of the Mohicans;* in its action sequences a lot of stock footage from Seitz's 1936 film version of *The Last of the Mohicans* was used.

"...seldom becomes convincing ... Weakly written characterizations ... a meandering script."—*Variety*

"There's an abundance of redcoats and Indians involved in double-crossing but the script never moves beyond the surface."—*The Motion Picture Guide*

Jamestown (Chronicle of America Pictures/Pathé, 1923)

Directed by Edwin L. Hollywood. Screenplay by Roswell Dague, based on *Pioneers of the Old South; A Chronicle of English Colonial Beginnings* by Mary Johnston. Length: four reels.

Cast: *Pocahontas* Dolores Cassinelli, *John Rolfe* Leslie Austin, *Sir Thomas Dale* Robert Gaillard, *Capt. George Yeardley*

Harry Kendell, *The Reverend Richard Buck* Leslie Stowe, and *Don Diego de Molina* Paul McAlister.

The story: In 1612, in addition to Indian and starvation problems the English in Virginia have troubles with their Spanish enemy in the South. To force the Indians in the area to join against the Spaniards, High Marshal Sir Thomas Dale holds Indian Princess Pocahontas as hostage. Her father Powhatan first refuses to cooperate, but love and marriage between John Rolfe and Pocahontas improve matters for the colonials. The British situation is saved by Indian intervention.

Notes: This production was part of the Chronicle of America series for the Yale University.

Janice Meredith (MGM, 1924)

Produced by Cosmopolitan Pictures. Directed By E. Mason Hopper. Screenplay by Lillie Hayward, based on Paul Leicester Ford's *Janice Meredith, a Story of the American Revolution* (Dodd, Mead 1899). Photography by Ira H. Morgan and George Barnes. Music score by Deems Taylor. Film length: 10 reels.

Cast: *Janice Meredith* Marion Davies, *Lord Clowes* Holbrook Blinn, *Charles Fownes* Harrison Ford, *Squire Meredith* Maclyn Arbuckle, *Mrs. Meredith* Hattie Delore, *George Washington* Joseph Kilgour, *Martha Washington* Maclyn Arbuckle, *Sir William Howe* George Nash, *Lord Cornwallis* Tyrone Power, *Patrick Henry* Robert Thorne, *Gen. Charles Lee* Walter Law, *Thomas Jefferson* Lionel Adams, *Lafayette* Nicolai Koesberg, *Colonel Rahl* George Siegmann, *a British sergeant* W.C. Fields, *Louis XVI* Edwin Argus, *Marie Antoinette* Princess De Bourbon, *Dr. Joseph Warren* Wilfred Noy, *Paul Revere* Ken Maynard, *Mrs. Loring* Helen Lee Worthing, *Squire Hennion* Spencer Charters, *Philemon Hennion* Olin Howland, *Susie* May Vokes, *Charles Mowbray* Douglas Stevenson, *Theodora Larkin* Harlan Knight, *Tabitha Larkin* Mildred Arden, *Benjamin*

Janice Meredith (MGM, 1924)—Lobby card.

Franklin Lee Beggs, *Arthur Lee* Joe Raleigh, *Parson McClave* Wilson Reynolds, *Cato* Jerry Peterson, *inn-keeper* Isadore Marcel, *servant* Keane Waters, *tailor* Edgar Nelson, *Captain Parker* Byron Russel, *Major Pitcairn* Colonel Patterson, *Trooper Heinrich Bruner* George Cline and *Alexander Hamilton* Burton McEvilly.

The story: After a disappointment in love, Lord Brereton assumes the name of Charles Fownes, arranges passage to the American Colonies as a bondservant, and finds a place with Squire Meredith, a wealthy New Jersey landowner. When Charles falls in love with the squire's daughter, Janice, she is sent to live with an aunt in Boston.

Janice learns about the planned British troop movement to the Lexington arsenal and gives the warning that results in Paul Revere's ride. Charles reveals his true station and becomes an aide to Washington. When captured by the British, Janice arranges his escape and later helps him learn the disposition of the British troops at Trenton. Janice returns home and agrees to marry Philemon Hennion, an aristocrat of her father's choosing.

Opposite: Janice Meredith—Top: Ira H. Morgan photographs Janice (Marion Davies). *Bottom:* A farewell party is set up for Janice when she is going to Boston with her school friend Tabitha; *left to right:* Susie, the maid (May Vokes), Squire Meredith (Maclyn Arbuckle), Janice Meredith (Marion Davies), Mrs. Meredith (Hattie Delore), and Tabitha Larkin (Mildred Arden).

51-64

Janice Meredith—Janice begs for mercy for Charles Fownes when he is captured at the headquarters of British Colonel Rahl after the American victory at Trenton. *From second from left:* Lord Clowes (Holbrook Blinn), Colonel Rahl (George Siegmann), Janice Meredith (Marion Davies), captured Charles Fownes (Harrison Ford), and Squire Meredith (Maclyn Arbuckle).

Charles and some Continental troops halt the wedding and confiscate the Meredith lands. Janice flees to Philadelphia, and Charles follows her. He is arrested but is freed when the British general, Howe, recognizes Charles as his old friend, Lord Brereton.

Janice and her father retire with the British to Yorktown, During the bombardment by Washington's forces, Lord Clowes binds Janice and abducts her in his coach; Charles rescues her. With peace restored, Janice and Charles meet at Mount Vernon, where they are to be married in the presence of President Washington.

Notes: Released in the same year as Griffith's costly production, **America**, another film dealing with the American Revolution.

William Randolph Hearst produced the movie and spent more than $1.5 million on it, a large sum at the time.

To balance Griffith's movie, this one recreated some historical events during the Revolution not covered by Griffith. Events such as the Boston Tea Party, Patrick Henry's speech before the Virginia House of Burgesses, Washington's crossing of the Delaware and the Battle of Trenton are recounted. It also covered events treated by Griffith: the Battle of Lexington, Valley Forge and the battle and surrender of Yorktown.

Washington's crossing of the Delaware

is one of the highlights in this production, as was Paul Revere's ride in Griffith's **America**. The depiction of the sneak attack on the Christmas-celebrating Hessians at Trenton following Washington's dramatic crossing of the Delaware is an event to remember.

When doing the movie Hearst realized that he had to compete with the "Master's" production of the same year. To do so he made **Janice Meredith** an epic, with a cast of thousands, exciting battle scenes and beautiful costumes and colonial settings. Even a few hundred feet at the end of the film was produced in color.

Critics' comparisons of the two pictures were indecisive on which one was better.

The New York Time favored **Janice** :

"The story is well told: in fact it is more inspiring than the love story in **America**."

Variety had another opinion:

"...Compared to '**America**' ... '**Janice**' is inferior..."

Generally, however, *Variety* appreciated the picture:

"Money has been spent without stint in some of the scenes, whereas in others a plainly painted backdrop looms up to spoil an otherwise perfect illusion ... and it is aided by the most musical score ever written for the movie..."

Photoplay in its review was more critical:

"**Janice Meredith** is fair to middlin'.... The story's chief fault is that it is repetitious. The hero is captured continually, only to be liberated by the heroine. The script is a wandering one and the direction loose."

Marion Davies in the title role generally won good notices for her emotional and dramatic acting, and the costumes suited her beauty. The legendary W.C. Fields added some comic touches to the picture in a role as a British sergeant who tries to flirt with Janice. Joseph Kilgour also made a superior appearance as George Washington, according to critics.

Janice Meredith, as did previous movies dealing with the American Revolution, ran into political problems. After censorial changes it was released in Britain as **The Beautiful Rebel**.

John Paul Jones (Warner Bros., 1959)

Produced by Samuel Bronston. Directed by John Farrow. Screenplay by John Farrow and Jesse Lasky, Jr., based on the story "Nor'wester" by Clements Ripley. Photography by Michael Kelber (Technirama, Technicolor). Music by Max Steiner. Running time: 126 minutes.

Cast: *John Paul Jones* Robert Stack, with Bette Davis, Marisa Pavan, Charles Coburn, Erin O'Brian, Macdonald Carey, Jean Pierre Aumont, David Ferrer, Peter Cushing, Susan Canales, Jorge Riviere, Tom Brannun, Bruce Cabot, Basil Sydney and John Crawford.

The story: John Paul Jones, American naval officer, repeatedly asks the Continental

John Paul Jones (Warner Bros., 1959)—American naval hero John Paul Jones (Robert Stack).

John Paul Jones—John Paul Jones (Robert Stack) entering an enemy ship during a sea battle.

Congress during the Revolutionary War to give him a ship command to fight the British Navy. He gets his reward and wins several sea battles, among them the battle between the American ship *Bon Homme Richard* and the British warship *Serapis*.

When the war ends, Jones suggests that the Congress to keep a strong navy for maintaining the nation's independence. Congress, however, turns down his suggestions, and Jones, the naval officer he is, instead goes to Russia to help Catherine the Great fight battles on the Black Sea.

Successful in his missions, Jones later returns to France to reunite with his love Aimee deTellison, in whose arms he dies at only 45 years old.

Notes: John Paul Jones was the best known American naval hero during the

Revolution. He was born in Scotland on July 6, 1747. At the age of 13 he joined the British merchant marine. After several years in the West Indies trade he immigrated to the colonies of North America.

At the outbreak of the Revolutionary War he obtained a lieutenant's commission in the Colonial Navy. His most famous undertaking in naval battles during the Revolution came on September 23, 1779, when in a bloody battle he captured the British ship *Serapis* on the North Sea off Famborough Head, England.

His life tended to be shrouded in mystery, and being a rather good-looking man he became involved in many love affairs. His ambition was to become a rear admiral in the American Navy, but in spite of his good personal relations with people like Thomas Jefferson, he had made many enemies who blocked his advancement. His chance came after the American Revolution, when he served as rear admiral in the service of Empress Catherine of Russia. In 1790 he returned to Europe and Paris, where he died at the age of 45 on July 18, 1792.

Johnny Tremain (Buena Vista, 1957)

Produced by Walt Disney. Directed by Robert Stevensen. Screenplay by Tom Blackburn, based on the novel by Esther Forbes. Photography by Charles P. Boyle. Running time: 80 minutes.

Cast: *Johnny Tremain* Hal Stalmaster, *Cilla Lapham* Luana Patten, *James Otis* Jeff York, *Jonathan Lyte* Sebastian Cabot, *Rab Silsbee* Dick Beymer, *Paul Revere* Walter Sande, *Samuel Adams* Rusty Lane, *Josiah Quincy* Whit Bissell, *Dr. Joseph Warren* Walter Coy and *Ephraim Lapham* Will Wright.

The story: Young Johnny Tremain takes up a job to become a silversmith in Boston in 1773. He burns one of his hands in molten silver and his career opportunities as a craftsman are destroyed. Johnny's true birthright is that of a noble family, Lyte. When Johnny goes to Jonathan Lyte with proof of his identity, he is accused of being a liar and is brought to court. With the help of Boston's best patriot lawyer he is exonerated. Johnny has trouble finding a job, and becomes interested in revolutionary ideas. He joins the Sons of Liberty and participates in The Boston Tea Party.

Because of the ongoing conspiracy activities by the patriots, General Gage, in

Johnny Tremain (Buena Vista, 1957)—Johnny Tremain (Hal Stalmaster, *right*) meets with Dr. Joseph Warren (Walter Coy), member of the "Sons of Liberty."

Johnny Tremain—Johnny (Hal Stalmaster, *left*) finds out from a British naval officer, who has come to collect his silver bottle at Lapham's silver shop, that the British fleet is leaving for Portsmouth. Ephraim Lapham (Will Wright, *right*) and Cilla Lapham (Luana Patten) are also pictured.

charge of the British interests in the colonies, threatens to take actions if they are not stopped. When the patriots reject him, British Colonel Smith assures Gage that he will take care of the matter. At Lexington Green the colonials are confronted by British troops, and when suddenly there is a shot the fighting is a fact. Using guerrilla tactics the colonials beat back the British. The shot at Lexington Green will be the flame that lights the revolution throughout the country.

Notes: Johnny Tremain was originally made as a two-part program for the Disney TV Show, but it was later decided to release it as a feature movie. The reason for this was basically financial.

"It takes some dramatic liberty with facts, but what is more important, it makes real and three-dimensional what most history books put down in a flat, hackneyed prose. It is an ideal film for young people."—Leonard Martin in *The Disney Films*

Keeping the Promise (Atlantic Films, 1997)

Produced by Martin Katz. Directed by Sheldon Larry. Screenplay by Gerald Dipego, based on the novel *The Sign of the Beaver* by Elizabeth Speare. Photography by Ron Stannet. Music by Peter Manning Robinson. Running time: 90 minutes.

Cast: Keith Carradine, Gordon Tootoosis, Brendan Fletcher, Maury Chaykin, David Cubitt, William Lighting and Annette O'Toole.

The story: Adventure teleplay about a young boy, caught in the wilderness, who becomes friends with Abnaki Indians. Set in Maine in 1763.

The Kent Family Chronicles (Universal TV mini-series, 1978-79)

Part I—"The Bastard"

Produced by Joe Byrne. Directed by Lee H. Katzin. Screenplay by Guerdon Trueblood, based on the novel *The Bastard* by John Jakes. Photography by Michael Hugo. Running time: 189 minutes.

Cast: *Phillipe Charboneau/Philip Kent* Andrew Stevens, *Benjamin Franklin* Tom Bosley, *Anne Ware* Kim Cattrall, *Benjamin Edes* Buddy Ebsen, *Bishop Francis* Lorne Greene, *Captain Plummer* Cameron Mitchell, *Alicia* Olivia Hussey, *Captain Caleb* Harry Morgan, *Lady Amberly* Eleanor Parker, *Solomon Sholto* Donald Pleasence, *Dan O'Brian* Noah Beery, Jr., *Girard* Peter Bonerz, *Lord North* John Colicos, *Samuel Adams* William Daniels, *LaFayette* Ike Eisenmann, *Marie Charboneau* Patricia Neal, *Paul Revere* William Shatner, *Abraham Ware* Barry Sullivan and *Johnny Malcolm* Keenan Wynn.

The Story: Living in France, Phillipe Charboneau is the illegitimate son of Lord Amberly, Duke of Kentland. In a robbery attempt, a young nobleman, Marquis De Lafayette, saves Phillipe from bandits. The two develop a friendship and become blood comrades. Lafayette teaches Phillipe the art of military fighting.

To establish his birthright, Phillipe and his mother travel to England to meet with his father. Arriving at the father's estate they are told that he is severely ill and that they cannot see him. When Phillipe and his mother claim Phillipe's inherited fortune, they incur the wrath of the father's wife and Phillipe's half-brother Roger. His brother's

"The Bastard" (Part I of *The Kent Family Chronicles*, MCA/Universal, 1979)—Phillipe Charboneau (Andrew Stevens, *right*) wards off an attack by his half-brother Roger Amberly (Mark Neely).

"The Bastard"—Phillipe Charboneau "Philip Kent" (Andrew Stevens, *left*) and Paul Revere (William Shatner).

fiancée, the aristocratic Alicia falls in love with Phillipe.

In exile they meet with the Sholtos, a family in London who care for them, and also teach Phillipe the printing business. In London Phillipe also meets with Benjamin Franklin, who talks about America and his thoughts about freedom.

To escape the threat from his father's family, Phillipe cannot stay in England any longer, and he and his mother leave for America. During the journey across the Atlantic his mother dies.

Arriving in Boston, Massachusetts, Phillipe, who changes his name to Philip Kent, starts a new life as a printer. At the print shop where he works the printers are helping Samuel Adams to publish political proclamations, which claim freedom from British rule. The liberty movement appeals to Philip and he decides to join the Sons of Liberty. His engagement in the cause gives

him the opportunity to meet with Paul Revere and several other liberty founders.

Benjamin Edes, the owner of the print shop, has a daughter Anne, who appeals to Philip, and the two fall in love. In his relation to Anne he develops an enemy in British Captain Stark.

In revenge for helping spread rebellious messages, the Tories burn the print shop. To demonstrate against British taxation, Philip participates in the Boston Tea Party, where he runs into trouble with Captain Stark and becomes wounded in a fight.

In his striving for liberty Philip joins the colonial militia and accidentally meets with his brother Roger, who has come to America as a British officer to participate in the fight against the colonial uprising. To protect Anne against violence from Roger he kills him in a duel.

Later an upset Anne looks up Philip in Concord to bring him a message from Alicia, who has arrived in the colonies and wants to meet with him. Philip goes to Philadelphia to see her. The old passion between the two awakes and they take up a joyful life together in Philadelphia.

During his stay in Philadelphia, Philip runs into Benjamin Franklin, who informs him that his father, Duke Amberly, is alive. Philip starts to realize that Alicia's love for him is just a cover-up, when she in reality is after his inheritance rights. He returns to Concord and takes up again with Anne, who is pregnant.

Part II—"The Rebels"

Produced by Gian R. Grimaldi and Hannah L. Shearer. Directed by Russ Mayberry. Screenplay by Robert A. Cinader and Sean Baine, based on the novel *The Rebels* by John Jakes. Camera by Frank Tackhery. Running time 190 minutes.

Cast: *Philip Kent* Andrew Stevens, *Judson Fletcher* Don Johnson, *Eph Tait* Doug McClure, *John Hancock* Jim Backus, *Duke of Kentland* Richard Basehart, *Mrs. Brumple* Joan Blondell, *Benjamin Franklin* Tom Bosley, *Breen* Rory Calhoun, *Dr. Church* Macdonald Carey, *Anne Kent* Kim Cattrall, *Henry Knox* John Chappell, *John Adams* William Daniels, *Mrs. Harris* Anne Francis, *George Washington* Peter Graves, *Charlotte Waverly* Pamela Hensley, *Peggy McLean* Gwen Humble, *General Howe* Wilfrid Hyde-White, *Baron von Steuben* Nehemiah Persoff, *Ambrose Waverly* Warren Stevens, *Thomas Jefferson* Kevin Tighe, *Sam Gill* Bobby Troup, *August Fletcher* Forrest Tucker, *Rachel* Tanya Tucker and *Seth McLean* Robert Vaughn.

The story: Set in 1776 in Virginia. Judson Fletcher is a rich young man who lives an untroubled life, far from the ongoing war. He runs into problems when he gets involved with a married woman, Charlotte Waverly. To defend his honor, Charlotte's husband Ambrose forces Judson into a duel. Judson kills Ambrose, but, threatened with revenge by Ambrose's brother, he decides to leave Virginia to join the Continental Army.

Anne, whom Philip Kent has married after learning that she was pregnant, becomes ill and dies giving birth to a son who is baptized Abraham, after her father.

Philip meets Judson in an army camp, while Washington is trying to assemble the militia into a fighting force. Washington assigns Philip and Judson on a special mission to join Captain Knox and go to Fort Ticonderoga to capture some cannons. The return trip with the captured cannons becomes a troublesome journey in hard winter weather. Philip becomes ill, and because he is burning up with fever his companions must leave him at a farmhouse on the route.

Rachel, who lives in the house with her son Abraham, helps Philip recover. Her husband, a Tory, is out in the war somewhere. During his convalescence, love develops between Philip and Rachel. In the spring Philip returns to Massachusetts.

Judson, who was wounded on the way back from Ticonderoga, goes into politics after his return and is elected a member of the Virginia delegation of the Congress. Washington is sending Philip on a new mission to meet Samuel Adams to confirm his support for a successful campaign against Boston. Adams promises his full support.

Benjamin Franklin reprimands Judson, who continues to live a joyful life with love affairs that have dishonored his reputation. Ambrose's brother returns for revenge on Judson. Peggy, his true love, also returns. She is captured by Judson's enemies, but saved by Philip who happens to be in the area.

Back in Cambridge, Philip is assigned a new mission by Washington to look up one of his spies in Boston, John Masters, to obtain his espionage information. During his mission the British capture Philip. In the meantime, Judson finds out that Peggy's father, Seth McLean, conspires against Washington. His discovery initiates a conflict with Peggy, and she leaves him.

In Boston, Philip is sentenced to death for his anti–British undertakings. Philip's father, the Duke of Kentland, arrives in the colonies and tries to postpone the execution. The Americans fortify Dorchester Heights and start to bombard the city. In the turmoil, Philip is released from prison by some of his friends. Threatened by the guns at Dorchester Heights, the British evacuate Boston.

In 1776 the war does not go well at all for the Americans. Washington retreats on all fronts. Help is needed, and Benjamin Franklin goes to France for negotiations. Judson looks up Peggy in Boston and finds out that she is pregnant; the two decide to take up their affair again. Lafayette arrives from France, eager to serve the course of liberty on the side of the Americans. Washington assigns Lafayette as a general and a member of his staff.

Judson has to return to Philadelphia and his work in Congress. The city is in danger, threatened by the British, and Washington takes his army for a winter rest at Valley Forge. To build up spirit and train the troops, Washington hires Baron von Steuben as drillmaster. The training turns out to be of great value later in the war.

Both Philip and Judson join Washington at Valley Forge and are assigned a mission to see General Gates in the North. On their route they are ambushed by a band of Tories, led by Ambrose's brother, who still hasn't forgotten Judson's "debt" for his brother. In the fight, Judson is wounded and dies. Philip is also seriously wounded in the leg.

Crippled by his wound, Philip is relieved from military service and returns to Boston to take up his printing business. Lafayette comes to visit Philip before he goes back to France on an important assignment. At night they attend a dinner party where Philip meets Peggy and tells her about a promise he has made to Judson that he would take care of all her needs.

The war comes to an end, and in 1781 Cornwallis surrenders the British Army to Washington in Yorktown, after six years of fighting. Philip marries Peggy and their children are destined to grow up with a new nation.

Part III—"The Seekers"

Produced by Gian R. Grimaldi and Hannah L. Shearer. Directed by Sidney Hayes. Screenplay by Steve Hayes, based on the novel *The Seekers* by John Jakes. Photography by Vincent A. Martinelli. Music by Gerald Fried. Running time: 189 minutes.

Cast: *Abraham Kent* Randolph Mantooth, *Elizabeth Fletcher Kent* Delta Burke, *First Mate* John Carradine, *Elijah Weatherby* Brian Keith, *Young Jarod* Marty Gold, *Hamilton Stovall* George Hamilton, *Ollie Prouty* Alex Hyde-White, *Harriet Kent* Harriet Karr, *Mr. Pleasant* Ross Martin, *Philip Kent* Martin Milner, *Leland Pell* Vic Morrow, *Jarod Kent* Timothy Patrick Murphy, *Andrew Piggot* Hugh O'Brian, *Daniel Clapper* Robert Reed, *Reverend Blackthorn* Stuart Whitman, with Edie Adams and Neville Brand.

The story: Philip Kent is running a successful printing business in Boston. In 1794, his son Abraham participates, as a cavalry lieutenant, in a campaign against the Indians in the Northwest Territory, led by General "Mad" Anthony Wayne. During the fighting Abraham kills his first enemy.

Back in Boston in 1796, Abraham is unsatisfied with his work in the print shop. He starts a love affair with his stepsister Elizabeth to the anger of his father. Thomas Jefferson's talks about the importance of settling the Western country appeal to Abraham, and he decides to go. Against the will of the family, Abraham and Elizabeth leave with a wagon train to break new ground.

On their route they face problems with renegades, and Abraham has to kill a man

---

Opposite, top: "The Seekers" (Part III of *The Kent Family Chronicles*, MCA/Universal, 1979)—Abraham Kent (Randolph Mantooth) and Elizabeth Fletcher (Delta Burke) on their way to the Northwest Territory. *Bottom:* Jarod Kent (Timothy P. Murphy) and his cousin Amanda (Sarah Rush), who is masquerading as a boy, in conflict with keelboat captain Isaac Drew (Neville Brand).

to save Elizabeth from being raped. Elizabeth gives birth to a son, Jarod, and the family settles in Ohio. Back in Boston, Philip Kent dies and leaves his printing shop to his youngest son, Gilbert.

When everything looks good for the family in Ohio, with Elizabeth pregnant again, they face Indian problems and Elizabeth is killed. After this Abraham and Jarod leave the frontiers and return to Boston.

Abraham for the first time in 1803 learns about his father's death. Abraham joins Gilbert in the print shop, but, unhappy about his situation, he takes up drinking, leading to problems with Gilbert and Gilbert's wife Harriet. In an accident caused by Abraham's drinking, Harriet has a miscarriage, which gives Abraham little choice but to leave. The custody of Jarod goes to Gilbert.

Growing up in an abusive household strengthens the relationship between Jarod and his cousin Amanda. Later Jarod cannot endure Harriet any longer, and in 1812 he joins the American Navy in the war against the British. The time in the navy is hard learning for Jarod, with several violent sea battles and harassment by a navy lieutenant.

When Jarod later returns to Boston, he runs into his disgusting father, who meets a violent death. His Uncle Gilbert also dies after a long sickness. Harriet remarries with a dreadful man who spends most of his time gambling. The calamitous circumstances cause Jarod and Amanda to flee Boston for the Western frontiers.

Notes: This TV mini-series was based on John Jakes's successful family saga *The Kent Family Chronicles*. The eight-volume series, published in conjunction with America's celebration of its Bicentennial, depicts American history through the lives of a fictional family. Jakes has won worldwide fame through his historical novels, and has been praised for his research and historical accuracy in his books. *The Los Angles Times* called him "the godfather of histor-

ical novelists," and *Reader's Digest* named him as "America's history teacher." In 1975 John Jakes managed to place three of his books on the *New York Times* bestseller list. In addition to the filming of the *Chronicles*, his novel series *North and South* also found its way to the screen.

Kings of the Sun (United Artists, 1963)

Produced by Lewis J. Rachmil. Directed by J. Lee Thompson. Screenplay by Elliott Arnold and James R. Webb. Photography by Joseph MacDonald (Panavision, De-Lux Color). Music by Elmer Bernstein. Running time: 108 minutes.

Cast: *Black Eagle* Yul Brynner, *Balam* George Chakiris, *Ixchel* Shirley Ann Field, *Ah Min* Richard Basehart, *Ah Haleb* Brad Dexter, *Ah Zok* Barry Morse, *Isatai* Armando Silvestre, *Hunac Ceel* Leo Gordon, *Ixzubin* Victoria Vettri, *Pitz* Rudi Solari, *The Chief* Ford Rainey, *Balam, the Elder* Angel Di Steffano and *The Youth* Jose Moreno.

The story: During an attack on the Mayan tribe by Hunac Ceel and his warriors from the North, their king is killed and his son Balam becomes the new chief. The threat from Hunac Ceel forces the tribe to leave the country. They resettle in what is now North America, but are attacked by a neighboring tribe led by Black Eagle. Black Eagle is wounded during the battle, but is nursed back to health by Ixchel, Balam's fiancée. The two leaders decide to bury the hatchet and live in peace.

Peace is broken when Hanuc Ceel, who has decided to destroy the Mayans, attacks again. With the help of Black Eagle's tribe the attackers are beaten, but Black Eagle is killed while saving his new friend's life.

Notes: "Motivations are simplistic, the script gives the actors plenty of "solemn" moments. The battle sequences are nicely together, but the rest of the drama lags."—*Motion Picture Guide*

Kiss of Fire (Universal, 1955)

Produced by Samuel Marx. Directed by Joseph Newman. Screenplay by Franklin Coen and Richard Collins, based on the novel *The Rose and the Flame* by Jonreed Lauritzen. Photography in Technicolor by Carl Cuthrie. Running time: 86 minutes.

Cast: *El Tigre* Jack Palance, *Princess Lucia* Barbara Rush, *Duke of Montera* Rex Reason, *Felicia* Martha Hyer, *Vega* Leslie Bradley, *Diego* Alan Reed, *Padre Domingo* Lawrence Dobkin, *Victor* Joseph Waring, *Pahvant* Pat Hogan, *Shining Moon* Karen Kadler, *Ship Captain* Steven Geray and *Acosta* Henry Rowland.

The story: Princess Lucia travels from Mexican territory to the coast of California for the purpose of boarding a ship to Spain to claim her throne when her grandfather, Philip III, is seriously ill.

Escorting the princess on the expedition is an ex-officer, El Tigre. The journey is not free of troubles. The party is attacked by Indians and continuously pursued by some traitorous countrymen led by the Duke of Montera. Along the way the princess falls in love with her helper, El Tigre, and she decides to relinquish the throne for her new love.

Notes: "Capable direction and production do not help a plodding script. Performances adequate, though Palance is a statuesque nobleman."—*Motion Picture Guide*

Lafayette (Copernic/Cosmos, 1961)

Produced by Maurice Jacquin. Writers: Jean-Bearnard Luc, Suzanne Arduini, Jacques Sigurd, Francois Ponthier, Jean Dreville and Maurice Jacquin. Directed by Jean Dreville. Photography by Claude Renoir and Roger Hubert in SuperTechnirama 70. Running time: 158 minutes.

Cast: *Lafayette* Michael Le Royer, *General Cornwallis* Jack Hawkins, *Benjamin Franklin* Orson Wells, *George Washington* Howard St. John, *Bancroft* Vittorio de Sica, *Silas Deane* Edmund Purdom, *Duc d'Ayen* Jaques Castelot, *Le Boursier* Folco Lulli, *Baron Kalb* Wolfgang Preiss, *Adri-enne Lafayette* Pascale Audret, *Vergennes* Georges Riviere, *Marie Antoinette* Liselotte Pulver, *Louis XVI* Albert Remy, *Duchesse d'Ayen* Renee Saint-Cyr, *Comtesse de Simiane* Rosanna Schiaffino, *Segur* Henri Amilien, *Monsieur* Gilles Brissac, *La Bergiere* Roger Bontemps, *Maurepas* Jean-Roger Caussimon, *Aglae* Silvie Coste, *General Philip* Christian Melsen, *Abbe de Cour* Claude Naudes, *Mauroy* Roland Rodier and *Lauzan* Rene Rozan.

The story: In 1776, Washington's army is in trouble. The soldiers are undisciplined and badly equipped, and there is a shortage of food. Washington is sending Silas Deane to France to negotiate for support.

In Paris he meets Benjamin Franklin and a young nobleman, Marquise de Lafayette, who is burning with enthusiasm for the cause of liberty. Lafayette goes to London to try to solve matters, where he meets with General Cornwallis. They develop sympathy for each other but they both realize that they soon will fight a war, but on different sides.

Unsuccessful in London, Lafayette returns to Paris and raises funds for a ship, *La Victorie*, which he sails to America with supplies. In America he offers his services to General Washington. Washington assigns him a commission as major general and makes him commander of the militia. During the battle at Monmouth, Lafayette proves himself as a fighter but is wounded. Later Lafayette helps in winning over the Iroquois to the American side.

The war takes a favorable turn for the Americans when the French fleet intervenes on the American side in the war. In a final battle at Yorktown in 1781, the British army is defeated. During the battle scenes, Cornwallis watches Lafayette from distance and expresses a bitter admiration for the young idealist.

Cornwallis surrenders to Washington and asks for permission to meet with Lafayette once more. Cornwallis tells Lafayette that he possibly had fought for the right cause. Lafayette bids a warm farewell

Lafayette (Copernic/Cosmos, 1961)—The Battle at Monmouth.

to Washington and leaves for France and his wife Adrienne.

Notes: Marquis de Lafayette was born on September 6, 1757, in Chavania in France. He came from a family of soldiers that brought him to studies at the Military Academy in Versailles. At the age of 16, Lafayette obtained a commission as a captain in the French Army in which he served from 1771 to 1776.

After the outbreak of the American Revolution he set sail for America to fight on the American side against the British. George Washington gave him a commission as a general in the Continental Army, and also assigned him as a member of his military staff.

Lafayette won several victories in the war leading American forces. In 1779 he returned to France and persuaded the French Government to grant financial and military aid to the Americans. In 1780 he returned to America and participated in the campaign that would lead to the surrender of the British at Yorktown. Returning home in Paris Lafayette was received as hero.

His belief in democracy and his efforts to work for political reforms in France, which later would lead to the French Revolution in 1791, caused him problems with French nobility and later also with the people. He came to be considered a traitor, and he had to flee the country. In Austria he was arrested and imprisoned until 1797.

After the fall of French emperor Napoleon I, Lafayette returned to politics and served as a member of the Chamber of Deputies, where he gave his support for making Louis Philippe a constitutional monarch. He would later regret his support of Philippe and started to work for a republic in France just before his death in 1834.

Lafayette—Marquis de Lafayette (Michael Le Royer) overtakes British fortifications at Yorktown.

The 1961 French-Italian co-production of **Lafayette,** intended as an international epic, is only interesting because of its star cameos.

Other movies about the American Revolution in which Lafayette appeared are: **The Spirit of '76** (1917), **Janice Meredith** (1924), and on television in **The Young Rebels** (1970-71, **The Kent Family Chronicles** (1978) and the **George Washington** mini-series from 1984.

The Last of the Buccaneers
(Columbia, 1950)

Directed by Lew Landers. Screenplay by Robert E. Kent. Running time: 79 minutes.

Cast: Paul Henreid, Jack Oakie, Karin Booth, Edgar Barrier, Mary Anderson, and John Dehner.

The story: A follow-up to **The Buccaneer** (Paramount versions 1938 and 1958).

With the help of Lafitte and his pirates, the Americans have defeated the British in New Orleans. After the war Lafitte takes up piracy again and the Americans do not interfere as long as he does not bother American ships.

One of Lafitte's captains, however, raids an American ship, which forces Lafitte and his fiancée Belle to escape to safety.

Last of the Mohicans (Powers, 1911)

Produced by Pat Powers. Adapted from Cooper's novel.

Last of the Mohicans (Thanhouser, 1911)

Directed by Theodore Marston. Screenplay by Theodore Marston from the novel by James Fenimore Cooper.

Cast: Frank Crane, William Russell, Alphonse Ethier.

Notes: This version of the Cooper's novel follows the original plot quite closely.

Last of the Mohicans (1914)

No information available.

The Last of the Mohicans
(Associated Producers, 1920)

Directed by Maurice Tourneur and Clarence Brown. Screenplay by Robert F. Dillon, based on the novel by James Fenimore Cooper. Photography by Carl Van Enger and Philip R. Dubois. Running time: six reels (72 minutes).

Cast: *Uncas* Albert Roscoe, *Magua* Wallace Beery, *Cora* Barbara Bedford, *Alice* Lilian Hall, *Hawkeye* Harry Lorraine, *Major Heyward* Henry Woodward, *Chingachgook* Theodore Lerch, *Captain Randolph* George Hackathorne, *David Gamut* Nelson McDowell, *Tamenund* Jack McDonald, *General Webb* Sydney Deane, with Joseph Singleton and Boris Karloff.

The story: In 1757, during the French and Indian War, British Colonel Munro's two daughters, Alice and Cora, are escorted by Major Heyward to rejoin their father at Fort William Henry. As a guide they have the Indian runner Magua, who in reality is a French spy. During their journey the party is assisted by Hawkeye, a British scout, and his two Mohican friends, Chief Great Serpent and his son Uncas, when Magua, joined by his Huron warriors, attacks them in a cave near Glenns Falls.

When finally the party arrive in the

The Last of the Mohicans (Associated Producers, 1920)—The grace and dignity of life in the wilderness: Alice Munro (Lilian Hall) playing with children at Fort Edward.

The Last of the Mohicans (1920)—The punishment of Magua (Wallace Beery): The start of his hatred of the British? (This scene is not in the movie.)

safety of Fort William Henry, they find out that French General Montcalm is preparing for an attack on the fort.

In Munro's headquarters the critical condition of the fort is discussed. The guns on the left rampart are useless. Captain Randolph, who proves to be a traitor, carries the information to Montcalm. Under a flag of truce, Montcalm summons Munro to a conference, in which he reveals that he knows about the poor situation of the fort. Munro agrees to surrender the fort to the French against a promise that women and children will go unharmed.

During the British departure, Montcalm cannot control his Indian allies, who attack and massacre those who have surrendered. Magua takes Cora with him to be his squaw. Uncas, who has fallen in love with Cora, follows their trail. Cora tries to escape from Magua, but he captures her at a high cliff precipice. She frees herself and jumps to her death from the cliff.

Uncas arrives and battles Magua. The combat ends with the death of Uncas. The life of Magua is put to an end by a bullet from Hawkeye's musket. Cora and Uncas are both buried in a beautiful sunny valley.

Notes: *The Last of the Mohicans* has been filmed several times. Scriptwriters and directors have frequently taken their own liberty with Cooper's original story.

The story in James Fenimore Cooper's *The Last of the Mohicans* centers around a small group of British people who are

The Last of the Mohicans (1920)—Troops leaving Fort Edward to support Munro at Fort William Henry.

pursued by hostile Hurons on the New York frontier during the French and Indian War. Magua, a vengeful spy and aid to French General Montcalm, leads his Hurons against the British intruders.

In the British group are Cora and Alice, daughters of Colonel Munro, commander of Fort William Henry. Cora is the older sister ready to protect Alice, who is more childlike and vulnerable.

Fort William Henry is under siege by Montcalm's troops. A British officer, Major Heyward, is on hand to protect the girls. Also with the group is an eccentric psalm singer, David Gamut. During the group's adventurous journey in the wilderness, they are continually saved from their pursuers by colonial scout Hawkeye and his two Mohican friends, Chingachgook and Un-

cas. Uncas is Chingachgook's son and the two are the last survivors of their tribe.

During Uncas's attempt to rescue Cora, in accordance with Cooper's story, love arises between Uncas and Cora.

Who was the last of the Mohicans? In line with Cooper's version, the final battle ends with Cora being stabbed by a Huron warrior. Magua angry over losing Cora, kills Uncas. Hawkeye quickly kills Magua with a couple of rifle shots from his long carbine. Surviving is Chingachgook, who is the last of the Mohicans.

In Cooper's tale there is no doubt about who the real heroes are. The heroic, wise and experienced problem solvers are Hawkeye and Chingachgook. The film versions sometimes took another track. In the 1920 version, Cooper's heroes were mar-

The Last of the Mohicans (1920)—At the abandoned blockhouse: Heyward (Henry Woodward) is saving Alice (Lilian Hall) from being killed by a Huron.

ginalized, and the picture focuses on a triangle drama among Uncas, Magua and Cora. Cora in this version, to escape Magua, takes her own life by throwing herself off a cliff.

The 1920 picture has by many been considered as the best film version of Cooper's story. French director Maurice Tourneur had started his film career in France before he came to America. In America he made most of his productions. At the time he made **The Last of the Mohicans**, he was considered one of America's best film directors, competing only with Griffith.

During the making of the movie, Tourneur had a bad accident which confined him to bed for several months. His co-director Clarence Brown took over the direction job and it is said that he actually directed most of the film.

The film was shot on location at Big Bear Lake and the Yosemite Valley in the California Sierras. A lot has been said about the photographic beauty of this film. It has brilliant photography of extraordinary natural settings of landscapes, forests and mountains that was unequalled for the period, except for work of the Swedish director Victor Sjostrom, who soon was to come to America himself.

"Tourneur's version of **Last of the Mohicans** was by far the best of the many versions of this James Fenimore Cooper tale."—G. Fenin and W. Everson in *The Western*

The Last of the Mohicans (1920)—Unwelcome guests: Hurons enter Alice's (Lilian Hall) bedroom. (This scene is not in the movie.)

As in Cooper's novel, the *Noble Savage*, in this production can only be found in the appearances of Cingachgoock and Uncas. The enemy Huron Indians were portrayed as barbaric and, given excessive drinking, their goal was only to kill white colonials.

"Much has been written about the photographic quality, beauty, exquisite composition, and breathtaking shots in this film. All of this did not help a film, which was less than inspired. Cooper's story has been translated into a series of static tableaus."—R. and N. Friar in *The Only Good Indian*

For Barbara Bedford, as Cora Munro, this picture not only brought her into a suc-

cessful movie career, but her love on the screen for Uncas also resulted in a private love for Albert Roscoe, who played Uncas.

Boris Karloff had a small role in the film as a marauding Huron. Karloff would later return in an Indian role in DeMille's **Unconquered.**

In spite of some negative reactions, generally critics were favorable:

"**The Last of the Mohicans** was wonderful virile and exiting fare, with never a dull moment. The camerawork was flawless ... but the real star of the whole film was director Maurice Tourneur, who, incidentally, was ably assisted by Clarence Brown."—Joe Franklin in *Classics of the Silent Screen*

Opposite: The Last of the Mohicans (1920)—*Top:* British military discipline. Unidentified actors. *Bottom:* Colonel Munro (James Gordon) consults with his officers about their critical situaion.

The Last of the Mohicans (1920)—*Top:* The traitor Captain Randolph (George Hackathorne) hides in the fort's gunpowder storehouse during the massacre. *Bottom, left:* The camera crew preparing for the dramatic finish. *Right:* Magua (Wallace Beery, *center*) gives his views of the setting while Clarence Brown instructs Cora (Barbara Bedford).

The Last of the Mohicans (1920)—Director Clarence Brown gives directions to Cora (Barbara Bedford) for the final takes at the precipice.

The Last of the Mohicans (Mascot Series, 1932)

Produced by Nat Levine. Screenplay by Colbert Clark, John Francis Netteford, Ford Beebe and Wyndham Gittens. Directed by Reaves Eason and Ford Beebe. Photography by Ernest Miller and Jack Young. Running time: 12 chapters, approx. 4 hrs.

Cast: *Hawkeye* Harry Carey, *Cora* Edwina Booth, *Sagamore* Hobart Bosworth, *Heyward* Walter Miller, *Alice* Lucille Brown, *Uncas* Junior Coughlin, *Magua* Bob Kortman, *DuLac* Walter McGrail, *Montcalm* Mischa Auer, *David Gamut* Nelson McDowell, with Chief John Big Tree, Yakima Canutt, John Gale, Edward Hearn and Tully Marshall.

Chapter 1: "Wild Waters"

In 1757, during the French and Indian War, Huron chief Magua tries to win over the Mohicans to the French side against the British. When the Mohicans refuse, the Hurons destroy the Mohican village. Only Sagamore and Uncas survive as the "Last of the Mohicans."

Acting pro–British, Magua escorts Major Duncan Heyward and Colonel Munro's daughters, Cora and Alice, and their singing teacher Gamut to Fort William Henry. On their way Magua's Hurons attack them. British scout Hawkeye together with Mohican friends Sagamore and Uncas try to help.

Chapter 2: "Flaming Arrows"

After several attacks by the Hurons the party is split and Cora and Alice are captured and brought to the Huron village. A French spy, DuLac, disguised as a trapper, steal a military dispatch from Hawkeye, which he is supposed to bring to Colonel Munro.

MAS-5-EP-1-46

The Last of the Mohicans (Mascot series, 1932)—From Chapter 1: "Wild Waters": British Major Heyward (Walter Miller, *center*), French-allied Huron Magua (Bob Kortman, *right*) and actor Chief Big Tree.

The Last of the Mohicans (1932)—From Chapter 2: "Flaming Arrows": Making up a plan to recapture Cora and Alice from the Huron village. *Left to right:* Sagamore (Hobart Bosworth), Uncas (Junior Coughlin), Hawkeye (Harry Carey) and David Gamut (Nelson McDowell).

Chapter 3: "Rifle or Tomahawk"

Hawkeye manages to recapture the dispatch from DuLac, and with Sagamore and Uncas he frees the captives from the Hurons. On their escape to Fort William Henry they are, however, again attacked and, except for the Mohicans, the party is taken prisoner.

Chapter 4: "Riding with Death"

The prisoners are brought to General Montcalm's camp, and Magua suggests that Montcalm should use Munro's daughters as hostage to obtain the surrender of Fort William Henry. Montcalm, however, refuses to use the women for war negotiations, to the annoyance of Magua. Again,

with the aid of the Mohicans, the party escapes from the Hurons. On the route to the fort, Hurons and French regulars continuously attack the party.

Chapter 5: "Red Shadows"

With the help of the Mohicans, the party reaches Fort William Henry. The French and Hurons attack the fort, and Munro is forced to surrender it to Montcalm. Montcalm gives the British favorable surrender terms, allowing Munro to evacuate his soldiers and colonials. This disappoints Magua, and the Hurons ambush and massacre many of the British during their retreat.

Chapter 6: "The Lure of Gold"

After the British defeat, Munro's daughters are again on the run from the Hurons. DuLac and some other renegades try to rob a French pay wagon, but fail. Cora Munro, who knows were the gold is hidden, is captured by Magua.

Montcalm, who promises Munro to help save his daughters from the Hurons, sends the conspirator DuLac to help. In reality DuLac wishes to find out where the gold is hidden. Also Hawkeye and the Mohicans also try to free the captives.

Chapter 7: "The Crimson Trail"

DuLac and French soldiers manage to free Cora and Alice from the Hurons. DuLac tries to force Cora to disclose where the gold is hidden.

Magua and the Hurons are still on the warpath. They attack Uncas when he tries to warn Hawkeye about a planned ambush the Hurons are setting up to recapture the Munro daughters, who now are with DuLac and the French.

Chapter 8: "The Tide of Battle"

During the ambush Uncas saves Cora from the Hurons. With Gamut and DuLac they take cover in an old log house, which the Hurons attack. DuLac promises to deal with the Huron "problem" in exchange for information about where the gold is hidden.

Magua captures Alice and threatens to burn her at the stake if the party in the log house does not surrender. The Hurons attack the house with burning arrows and set it on fire. Hawkeye rescues Alice from being burned.

Chapter 9: "A Redskin's Honor"

Hawkeye and Sagamore save the party through a secret tunnel attached to the log house. Cora is again captured by Magua and brought to the Huron village. French renegade DuLac captures Heyward and Alice. DuLac wants to use Alice to have Cora disclose the place of the hidden gold. In a canoe race, the Hurons overrun Hawkeye and the Mohicans.

Chapter 10: "The Enemy Stronghold"

The Hurons believe that Hawkeye and the Mohicans have been eliminated, but in reality they have tricked their pursuers.

In the Huron village, Magua wants to make Cora his squaw. Disguised, Uncas infiltrates into the village to free Cora, but he is unmasked and threatened with burning at the stake. Sagamore goes to the village to exchange himself for saving the life of Uncas.

Chapter 11: "Paleface Magic"

When Sagamore and Hawkeye arrive at the Huron village, they are imprisoned by Magua, and with Uncas they are tied to a pole to be burned.

General Munro and a troop of British soldiers save Alice from attacking Hurons. When Alice tells her father that Magua has brought Cora to the Huron camp, the British troop attacks the village. Magua escapes from the village with Cora and Alice as captives. Before leaving, Magua ignites a fire to burn Hawkeye and the Mohicans at the stake.

Chapter 12: "The End of the Trail"

In the last minute, Munro and Heyward save Hawkeye and the Mohicans. The party sets off after Magua. Alice escapes from Magua, and is reunited with her father.

In the final battle, which takes place on a high cliff, Cora is saved. Sagamore and Uncas kill Magua. DuLac, still eager to find out about the hidden gold, has been following the party and puts an end to Sagamore with a musket bullet. Hawkeye kills DuLac. With the death of Sagamore, Uncas is now the Last of the Mohicans.

Notes: "This appalling nonsense has to be seen to be believed ... (Cora and Alice undergo at least twelve chapters and rescues, the dispatches do only marginally better, and we could not keep count of the number of 'plans' and ambushes)."—Martin Barker and Roger Sabin in *The Lasting of the Mohicans*

The Last of the Mohicans (United Artists, 1936)

Produced by Edward Small and Harry M. Goetz. Director: George B. Seitz. Screenplay by Philip Dunne, based on the book by James Fenimore Cooper. Photography by Robert Planck. Music by Roy Webb. Running time: 91 minutes.

Cast: *Hawkeye* Randolph Scott, *Alice Munro* Binnie Barnes, *Cora Munro* Heather Angels, *Colonel Munro* Hugh Buckler, *Major Duncan Heyward* Henry Wilcoxon, *Magua* Bruce Cabot, *Chingachgook* Robert Barrat, *Uncas* Philip Reed, *Captain Winthrop* Williard Robertson, *David Gamut* Frank McGlynne and *Jenkins* Will Stanton.

The story: The year is 1757 and the background is the war between the British and the French and their Indian allies. The French General Montcalm is preparing for a campaign against Fort William Henry.

Colonel Munro, English commander, orders army scout Hawkeye and British Major Heyward to escort his two daughters, Alice and Cora, to Fort William Henry. As guide, the Huron Magua is engaged, who in reality is a spy working inside British lines.

Alice falls in love with Hawkeye, to the chagrin of Major Heyward, who would prefer she loved him. Accompanying Hawkeye are Chingachgook and Uncas, his son, the last survivors of the Mohican tribe, which has been wiped out by the Hurons.

On their way, the savage French-allied Hurons attack the party on several occasions. The Hurons are led by Magua, who now has joined his kinsmen. Hawkeye and the two Mohicans succeed in bringing the party to the safety of the fort. The situation at the fort is desperate for the British. When reinforcement fails to arrive, the French General Montcalm prepares for an attack. When Hawkeye helps the Colonists escape from the fort, he is arrested as a traitor. French and Indian forces overwhelm the fort. Alice and Cora are taken prisoners and carried away.

Cora escapes but is trapped by Magua on a high rock peak, and rather than submit to him she flings herself from the rock to a self-chosen death. The two Mohicans put an end to Magua, but the young Uncas falls to his death. Hawkeye catches up with the Hurons and volunteers to die at the stake in exchange for Alice's life. In the last second he is, however, rescued by a troop of Colonists.

A military Court acquits Hawkeye of all accusations, and he joins the army as a scout. Alice swears him her love and promises to await his return.

Notes: Director George B. Seitz had previously filmed Cooper's classics for the silent 1924 series **Leatherstocking.**

James Fenimore Cooper has been considered the first major American novelist. He was born in Burlington, New Jersey on September 15, 1789, as the eleventh of 12 children born to Judge William Cooper and his wife.

In 1790 the family moved to upstate New York at the head of the Susquehanna River, where his father founded a settlement he named Cooperstown. After being expelled from Yale because of a prank, Cooper joined the American Navy for a few years. His father's death in 1809 made him financially independent, and he could settle down for a quiet life. A series of family tragedies, however, left him deeply in debt, and he took up writing as a source of income.

His second book *The Spy*, a story dealing with the Revolutionary War, brought Cooper international fame. Cooper is best known for his stories dealing with New York frontier life. His five *Leatherstocking* novels depict the adventures of Natty Bumppo (also called Leatherstocking, Hawkeye, Pathfinder and The Long Carbine) and his Indian friend Chingachgook. Chronologically the *Leatherstocking Tales* starts with *Deerslayer* (1841), which depicts Natty's adventures as a young man in the 1840s. *The Last of the Mohicans* (1826) and *The Pathfinder* (1840) are both set during the French and Indian War. The first

ADVERTISING

THE MIGHTIEST DRAMA OF THE CENTURIES...
the hand-to-hand struggle for a nation still unborn!

HARRY M. GOETZ
and
EDWARD SMALL,
the makers of
"Count of Monte Cristo"
Present
THE JAMES FENIMORE
COOPER CLASSIC

The LAST
OF THE MOHICANS

See the death-leap of Cora and the man she loved from the heights of Lovers' Cliff!

See the amazing shooting contest where the winner loses his life!

See the valiant defense of Fort William Henry against the onslaught of the French legions...

See the race for life as Hawkeye wings his canoe through a rain of enemy bullets.

See the most thrilling motion picture event of recent years!

RANDOLPH BINNIE HENRY
Scott · Barnes · Wilcoxon

and
BRUCE CABOT · HEATHER ANGEL · HUGH BUCKLER
ROBERT BARRAT · PHILIP REED · WILLARD ROBERTSON

Directed by GEORGE B. SEITZ · A Reliance Picture   Released thru UNITED ARTISTS

THEATRE

The Last of the Mohicans (1936)—Uncas (Philip Reed) is about to rescue Cora (Heather Angel, *left*) and Alice (Binnie Barnes) from captivity by the Hurons.

book in the series, *The Pioneers* (1823), deals with events in Otsego County in 1793, and *The Prairie* (1827) is set in 1804 when Natty joins the westward movement.

The 1936 version of *The Last of the Mohicans* stayed close to the characters in Cooper's story. They are all there: Hawkeye, Chingachgook, Uncas, Heyward, Cora, Alice and Magua. The only missing link is psalm singer David, although he appears during a short sequence during the massacre of Fort William Henry.

The love story is correct. It's Uncas and Cora, and they both die. Not following Cooper's story, Chingachgook instead of Hawkeye kills Magua, but he survives as the "Last of the Mohicans." Several **Mohi-can** scriptwriters would later take up this story line. Also departing from Cooper's original story, Hawkeye has a love affair with Alice, the older sister of Cora, in this version.

The film was shot at Sherwood Forest and at Cedar Lake in California. The production values of the movie are convincing. Even if there were numerous studio shots, the viewers have a feeling of being removed to upstate New York during the French and Indian War. Initially the plan was to shoot the film in Technicolor, but cost restraints changed this.

The film's production during the Great Depression resulted in some problems with the casting. Indians were underbidding

Opposite: The Last of the Mohicans (United Artists, 1936)—From the pressbook.

each other to get roles as extras, and a special union was created to deal with the matter. For authenticity, the producer had to hire local Boy Scouts to teach the Indian actors to whoop and holler in an acceptable Cooper manner.

The massacre at Fort William Henry is a bloody, terrifying event in the film. It is said that Remington Schuyler's painting *Custer's Last Stand* served as a model for the massacre and scalping scenes.

For the leading role as Hawkeye, Randolph Scott was borrowed from Paramount. Scott's appearance as Hawkeye was a step up in his movie career. Prior to doing **Mohicans**, he had appeared in a series of B-westerns based on Zane Grey stories for Paramount. He later managed to keep up a steady and profitable acting career for the rest of his life.

When the film was released, United Artists, the releasing company, heavily advertised it. From the original 1936 pressbook:

"Towering in its exciting drama above the screen achievements of all time, the Reliance picturization of James Fenimore Cooper's—"The Last of the Mohicans"—comes to life on the screen to thrill millions with the drama of a country in the making."

To advertise the movie, the company released a series of sound records for radio release to the movie theaters.

"The Last of the Mohicans" the most thrilling, romantic and suspenseful of James Fenimore Cooper's classics and now a sure box-office winner for you, has been made into a complete series of 13 electrical transcriptions, telling the classic with vivid drama and genuinely fine acting."

Well-known artists such as Russell Arrows, Larry Sobel, Samuel Mirsky, Robert Benny, Willard Down and Gene Aiello were also hired to illustrate scenes from Cooper's story and the movie. On the front cover of the pressbook, one of the classic illustrations for the 1919 edition of Cooper's novel by N.C. Wyeth was used.

The script in this "Mohican" version by Philip Dunne would later partly be used in the making of Michael Mann's 1992 filming of *The Last of the Mohicans*.

The movie was well received by viewers as well as by critics:

"Like some of its late silent film predecessors of American pioneer days, the picture has its spectacular moments, but it will be remembered mostly for its moving story. George B. Seitz's megging is aces...."—*Variety*

"The whole film is a flow of excitement and movement, with an intelligent script by Philip Dunne, crisp direction by George Seitz, and sharp photography ... picture-making of the old romantic-heroic school, and the lack of anything like it in contemporary Hollywood is regrettable."—Tony Thomas in *The Great Adventure Films*.

Last of the Mohicans (BBC TV series, 1971)

Produced by John McRae. Directed by David Maloney. Screenplay by Harry Green. 8 episodes @ 45 minutes.

Cast: *Hawkeye* Kenneth Ives, *Chingachgook* John Abineri, *Uncas* Richard Warwick, *Magua* Philip Madoc, *Alice* Joanna David, *Heyward* Tim Goodman, *Cora* Patricia Maynard, *Gamut* David Leland, and Andrew Crawford.

Episode 1

Set in 1757 on the New York frontier during the French and Indian War. British Colonel Munro, commander at Fort William Henry, longs to see his two daughters, Cora and Alice, who are in England. Hawkeye and his two Mohican friends, Chingachgook and Uncas, are scouting for the British.

In England Cora and Alice are deciding to meet with their father in the American colony. General Webb is commander at Fort Edward and Munro's superior. A young psalmist, Gamut, arrives and starts teaching the soldiers his psalms. Major Heyward arrives at Fort Edward to request military aid to Munro at Fort William Henry, which is threatened by French troops.

On their way from England to join

their father, Cora and Alice stop at Fort Edward. Heyward is immediately attracted to Alice. As a lesson to others, Munro orders the execution of deserters at Fort William Henry.

Munro receives news of his daughters' arrival in the colonies. General Webb orders Mohawk scout Magua to lead Munro's daughters to their father. Magua leaves with the two Munro daughters, Major Heyward and Gamut. During a rest on their journey, Hurons attack them. Hawkeye and the Mohicans save the party. Magua, who in reality is no Mohawk, but Huron, is exposed as a traitor. The white party continues its journey, followed by the Hurons.

Episode 2

In canoes the escaping party reaches a desolate cave. At the fort, Munro, worrying about his daughters, sends Major Grant with some men to scout for the party. On their way Grant's party is ambushed and massacred by the Hurons.

The Hurons attack the cave. The defenders run out of powder. Still, Cora insists that Hawkeye use his last shot in an act of mercy to relieve a wounded Huron of his suffering. The party realizes its desperate situation, and it is decided that Hawkeye and the Mohicans should try to escape to get help. Uncas hesitates to go because he has fallen in love with Cora. After the scouts have left the cave, Magua and his warriors appear and capture the party.

Episode 3

Magua brings the party downriver by canoes. Hawkeye and the Mohicans are following at a distance. General Webb also sends a search party after Munro's daughters. They fail in their mission and return to Fort Edward.

Among the captives, Heyward tries to persuade Magua to free the women. Magua will not accept this, and claims Cora for his squaw. The conflict escalates and the Munro daughters and Heyward are tied to trees and are harassed by tomahawk throwing. Gamut, considered mentally deranged

by the Indians, manages to kill one of the Hurons. In the last minute, Hawkeye and the Mohicans arrive to save the captives.

The party is heading toward Fort William Henry and spends the night at an abandoned blockhouse at an old burial ground. During the night the Hurons approach.

Episode 4

Fearing the spirit of the burial ground, the Hurons leave. The party splits and Heyward, under cover of fog, leads Munro's daughters to the fort, now under siege by French General Montcalm's troops.

General Webb at Fort Edward sends a scouting party to evaluate Montcalm's strength. When intelligence confirms the weak position of Munro, Webb sends dispatches advising Munro to surrender Fort William Henry.

Cora and Alice adjust to the war situation at the fort and persuade their father to help the sick and wounded, contrary to the will of the regiment's doctor.

In the meantime, Hawkeye and the two Mohicans have been captured by the Hurons in the forest and are subjected to torture. Montcalm's soldiers, however, intervene and save them. The French send them to Fort William Henry to deliver captured dispatches written by Webb to suggest the surrender of the fort. Colonel Munro realizes that he cannot expect any help from Webb, and decides to parley with Munro about surrender.

Episode 5

Montcalm offers Munro surrender with full honor. Munro asks for a 24-hour truce to discuss the terms with his officers.

Elsewhere in the woods Uncas, Chingachgook and Hawkeye are healing their wounds after the torture. During the night Munro and Montcalm observe each other at a distance. Magua, who has a deeprooted hate for Colonal Munro, aims at him with his musket but before he fires he is hindered by Montcalm.

The next day Munro, in the shadow of the serious situation, arranges a feast with dancing to cheer up the defenders. Hey-ward, whose affection for Alice has grown, explains his feelings to her and she agrees to consider his proposal when matters are more stable.

Munro and his officers discuss their ex-posed situation. Heyward and most of the officers are in favor of continuing the fight-ing. Munro, however, as the old loyal Scot-tish officer he is, decides to follow his com-mander's order to surrender the fort.

The next morning Munro agrees on surrender of the fort to Montcalm. Magua explains his disappointment to Montcalm about letting the British leave in peace. His warriors own the reward of scalps for sup-porting their "Canadian father" during the siege. Returning after scouting on the Huron village, Uncas informs Hawkeye and Chingachgook that the Hurons are preparing for war.

The British are leaving the fort and the French flag is raised over the ramparts of Fort William Henry.

Episode 6

When the British depart the fort, Magua and his warriors attack and mas-sacre the troops. Magua captures Cora and Alice. Uncas tracks their path north toward Canada. With Hawkeye and Chingachgook he sets off after the escapees by river to ad-vance faster than Magua and his party can do in the woods.

On their way they are attacked by a war party of Hurons in canoes. Hawkeye with his long carbine beats back the attack. Magua's escaping party is splitting. Magua sends Cora to "the people of the turtle," a Delaware village, while he brings captives Alice and Gamut to a Huron village.

Uncas and company find David in the forest, dressed as a "French Indian." The Indians consider Gamut mentally disor-dered because of his behavior, which has simplified his escape.

The party decides to divide to follow the captured women. Heyward and Gamut go after Alice in the Huron village. At the village, Heyward claims that he is a healer.

One of the chiefs has a daughter who is badly ill and it is decided that he can prove his credibility by curing the woman.

A hunting party of Hurons arrives with Uncas, who has been captured. Mean-while in the woods, Colonel Munro, wor-rying about his daughters, reveals to Hawk-eye that Cora is the daughter of a black slave woman whom he met during one of his military undertakings in the West In-dies.

In the Huron village Magua accuses the captured Uncas of being a traitor to the Indians and wants him killed.

Episode 7

Hawkeye and Chingachgook leave Munro in the forest to go after the captives in the Huron village. In the village, Hey-ward realizes that his trick can be un-masked when the woman dies. By claming that the Indian woman must be brought into the woods to meet "The Great Spirit" to recover, Heyward, Gamut and Alice manage to escape.

Hawkeye and Chingachgook arrive at the village and free Uncas. United with her father in the woods, Alice and the rest of the party set off after Cora in the Delaware camp. Magua returns to the "village of the turtles" to claim Cora. Old Sagamore of the tribe is to decide about the fate of the intruders. Reputation has brought word of the "Long Carbine" to the Delawares. Hey-ward is claiming that he is the Long Car-bine. In a shooting contest, Hawkeye proves he is the Long Carbine. Uncas ar-gues against Magua's claim of Cora as his squaw. Sagamore questions the young Mo-hican's truthfulness, but when it is revealed that Uncas and Chingachgook are descen-dants of the old Delaware Chief Tam-maron, Sagamore decides to let them go in peace. Magua, however, in accordance with his "right of conquest," is allowed to leave with Cora. When they depart, Uncas in anger declares to Magua that he will follow them to free Cora when the sun rises.

Episode 8

Magua departs with Cora for the

Huron village. In the Delaware village a plan is set up to go after Magua and the Hurons. The Delawares agree to make war on the Hurons because of Magua's "bad blood." The war plan is to strike the Huron village on three flanks. Colonal Munro will lead one group, Hawkeye and Heyward accompanied by Daniel will lead the second, and Uncas will strike with a third force of Delawares. Magua returns to the Huron village and announces that the Yankees will attack. Cora is put under guard.

The Hurons sets up an ambush for the advancing war party of Delawares. In a furious fight the Hurons are beaten. In the Huron village Cora escapes and leaves in a canoe. Magua with some of the Huron warriors sets off in pursuit.

At the Delaware camp, Munro, wounded during the battle, is left behind, and the others go after Magua to save Cora. Magua tracks and captures Cora. On their escape, beside a waterfall, Cora refuses to go any farther. In the confused situation, Uncas arrives and is stabbed by Magua. A Huron warrior kills Cora with his knife. An enraged Magua kills the warrior. Chingachgook, not far away, arrives and challenges Magua. During a deadly fight, Chingachgook kills Magua.

In the final scene, Uncas and Cora are buried. Chingachgook calls out that he is now alone. Hawkeye assures him that they will stay together also in future.

Notes: This BBC series was filmed in Scotland. It is an adventurous series, with beautiful scenery. It is possibly the "**Mohican**" version that is most faithful to the James Fenimore Cooper classic novel. Possibly the only deviation from Cooper's original story is that Chingachgook kills Magua in the final fight, not Hawkeye. Otherwise the story follows the original conclusion, love affairs and characters, and Chingachgook is the "Last of the Mohicans."

"The BBC version is an important one ... in all this version's details there is a real hunt for "authenticity" ... With this **Mohican** miniseries Britain thus offered America a view of its soul, a soul scarred by its 'mistake' in invading Vietnam."—Martin Barker and Roger Sabin in *The Lasting of the Mohicans.*

The Last of the Mohicans (Hanna-Barbara Productions for CBS, 1975)

Produced by Joseph Hanna and William Barbera. Story by Draper Lewis, based on James Fenimore Cooper's novel. Running time: 60 minutes.

Voices: John Doucette, Paul Hecht, Kristina Holland, Casey Kasem, Mike Road, John Stephenson, Joan Van Ark and Frank Welker.

Animated famous classic tale for television.

Last of the Mohicans (Schick Sunn Classics, 1977)

Produced by Robert Stabler. Directed by James L. Conway. Screenplay by Stephen

Last of the Mohicans (1977)—The ferocity of battle.

Last of the Mohicans (Schick Sunn Classics, 1977)—Hurons wait to attack.

Lord. Photography by Henning Schellerup. Running time: 97 minutes.

Cast: *Hawkeye* Steve Forrest, *Chingachgook* Ned Romero, with Andrew Prine, Don Shanks, Michele Marsh, Jane Actman, Robert Tessier, Robert Easton, Whit Bissell, Dehl Berti, John G. Bishop, Coleman Creel, Beverly Rowland, Rosalyn Mike and Reid Sorenson.

Notes: TV-movie remake of Cooper's novel. Steve Forrest and Ned Romero repeated their Hawkeye and Chingachgook roles in a follow-up, **The Deerslayer.**

The story takes liberties with the original story; for example, Magua is killed in combat with Chingachgook, and Cora survives.

The Last of the Mohicans (Burbank Studios, 1987)

Screenplay by Leonard Lee.

Animated version produced in Australia by Burbank Studios for Family Home Entertainment.

The Last of the Mohicans (Morgan Creek International, 1992)

Produced by Michael Mann and Hunt Lowry. Directed by Michael Mann. Screenplay by Michael Mann, Christopher Crowe and Philip Dunne (from Dunne's 1936 screenplay based on the adaptation by John L. Balderson, Paul Perez and Daniel Moore of the novel by James Fenimore Cooper). Photography by Dante Spinotti. Music by Trevor Jones and Randy Edelman. Running time: 122 minutes.

Cast: *Hawkeye* Daniel Day-Lewis, *Cora Munro* Madeleine Stowe, *Chingach-*

The Last of the Mohicans (Morgan Creek International, 1992)—Hawkeye (Daniel Day-Lewis, *left*) and Uncas (Eric Schweig).

gook Russell Means, *Uncas* Eric Schweig, *Alice Munro* Jodhi May, *Major Duncan Heyward* Steven Waddington, *Magua* Wes Studi, *Colonel Munro* Maurice Roeves, *General Montcalm* Patrice Chereau, with Edward Blatchford, Terry Kinney, Tracey Ellis, Justin M. Rice, Dennis J. Banks, Pete Postelthwaite, Colm Meany and Mac Andrews.

The story: In 1757 during the French and Indian War, frontier woodsman Hawkeye and his two Mohican friends, Chingachgook and Uncas, are hunting in the New York forests. At night they rest with the trapper Cameron's family at a frontier log cabin where they are well received. Information is spread that the English are forming a colonial militia against the advancing French troops.

In Albany, Major Duncan Heyward arrives with dispatches to General Webb. He meets with Cora and Alice Munro, daughters of Colonel Munro, who is stationed as commander of Fort William Henry. Heyward is in love with Cora and wants to marry her. Heyward with some British soldiers is assigned to escort Cora and Alice to their father.

In the wilderness they are attacked by French-allied Hurons led by Magua. At the last moment Hawkeye and the two Mohicans arrive to rescue Cora, Alice and Heyward. To prepare for the night they seek protection at the Camerons's, but find the log cabin burned out and the whole family massacred. To the annoyance of Cora, they leave the place without burying the massacred bodies. Hawkeye, however, later explains to Cora that this is done only to protect them from being detected by hostile war parties. Cora, who first was repelled by Hawkeye, begins to fall in love with him.

When darkness falls, they hide at an old burial ground. A war party of French-allied Ottawas is approaching in the forest. The intruders leave, however, because they do not want to desecrate the sacred ground.

The party makes it to Fort William Henry, which is under siege by Montcalm's French troops. The fort is under heavy bombardment from the French. Some colonial support troops decide to leave the British because they would rather go to protect their families on the burning frontiers. In this connection Munro puts Hawkeye in irons because of his support for the colonials.

At the fort the love between Hawkeye and Cora is strengthened. Munro realizes his weak position, and when no help is to be expected from General Webb at Fort Edward, he surrenders the fort to Montcalm. When the British troops march out from the fort into the wilderness, Magua and his warriors break the agreement to allow the defeated British to leave in peace, and attack and massacre the British. Colonel Munro is killed and Magua, with vengeful hate for him, cuts out his heart.

Hawkeye and the Mohicans again save Alice, Cora and Heyward. Magua with some of his warriors pursues the group and finally captures them under a waterfall. Hawkeye and the Mohicans, however, escape with the intention of later returning to save the captives.

Magua brings the captives into the Huron village in front of their elderly Sachem. Hawkeye makes his way to the Huron encampment to offer his life in exchange for those of Cora and Alice. Instead Heyward preempts Hawkeye's offer, which costs him his life. The Sachem gives Alice to Magua and allows the others to go in peace. When Magua leaves with Alice, Hawkeye's party pursues him.

At a high mountain pass they catch up with the Hurons. Alice commits suicide rather than to continue with Magua. Uncas tries to avenge her death but is killed by Magua. Chingachgook in revenge tomahawks Magua to death.

In the final scene, Chingachgook takes farewell of his son Uncas during a burial in the mountains. Hawkeye and Cora presumably will live happily ever after.

Notes: Director Michael Mann was best known for his TV productions **Starsky and Hutch** and **Miami Vice**. He started directing feature movies in 1981 with **Thief**, followed by **Manhunter** in 1986, before doing **The Last of the Mohicans** in 1992.

Mann bought the film rights to Philip Dunne's 1936 script in 1989. The **Mohicans** from 1936 had captured Mann's interest early in his life; in fact, it was his first childhood filmgoing experience when he stumbled upon a screening of it in a basement of a church. The script takes great liberties with the original Cooper novel.

The love affair is much different in this version of the tale. In Cooper's story Uncas and Cora are the lovers. Here the story is built up as a passionate love affair between Hawkeye and Cora. This is not only unfaithful to Cooper but also to Dunne's 1936 script in which Hawkeye loved Alice. Following Dunne, but not Cooper's original, Chingachgook rather than Hawkeye kills Magua. Nevertheless, Chingachgook is still the last of his tribe.

To do the film Mann wanted Daniel Day-Lewis for the role as Hawkeye but he wasn't easy to get. Day-Lewis had recently enjoyed remarkable success with his Oscar-winning role in **My Left Foot**. After a face-to-face meeting in London in October 1990 with Mann, Day-Lewis decided to take the part.

Getting Lewis on board in the casting was not the end of Mann's troubles with actors. With the white roles settled, he needed a Native American in the role as Chingachgook. In choosing between Native activists Dennis Banks and Russell Means, the role went to Means. Activist Russell Means, a Sioux, was very critical of the recently made Kevin Costner film **Dances with Wolves**. He felt it got the Sioux folkway and hunting practices completely wrong. He had, however, fewer problems

The Last of the Mohicans (1992)—Hawkeye (Daniel Day-Lewis) on his way to rescue Cora during the massacre.

accepting the role as Chingachgook, and after the film was finished he thought the treatment of the Natives in **The Last of the Mohicans** was basically positive.

The filming of the movie was done on location in the Blue Ridge Mountains in North Carolina. Before entering into filming, Day-Lewis had to be taught about 18th century frontier survival. This brought him and Michael Mann together, who also joined the training course in woodland survival and weapon training.

Madeleine Stowe (Cora) commented on the Mann–Day-Lewis relationship during the making of the movie in *Premiere*:

"Daniel was unique. He did not question or challenge Michael.... It's a real deep, unspoken agreement I think they had—a real male thing—that Michael was a general and Daniel was going to fulfill his orders. I think they really care about each other a great deal, those two."

Great efforts were made to have bewigged British Redcoats, colonials, Natives and Coureurs de Bois to look as authentic as possible on the scene. Every small arm fired during the filming was charged with black powder. Every gun fired was an actual flintlock. Some were even original weapons of the early to mid–18th century.

Author and reenactor Mark Baker spent the whole summer of 1991 with the production team as an instructor in woodland tracking and wilderness warfare. His initial responsibility fell to train Daniel Day-Lewis to run while loading his rifle, Killdeer. Madeleine Stowe would later comment on Daniel Day-Lewis' relation to his gun in an interview for *Empire*:

"Daniel would carry his gun around all the time, when we went to lunch he'd have that gun with him, when he went to the bathroom he'd have that gun with him. He's sort of not of this world, Daniel."

Mark Baker concluded his experiences from the film job in an article in *Muzzle-loader*:

"Working with **The Last of the Mohicans** was undoubtedly the best summer job I have ever endured, but after several weeks of mostly all-night shooting, I was physically drained. I could fall asleep anywhere, in any position and had lost approximately ten pounds."

The film production did not go smoothly. Fed up by long hours, bad food and not the best pay, virtually the entire production crew went on strike. The Native American extras also came up with their own protest against their bad living and working conditions, and they used activist Russell Means, playing Chingachgook, in their efforts when negotiating with the production management.

The final scenes of the film were completed on October 10, 1991, after almost four months of filming. The filming had been hard on crew and actors:

"After months of the Blue Ridge Mountains, I came away saying, 'Give me lights, give me some rock 'n' roll, I am out of there.'"—Michael Mann, in *Premiere*

"When you have lived in the mountains for five or six weeks it's not something you readily let go of and the shock of being back in the city was really acute."—Daniel Day-Lewis in *Movies*

Generally the reception of the movie was positive. There is some spectacular scenery in the film from the mysterious Smoky Mountains, which stood for the New York wilderness in Cooper's story.

"The North Carolina locations, framed in 'Scope' are certainly pretty, but the period ambiance is undermined by a tacky wallpaper score by Trevor Jones and Randy Edelman."—*Chicago Reader*

Jones's and Edelman's music, however, gave the film its only Oscar, even if more were expected.

"Mann's film is quite an improvement on Cooper's all but unreadable book.... **The Last of the Mohicans** is not as authentic and uncompromised as it claims to be—more a matinee fantasy than it wants to admit—but it is probably more entertaining as a result."—Roger Ebert in *Chicago Sun-Times*

The film has, however, been accused of some extreme violence:

"Many of the scenes, the massacre among them, are not for the squeamish; tomahawks and hunting knives leave especially gruesome wounds. Scalping is also graphically depicted, as is a particularly nasty form of heart surgery reminiscent of Indiana Jones and the **Temple of Doom**."—Rita Kempley in *The Washington Post*

On the violence in **The Last of the Mohicans** Day-Lewis made a comment in an interview for *Movies*:

"I was quite stunned by the ferocity of some of the violence.... Even though I'd been a part of some of it at the time we were filming. It doesn't feel like that when you are involved in it."

Commercially the film did well. When it was released in United States it grossed $11.4 million during the first weekend of distribution.

Last of the Redmen (Columbia, 1947)

Produced by Sam Katzman. Directed by George Sherman. Screenplay by Herbert Dalmas and George H. Plympton, based on the book *The Last of the Mohicans* by James Fenimore Cooper. Photography in Vitacolor by Raoul Fernstrom and Ira H. Morgan. Music by Mischel Bakaleinkoff. Running time: 78 minutes.

Cast: *Major Heyward* Jon Hall, *Hawkeye* Michael O'Shea, *Alice Munro* Evelyn Ankers, *Cora Munro* Julia Bishop, *Magua* Buster Crabbe, *Uncas* Rick Vallin, *Davy* Buzz Henry, *Gen. Munro* Guy Hedlund, *Gen. Webb* Frederick Worlock, *Bob Wheelwright* Emmet Vogan, and Chief Many Treaties.

The story: During the French and Indian War, Montcalm's army is threatening British outposts along the Hudson and St. Lawrence rivers. General Webb, commander at Fort Edward, sends Major Heyward to

Last of the Redmen (Columbia, 1947)—Trouble ahead: Magua (Buster Crabbe, *foreground*) has just spotted hostile Indians and warns Davy (Buzz Henry, *left*), Cora (Julie Bishop), Alice (Evelyn Ankers) and Heyward (Jon Hall) of the danger.

escort General Munro's two daughters, Alice and Cora, and their 12-year-old brother Davy, to join their father at Fort William Henry. But there is trouble. The renegade Iroquois warrior, Magua, who is scouting the party, plans to kidnap and hold them for ransom.

Along the way they encounter a number of adventurous obstacles. Magua aided by his warrior tribesmen attack the party again and again. Help, however, appears from British scout Hawkeye and his Indian friend Uncas, the last survivor of the eliminated Mohican tribe.

When the party finally approaches Fort William Henry, it meets General Munro's troops, who have been forced to surrender the fort to Montcalm. Magua and his warriors attack the retreating military column. Uncas goes after help, but is followed by Magua. In the final battle Uncas is mortally wounded but manages to put an end to Magua.

Notes: This is a **Last of the Mohicans** version intended for children. Therefore a new character was introduced into the script, Davy, the Munro sisters' younger brother. The story takes great liberties with Cooper's original. There is no Chingachgook in this version and not much in the way of love affairs. In the final battle Uncas, not Hawkeye, kills Magua but Uncas dies of his wounds.

Last of the Redmen—A ritual haircut: a dead Indian scout, who has been carrying a military dispatch, is about to be scalped by Huron braves.

"**The Last of the Redmen** is showing ... to the accompaniment of war whoops, flying arrows, swinging hatchets, belching muskets and thundering hoof beats. And in color too! ... Some fun, eh! Go to it kids and squirm with excitement the way we once used to do on Sunday afternoon."—T.M.P. in *The New York Times*

"A dressing up of a classic tale may thrill the kids, but adults might give it a dressing down for some plot manhandling that Natty Bumppo would not have liked."—*The Motion Picture Guide*

Leatherstocking (Biograph Co., 1909)

Produced and directed by D.W. Griffith. Photography by G.W. Bitzer and Arthur Marvin. Screenplay by Stanner E.V. Taylor, based on the Leatherstocking series of books by James Fenimore Cooper. Photography by G.W. Bitzer and Arthur Marvin. Length: 372 feet.

Cast: George O. Nicholls, Marion Leonard, James Kirkwood, Linda Arvidson, Mack Sennett, Owen Moore, William A. Quirk, Werner Clarges, and Adele De Garde.

The Story: Indian scout Magua is guiding a party of two soldiers and two women on a trek through the wilderness. Magua turns out to be a renegade and, joined by his tribesmen, he attacks the group. The party is saved, however, by British scout Hawkeye and his Indian friend Chingachgook.

Pursued by Magua and his warriors,

the party manages to escape into an abandoned fort, and closes the gate just in time to prevent the Indians from entering.

In the fort the group is continuously attacked by the Indians, and in the end they are captured and taken away. In the forest, Chingachgook is tied to a tree to be tortured. British troops arrive in time to save him and the rest of the party.

Notes: This is one of Griffith's hidden movies, and it was mostly photographed outdoors on location at Cuddebackville in New York.

In his early career, being the main producer of film for Biography, Griffith made almost 450 films for the company. **Leatherstocking** is a short version of *The Last of the Mohicans*. The 15 minute-length of the film is not a long time to expend on interrelations among Cooper's fictional characters. No love affairs, no Uncas and there is no "Last of the Mohicans" in this story. Therefore the plot is straightforward. The focus is to tell an adventure story, and it is done well in short time.

Leatherstocking (Pathé serial, 1924)

Directed by George B. Seitz. Screenplay by Robert Dillon.

Cast: *Natty (Leatherstocking)* Harold Miller), with Edna Murphy, Frank Lackteen and Whitehorse.

Unfortunately information on plot summaries for chapters 2 and 3 is missing.

Chapter 1: "The War-Path"

Leatherstocking is a white man who has been living among the Delawares for ten years and who has learned their language and customs. The Delawares live in peace with their white brothers.

Chingachgook, a brave, loves Wah-ta-wah, who has been taken away by Briarthorn. To search for Briarthorn, Chingachgook and Leatherstocking take separate trails and decide to meet at Glimmerglass Lake in seven moons.

During the search Leatherstocking meets Henry March, a hunter known as "Hurry Harry." When they reach Glimmerglass Lake they run into a French-allied Huron attack on Muscrat Castle, the strange home of Tom Hutter on Glimmerglass Lake. Hutter is an ex-pirate living with his two daughters, Judith and Hetty.

Leatherstocking and Hurry Harry help drive off the attackers, but when they attempt to land, Hurons hidden in trees jump onto the ark, the craft Hutter uses to carry him from Muskrat Castle to the shore.

Chapter 2: "The Secret Trail"

Chapter 3: "The Hawk's Eye"

Chapter 4: "The Paleface Law"

Hetty, the religious daughter of mysterious old Tom Hutter, is held captive in Rivenoak's Huron camp. She tries to teach the Huron chief and his braves the law of the whites.

Hetty's faith in God's teachings is so great that she tries to teach the Hurons to love their enemies and do good to them. This is difficult for the Indians to understand, when the paleface himself does not live by this law. When trying to rescue Hetty, the Hurons imprison Tom Hutter and Hurry Harry.

Chapter 5: "Ransom"

When all efforts to free Tom Hutter and Hurry Harry fail, Leatherstocking and Chingachgook seek something to offer as ransom. They search Hutter's treasure chest, but there seems to be nothing that Chingachgook thinks the Hurons would prize except some ivory chessmen carved in the forms of elephants.

Rivenoak and his braves with their prisoners approach Muskrat Castle on rafts to bargain for ransom. Leatherstocking, knowing the cunning of the Indians, is prepared for treachery.

Chapter 6: "The Betrayal"

Hurry Harry March is disclosed as a traitor. He has watched, with smoldering passion, the love in Judith's eyes when she looks at Leatherstocking. Taking advantage of Leatherstocking's absence in his search to rescue Wah-ta-wah, Hurry Harry tries to force his attention and unwelcome kisses on Judith. She repels his advances.

Chapter 7: "Rivenoak's Revenge"

Leatherstocking is captured and imprisoned by the Hurons. Fearing that the Indians will accept the ivory elephants as ransom for Leatherstocking, Hurry Harry commits another act of treachery and Leatherstocking is doomed to death. First, however, he is tortured by being forced to look on while the Hurons attack Muskrat Castle. What is to be the fate of Judith Hutter, the girl he loves?

Chapter 8: "Out of the Storm"

Tom Hutter makes his last stand against the Indians. Before he dies he tells Judith and Hetty that they are not his daughters. Their mother was one of the women captured by the pirate crew of which he was a member, but he never knew their father.

A golden casket contains information about him, but the Hurons have stolen this. Hutter dies. Hurry Harry plans to take Judith, even against her will, back to the settlements with him.

Chapter 9: "The Panther"

Leatherstocking is permitted a parole by his captors for the purpose of delivering Hurry Harry March, who has killed an Indian maid. Otherwise Judith and Hetty must pay the price of March's treachery with their honor. March reveals himself as a coward. Leatherstocking decides to let him go, hoping for a miracle to be able to save the girls from their fate. He is able to protect the girls, but he is captured himself and doomed to torture. Judith, realizing his great peril, starts out for the nearest English garrison to get soldiers to rescue her sweetheart. But she sprains her ankle and is unable to walk.

Chapter 10: "Mingo Torture"

Leatherstocking is bound to a tree and tortured with thrown knives and tomahawks. He realizes that death is near. How-

ever, Judith sends British soldiers to the rescue, and the Indians are beaten. Hetty is mortally wounded. Chingachgook and Wah-ta-wah return to their tribe and Leatherstocking and Judith go to the white settlement.

Notes: This silent series was based on the 1841 novel *The Deerslayer* from the Leatherstocking Tales by James Fenimore Cooper. George B. Seitz later used the experience from this work when he in 1936 directed a film version of another of Cooper's novels, *The Last of the Mohicans*.

This is most probably a lost picture, and the chapter guide presented here originates from information in the 1924 Campaign Book for the series.

Lederstrumpf (Leatherstocking)
(Aura Film for ZDF/ORF, 1968)

Produced by Georg Glass. Directed by Jean Dreville. Screenplay by Walter Ulbrich and Pierre Gaspard-Huit. Photography by André Zarra. Music by George Grigorin and Robert Mellin.

Cast: Pierre Massimi, Helmut Lange, David Alexander, Loumi Jacobesco, Otto Ambros, Ali Raffi, Jack Brunet, Sylvie Maas, Roland Ganement, Juliette Villard, Daniel Crohem, Christian Duroc, Gilbert Normand, Czach Szabolcs, Helmuth Schneider, Catherine Jourdan, Robert Benoit, Gabriel Gason, George Demetry, Victoria Medea, Mircea Pascu, J.P. Compain, and Ion Dichiseanu.

The Story: A Karl May–inspired adoption of James Fenimore Cooper's *Leatherstocking Tales* in a German-French co-production for television. Four episodes: 1) "**Der Wildtöter**" ("**The Deerslayer**"); 2) "**Der Letzte Mohikaner**" ("**The Last of the Mohicans**"); 3) "**Das Fort am Biberfluss**" ("**The Fort on Beaver River**," "**The Pathfinder**"); 4) "**Die Prärie**" ("**The Prairie**").

Der Letzte Mohikaner (The Last Tomahawk) (International Germania-Balcazar, 1965)

Directed by Harold Reinl.

Cast: Joachim Fuchsberger, Karin Dor, Anthony Steffen, Dan Martin, and Ricardo Rodriguez.

A German-Italian-Spanish co-production. Following a German Karl May tradition the story was transferred from that of the Colonial period to the "Wild West" in the 1870s.

The Light in the Forest (Buena Vista, 1958)

Produced by Walt Disney. Directed by Herschel Daugherty. Screenplay by Lawrence E. Watkin, based on the novel by Conrad Richter. Photography in Technicolor by Ellsworth Fredericks. Music by Paul J. Smith. Running time: 93 minutes.

Cast: *Johnny Butler* James MacArthur, *Shenandoe* Carol Lynley, *Del Hardy* Fess Parker, *Wilse Owens* Wendell Corey, *Milly Elder* Joanne Dru, *Myra Butler* Jessica Tandy, *Chief Cuyloga* Joseph Calleia, *John Elder* John McIntire, *Half Arrow* Rafael Campos, *Harry Butler* Frank Ferguson, *Niskitoon* Norman Fredric, *Kate Owens* Marian Seldes, *Colonel Henry Bouquet* Stephen Bekassy and *George Owens* Sam Buffington.

The story: A peace treaty in 1764 between the British and the Delaware Indians demands that all white prisoners be re-

The Light in the Forest (Buena Vista, 1958)—Lobby card: Del Hardy (Fess Parker) in the river fight with a Delaware warrior.

The Light in the Forest—After the fistfight: a handshake of friendship between Wilse Owens (Wendell Corey, *left*) and Johnny Butler (James MacArthur).

leased and returned to their people. One of the prisoners is a boy named Johnny Butler, who is now more Indian than white.

Del Hardy, who is an Army scout, has been assigned to help Johnny through his readjustment period. As Johnny is bitterly anti-white, he rebels against his real parents when they try to incorporate him to their way of life.

Conflict arises when Johnny understands that his uncle Wilse is the leader of a band of men who raid and murder Indians. Shenandoe, a servant girl of Wilse's, whose parents have been killed at the hands of an Indian party, is first frightened of Johnny because of the nightmarish memories of her parents' death. She and Johnny, however, soon fall in love. Johnny's feeling for Shenandoe influences his attitude to-

ward the whites and he starts to behave more and more like a white man.

One night Wilse kills an Indian friend of Johnny who is coming for a visit. This causes Johnny to return to his tribe, more embittered than ever. When the Indians want to use him as a decoy to lure an innocent party of whites into an ambush he decides not to do it. He returns to the white settlements intent to fight Wilse, in the white man's way, with his fists. In the fight Johnny beats Wilse. He and Shenandoe find an idyllic place in the forest where they decide to settle down and live with the nature. In town, Del Hardy also settles down with Milly, the daughter of the local clergyman.

Notes: "...is an absorbing and fairly intelligent film with an enlightening moral for young viewers, showing that there are good and bad men in every part of life, and that before one can be at peace with others, one must be at peace with oneself.—Leonard Maltin in *The Disney Films*

"...the whole thing is talky (much of which is quite hard to understand) and the dramatic incidents are less viewed than they ordinarily are in Disney films ... [but it] is wholesome, in a nice, simple, outdoor way, and the scenery is pretty in color. It should entertain kids."—Bosley Crowther in *The New York Times*

Many Rivers to Cross
(MGM, 1955)

Produced by Jack Cummings. Directed by Roy Rowland. Screenplay by Harry Brown and Guy Trosper, based on a story by Steve Frazee. Photographed in Cinemascope and Eastman Color by John Seitz. Music by Cyril J. Mockridge. Running time: 92 minutes.

Cast: *Bushrod Gentry* Robert Taylor, *Mary Stuart Cherne* Eleanor Parker, *Cadmus Cherne* Victor McLaglen, *Fremont* Jeff Richards, *Shields* Russ Tamblyn, *Esau Hamilton* James Arness, *Luke Radford* Alan Hale, Jr., *Hugh* John Hudson, *Lige Blake* Rhys Williams, *Mrs. Cherne* Josephine Hutchinson, *Spectacle Man* Sig Ruman, *Lucy Hamilton* Rosemary DeCamp, *Banks* Russel Johnson, *Sandak* Ralph Moody and *Slangoh* Abel Fernandez.

The story: In 1798, Kentucky trapper Bushrod Gentry, en route to the Ohio hunting grounds, rescues a girl, Mary Stuart Cherne, from Shawnee Indians. The girl is only too willing to show her gratitude but the unromantic Bushrod prefers to go it alone. Mary decides that Bushrod is the man for her, and his fate is sealed. She goads her ex-boyfriend into fighting Bushrod in the hopes of subduing him, but Bushrod flattens the toughie out. When she pretends that Bushrod has betrayed her, her father,

Many Rivers to Cross (MGM, 1955)—From the pressbook.

Cadmus, and her four strapping brothers force Bushrod at rifle point to marry Mary. The ceremony over, he takes off into the wilderness alone, followed by Mary.

Tarrying too long in a small inn, Bushrod is thrown into jail, only to be freed by Mary, who floors the jailer. But she still cannot convince Bushrod to settle down. He is further encouraged to leave her by Esau Hamilton, a giant of a man and fellow roisterer. Bushrod is about to leave Mary again when a crisis in Esau's family shows him the joys of domesticity. But this time, Mary is ahead of him on the trail. Bushrod overtakes her just as Indians trap her. He subdues the Indians and has come down to Mary's way of thinking when the irate father and brothers arrive to avenge Mary's honor. Mary intervenes and points out that she is happily married and intends to stay that way.

Many Rivers to Cross—Bushrod (Robert Taylor) is in trouble with the Shawnee warrior Slangoh (Abel Fernandez).

Notes: "...an extremely broad, sometimes funny, comedy about the romantic di-does of settlers in early Kentucky ... The slapstick treatment, in itself, is well enough handled by Roy Rowland's direction.... Buckskin-clad Taylor displays a sense of humor in trouping the role as a trapper..."—*Variety*

"The first review of a double feature movie at one theater made about the same time of *Seven Brides for Seven Brothers*, is as inane, raucous and clumsy an attempt at Western satire as has snaked out of the Hollywood brush in a long time."—H.H.T. in *The New York Times*

"The script is well-balanced, tying comedy in with drama and featuring a cast that gives entertaining caricatures of backwoods types."—*The Motion Picture Guide*

Marguerite Volant (Telfilm Canada 1996, TV mini-series)

Produced by Lorraine Richard. Directed by Charles Biname. Screenplay by Jacques Jacob and Monique H. Messier. Photography by Pierre Gill. Music by Richard Gregoire. Canadian produced TV mini-series in 11 episodes.

Cast: *Marguerite Volant* Catherine Senart, *James Elliot Chase* Michael Saphieha, *Laval Chevigny* Normand d'Amour, *Claude Volant* Gilbert Sicotte, *Isabeau* Veronique Le Flaguais, *Élénore Volant* Pascale Bussieres, *Lambert Volant* Stephane Gagnon, *Renaud Larochelle* Pierre Curzi, *Éugénie Beaubassin* Angele Coutu, *Antoine De Courval* Philippe Cousineau, *Jeanne Lettellier* Pascale Montpetit and *Blaise Melanson* Benoit Briere.

Episode 1

In the spring of 1763, after the peace treaty between England and France settling the French and Indian War, Claude Volant and his 20-year-old daughter Marguerite, fearing the new British rule, set up plans to return to France with the family. Claude Volant's wife Isabeau, however, refuses to leave.

Life at the Volant Manor adjusts to a "normal," peaceful situation. Marguerite's brother Lambert decides to leave the country life and become a poet. A catastrophe hits the family when Claude's wife becomes sick and dies.

Episode 2

In late summer of 1763, at the death of his wife Claude Volant becomes disoriented. Marguerite takes over as head of the family at the manor. A French neighbor, Antoine de Courval, who is interested in the Volant resources, requests Claude's permission to marry Marguerite. He agrees, on the condition that Marguerite accepts the proposal.

British forces arrive at the manor. Captain James Chase has been sent to the region to establish British rule. The British bring French wounded from the war, including a Volant servant, Blaise. To the distress of the family, Marguerite's sister Élénore's husband, who has been in the war, is not among the prisoners.

Episode 3

The Canadian nobility amuse themselves in autumn, 1763. For once, to escape the obligations at the manor, Marguerite attends a ball in Montreal. Captain Chase, who is becoming interested in Marguerite, asks her for a dance. Marguerite, who has been hesitating to act on Chase's courtesy, accepts his request and accompanies him after learning that Antoine does not really care for her, but that his real interest is the Volant estate. Antoine does not give up his plan for Marguerite, and sends her countless letters, which she refuses to answer. When Antoine later finds an occasion to explain his "misunderstood" behaviors, Marguerite wonders if she possibly has misjudged him.

Episode 4

In autumn 1763, the British gather the people at the Volant Manor to proclaim British rule. The French crowd protests, which causes the British troops to raise arms. Claude Volant expresses his dislike and anger against the British. When he realizes the impossibility of the new situation, he takes his own life. Marguerite, full of grief, finds a pistol and aims it at Captain Chase and fires, but the shot misses. She is arrested for her murder attempt.

Episode 5

Still in autumn 1763, Marguerite is kept prisoner in her room at the manor. Antoine, still interested in the Volant property, tries to persuade Captain Chase to release Marguerite. He suggests that she make a public apology and enter into a marriage with him. Marguerite, however, refuses, and her case is turned over to the governor in Quebec to decide.

A messenger arrives and orders Marguerite's transport to Quebec for a legal trial. During the night before the departure, Lambert and her sister Élénore arrange her rescue. When they leave the house, Captain Chase, who is starting to fall in love with Marguerite, observes their escape but does not try to stop them. Lambert brings her to his friend Laval Chevigny, a defender of French interests in Canada.

Episode 6

In late autumn 1763, Marguerite and Lambert join Laval on a journey down the Hudson River to deliver weapons for the support of Pontiac's rebellion against the British. Captain Chase leaves the manor to be stationed in Quebec. Marguerite's sister Élénore asks him to appeal to the governor about Marguerite, but in her absence she is sentenced to death.

During their adventurous trip affection grows between Marguerite and Laval. Laval's rebellious attitude has its roots in his family's slaughter in a raid by the British. One of the officers of the occupation force at Volant's manor, Lieutenant Kingsford, was responsible for the raid.

Episode 7

In winter 1763, Laval's party runs into problems with gun trader Brady; Brady and his Indian allies attack them in the forest. Marguerite saves the life of Laval. He is wounded, and Marguerite nurses him at a trading post in the wilderness. Affection now grows into love between the two.

Back at the manor, Antoine continues his intrigues to gain possession of the property. With Marguerite gone, he now concentrates on Élénore. He manages to win her affection, and in spite of warnings, she decides to marry him.

Episode 8

In spring 1764, Antoine takes over as patron of the manor. The financial situation is critical and it seems that the only solution would be to sell the property. A long-kept secret is unveiled: Renaud Larochelle, an old friend of the family, is the real father of Marguerite.

Laval leaves Marguerite to seek Lieutenant Kingsford for revenge. When he finally finds him, Kingsford prevents his revenge by shooting himself. Marguerite goes after Laval. During her forest journey she is exposed to a rape attempt.

Episode 9

That same spring, Marguerite leaves for Quebec to find Laval. Antoine continues his conspiracy to become rich on the Volant manor. Through a lawyer he makes an agreement to sell the manor to an unknown person named McDonalds in London, and he also talks Élénore into moving to Quebec.

Marguerite finds Laval at his settlement in the forest. Her world tears apart when she realizes that Laval's wife is alive and he has decided to stay with her. Broken, she leaves him and returns to the manor. Her despair increases when she receives the message that the property has been sold.

Episode 10

That summer, Marguerite is recognized in Quebec and she is imprisoned. To save her life, Captain James Chase, now a civilian, suggests Marguerite marry because husbands are not allowed to witness against their wives. After their wedding Marguerite and Chase leave Quebec for the manor.

At the manor everyone is happy about the return of Marguerite. She finds out that she is pregnant by Laval. It is also disclosed that Chase is the English buyer of the manor, and that he has done it for his love of Marguerite.

Élénore starts to realize Antoine's treacheries. It is becoming clear that he is a gambler and his debtor's crime causes his imprisonment. Marguerite, uncertain of Chase's reaction to her pregnancy, lets him believe he is the father.

Episode 11

This episode takes place in the winter of 1764 and spring of 1765. Chase finds out that Laval is the father of "his" child. Disappointed and broken, he leaves for Quebec, but he returns when he understands that his love for Marguerite is all that matters.

Renaud is mortally wounded in an accident, but before he dies, he and Marguerite are united as father and daughter.

Marguerite receives a letter from Laval, now free of his wife; he wants to meet her in Quebec. In Quebec, Laval declares his love for her, but Marguerite realizes that her true love is Chase, and she returns to the manor and Chase.

Mission of Danger (MGM, 1959)

Produced by Adrian Samish. Directed by George Waggner and Jacques Tourneur. Screenplay by Gerald Drayson. Photography in Metrocolor by William W. Spencer. Music by Raoul Kraushaar. Running time: 78 minutes.

Cast: *Major Robert Rogers* Keith Larsen, *Hunk Marriner* Buddy Ebsen, *Langdon Towne* Don Burnett, *Audrey Bonay* Taina Elg, *Colonel Trent* Patrick MacNee, and *Sam Beal* Alan Hale, Jr.

The story: The year is 1759. Major Robert Rogers and his colonial Rangers fight together with the regular British militia against the French and their Indian allies.

On a mission to capture a French general, Roger and his Rangers find out that a British compatriot has been taken prisoner by the French and is being held captive in the enemy's fort at Quebec. It is believed this Englishman has found a secret entrance to the fort.

On the route to Quebec, Rogers, Hunk Marriner and Langdon Towne are captured by the French and thrown into a stockade. During their imprisonment, the Rangers meet the lovely French girl, Audrey Bonay, whom the French believe to be on their side. Actually, she's a spy for the British. The Rangers escape by digging a tunnel from their cell beneath the stockade wall.

By the time the party arrives in Canada, Rogers has fallen in love with Audrey. Although disguised as Frenchmen, the Rangers are exposed and are forced to duel their way to freedom. In the process they learn that the prisoner in Quebec has indeed discovered a secret entrance to the stronghold. Rogers must now quickly return to the British headquarters to tell what

Mission of Danger (MGM, 1959)—From the pressbook.

he has learned. There is time for only a moment of parting between him and Audrey, but long enough to express hope that the future will bring them together again.

Notes: This is one of three feature films for release in Europe which were cut together from MGM's TV series **Northwest Passage**, based on Kenneth Roberts's novel and the 1940 feature film version by King Vidor. This one contains material from the episodes: "The Red Coat," "The Break Out," and "The Secret of the Cliff." The two other European feature releases were

Frontier Rangers (1959) and **Fury River** (1959).

Mission to Glory (Western World, 1980)

Directed by Ken Kennedy. Running time: 100 minutes.

Cast: Richard Egan, John Ireland, Cesar Romero, Ricardo Montalban, Rory Calhoun, Michael Ansara, Keenan Wynn, and Aldo Ray.

The story: Father Francis "Kino" Kin

was a 17th-century priest in California who took on Apaches and Conquistadors in defense of his people. This is his story.

Mohawk (20th Century–Fox, 1956)

Produced by Edward L. Alperson. Directed by Kurt Neumann. Screenplay by Maurice Geraghty and Milton Krims. Photography in WideVision and Eastman Color by Karl Strauss. Music by Edward L. Alperson, Jr. Running time: 79 minutes.

Cast: *Jonathan Adams* Scott Brandy, *Onida* Rita Gam, *Rokhawah* Neville Brand, *Cynthia Stanhope* Lori Nelson, *Greta* Allison Hayes, *Butler* John Hoyt, *Aunt Agatha* Vera Vague, *Clem Jones* Rhys Williams, *Kowanen* Ted DeCorsia, *Minikah* Mae Clark, *Captain Langley* John Hudson, *Kooga* Tommy Cook, *Priest* Michael Granger, *Sergeant* James Lilburn and *Dancer* Chabom Jadi.

Mohawk (20th Century–Fox, 1956)—From the pressbook.

The story: Jonathan Adams, a young artist from Boston, has come to the Mohawk Valley to paint landscapes for the Massachusetts Indian Society. Jonathan's fiancée, the lovely Cynthia Stanhope, and her aunt Agatha arrive at Fort Alden to find that Jonathan has taken up with the vivacious Greta, daughter of the storekeeper, Clem Jones.

The greedy land-grabber Butler is trying to set up the Iroquois against the settlers in the Mohawk Valley. The real trouble starts when Butler kills a son of a Mohawk chief and puts the blame on the settlers. The Mohawks take Jonathan as prisoner. With the help of Onida, a young Mohawk woman, Jonathan makes his escape in time to warn the fort of the planned Indian attack.

The Indians attack the fort but the garrison manages to repulse the attackers, and with the arrival of reinforcement, peace is restored. The Mohawk chief, Kowanen, learns the truth that Butler had killed his son and that the settlers only wish to live in peace with the Indians. Jonathan returns to painting and marries his hometown girl, Cynthia.

Notes: "Foppish artist proves his manliness and brings peace between whites and Indians in Pre-Revolutionary upper New York. Silly foolishness."—Brian Garfield *Western Films: A Complete Guide*

Mohawk—After the battle, Kowanen (Ted DeCorsia) learns about Butler's treachery.

"Unintentionally hilarious hokum of devil-may-care painter Brady attempting to thwart Iroquois uprising while tangling with squaw Gam, among other femmes. There's plenty of heavy breathing, 1950-style, here."—Leonard Maltin's *Movie and Video Guide*

"Cornball story about love between settler Scott Brady and Indian Rita Gam and their efforts to bring their people together must have been inspired by excess footage from John Ford's classic **Drums Along the Mohawk.**"—Mick Martin and Marsha Porter *Video Movie Guide*

A Mohawk's Way (Biograph, 1910)

Directed by D.W. Griffith. Screenplay by Stanner E.V. Taylor, based on James Fenimore Cooper's work. Photography by G.W. Bitzer. Length: 991 feet.

Cast: Clair McDowell, Mack Sennett, Dorothy Davenport, Adele DeGarde, George Nicholls and Alfred Paget.

The story: A white medicine man is called to a Mohawk village to take care of a sick papoose. His dislike for the Indians results in his brutal attack on the Mohawk messenger. The Mohawks, in revenge, plan to kill his wife. A woman from the tribe, however, comes to her rescue. Utilizing her medicine herbs the white wife cures the fever of the sick papoose and peace is restored.

Notes: This story has its basis in James Fenimore Cooper's works and his appreciation of the "Noble Savage." D.W. Griffith, in his early motion picture career, directed on location at Delaware Water Gap in New Jersey.

"There is enough human nature in the picture to make it appeal to the audience."—*Variety*, September 10, 1910

Mutiny (United Artists, 1952)

Directed by Edward Dmytryk. Screenplay by Philip Yordan and Sydney Harmon. Running time: 77 minutes.

Cast: Mark Stevens, Angela Lansbury, Patric Knowles, Gene Evans, and Rhys Williams.

The story: In the War of 1812, the crew on an American ship, carrying French gold to the American war effort, fight among themselves for the gold.

Northwest Passage (MGM, 1940)

Produced by Hunt Stromberg. Directed by King Vidor. Screenplay by Laurence Stallings and Talbot Jennings, based on the novel *Northwest Passage* by Kenneth Roberts. Photography in Technicolor by Sidney Wagner and William V. Skall. Music by Herbert Stothart. Running time: 125 minutes.

Cast: *Major Robert Rogers* Spencer Tracy, *Langdon Towne* Robert Young, *Hunk Marriner* Walter Brennan, *Elisabeth Brown* Ruth Hussey, *Cap Huff* Nat Pendleton, *Reverend Browne* Louis Hector, *Humphrey Towne* Robert Barrat, *Lord Amherst* Lumsten Hare, *Sergeant McNott* Donald McBride, *Jennie Colt* Isabel Jewell, *Lieutenant Avery* Douglas Walton, *Lieutenant Crofton* Addison Richards, *Jesse Beacham* Hugh Sothern, *Webster* Regis Toomey, *Wiseman Clagett* Montague Love, *Sam Livermore* Lester Matthews, and *Captain Ogden* Truman Bradley.

The story: In 1759, Langdon Towne, a talented artist, arrives home in Portsmouth, New Hampshire, after having been expelled from Harvard University for the snide political comments inserted into his cartoons. Because of his criticism he has to run away into the woods to escape arrest.

Mutiny (United Artists, 1952)—Eagerness for gold causes mutiny among the ship's crew.

Northwest Passage (MGM, 1940)—Major Robert Rogers (Spencer Tracy, *center*) and Langdon Towne (Robert Young, *right*) are planning for the St. Francis expedition.

Accompanied by his friend Hunk Marriner, Langdon joins Major Rogers's Rangers at Crown Point as a map maker. With a force of 200 men, Rogers embarks on a mission to obliterate the village of hostile French-allied Abnakis at St. Francis in Canada.

The journey through the wilderness becomes adventurous and troublesome. Sometimes the Rangers have to proceed on foot in the woods, and sometimes in heavy whale boats on lakes and rivers. They have to pass rough swamps and occasionally must carry the heavy boats through the woods. The journey is further aggravated by the risk of being discovered by French troops searching for the Rangers.

At last they arrive at St. Francis. At dawn Rogers and his men advance against the village. The Abnakis are surprised by the morning attack and are overrun and massacred in the battle that follows. With the loss of only a few men Major Rogers's company destroys and burns the village.

The Rangers start their return to British lines now almost lacking food and supplies. When they reach Lake Memphremagog, where they expect to find supplies, they find no food or British troops. Now they push on toward old Fort Wentworth. When they at last stumble into the abandoned fort, they find nothing. The men, exhausted and demoralized, are hard for Rogers to inspire. However, at this time British troops arrive and the party is saved.

Later, back in civilization, Rogers informs his men that as a reward for their successful campaign he has been appointed to command an expedition to find a route through the wilderness to the Pacific. That story is, however, not told.

Notes: Except for the many film versions of James Fenimore Cooper's *The Last of the Mohicans*, perhaps the best-known movie dealing with the French and Indian War is King Vidor's **Northwest Passage**.

The movie became a great box – office success with the public. The critics were also mainly benevolent. Some considered it one of Vidor's masterpieces.

Kenneth Roberts devoted his novels to Colonial American history, with a special focus on New England. He won admiration with books like *Arundel*, *Rabble in Arms*, *Captain Caution*, *Oliver Wiswell* and *Lydia Baily*. His most successful novel is *Northwest Passage*, which first appeared as a serial in *The Saturday Evening Post*.

Northwest Passage deals with one of the most colorful persons in colonial warfare on the American frontiers, Major Robert Rogers. Rogers and his Rangers are best known for their scouting for the British along the Lake Champlain Corridor during the French and Indian War. His revenge attack on the French-allied Abnaki village at St. Francis in Canada is possibly his most famous undertaking.

Rogers had a life dream to explore a route through the American continent to the Pacific, a task he never was able to accomplish. Vidor's **Northwest Passage** deals only with part one of Roberts's novel, and its basic story concerns the advance of the Rangers and their attack on the Abnakis in St. Francis.

MGM gave director King Vidor a $2 million budget to do the film. Without a complete script he brought his cast and crew into the wilderness of Idaho, around Lake Payette, where most of the outdoor scenes would be shot. When searching for backwoods areas similar to the mountains of Vermont and upstate New York in the 18th century, MGM had problems finding a suitable location for shooting the picture. On location in the Idaho wilderness, the stage people built a replica of Fort Crown

Point close to Lake Payette, and also an Abnaki village with more than 100 buildings.

More than 300 local natives from the Nez Percé reservation were hired as extras for the movie. It is said, even if it's hard to believe, that they claimed a $10-per-day fee for acting, but that they accepted a $5-per-day fee from Vidor (on advice of Tracy) because he said they were only cast as half-breeds.

For ten weeks, Vidor worked his crew and cast nonstop under hard conditions to produce as realistic as possible a story. Spencer Tracy, cast as Major Robert Rogers, who had a previous Hollywood experience of "not too hard" physical work, changed his perspective after a few days in the Idaho wilderness with Vidor.

During the shooting of the picture, Vidor marched his cast in possibly almost the same way as Rogers would have his Rangers, through swamp lands, forests, mountains and swift rivers. One of the most famous scenes in the movie is the crossing of the Saint Francis River, where the Rangers crossed by making a human chain. The shooting of the "the human chain" sequence was first done on location at Payett, but because of the treacherous conditions the last part of the crossing was done at a MGM backlot exterior "tank" at Culver City.

Tracy was later reported to refuse to do the second part of Roberts's story with Vidor because of his slave-driving manner during the filming of the first part. Producer Hunt Stromberg in Hollywood had problems making up his mind about doing the second part, even if Vidor already had started some shooting in Idaho.

The war economy of 1940 gave MGM a good excuse for not continuing with the second part. This might well have been an unlucky decision, especially since Spencer Tracy gave a splendid performance in the first part. Book II of Roberts's novel would most likely have been an interesting role for Tracy, because in this part he would have been able to explore Rogers's egocentricity even more in his attempts to gain

Northwest Passage—The hardship of war: Hunk Marriner (Walter Brennan, *right*) supports wounded Langdon Towne (Robert Young).

funds to explore the Northwest Passage to the Pacific.

Despite its generally good reception by the public, Vidor's **Northwest Passage** has also been accused of being one of the most anti–Native American films ever made. The motive for the cruel attack on the Abnaki village is purely revenge for French-allied Indian attacks on colonial settlements. The Native side of the story is never presented. Kim Newman, in *Wild West Movies*, alludes to the racism in **Northwest Passage**:

"...the modern viewers will find they [can] hardly justify in dramatic terms the brutal massacre of Indians Rogers supervises."

Michael Hilger elaborates the racist tone in **Northwest Passage** in his book *From Savage to Nobleman*:

"...virtually all the Native American characters are diminished to the image of savage ... Rogers has only disdain for Native Americans and even looks down on his devoted but drunken Stockbridge guide, Konapot ... for the Abnaki..., Rogers has the deepest hatred."

"...one of the most viciously anti–Indian films ever made. Hatred for the Indians is apparently justified only by a sequence in which Indian tortures of a particularly revolting nature are described by a member of Rogers' Rangers..."—G. Fenin and W. Everson in *The Western*

"Visually **Northwest Passage** is remarkable. Director King Vidor tackled the project with a passion, although he found himself on location without completed script. The scenarists had found the Roberts book extremely hard to translate exactly—another reason why MGM backed away from the sequel."—Tony Thomas in *The Great Adventure Films*

During the time of its release critics mostly were positive:

"...will be pointed to as a great picturization of American history by critics and educators. These factors should provide wide publicity and exploitations for the picture to hit audiences that seldom attend theatres.... King Vidor's direction is masterful..."—*Variety*

Northwest Passage (MGM-TV, 1958-59)

Produced by Adrian Samish. 26 episodes @ 26 minutes.

General cast: *Robert Rogers* Keith Larsen, *Hunk Marriner* Buddy Ebsen, *Langdon Towne* Don Burnett and *General Amherst* Philip Tongue.

These are some of the episodes:

"The Assassin"

Cast: *Joseph Savatfor* Jacques Abourdon, and *Jacques Chevaz* Pernell Roberts.

In 1759, at the French headquarters in Montreal, Captain Jacques Chevaz is given a mission to kill Major Rogers, leader of the British Rangers. Rogers and his Rangers have made several raids along the French lines.

The French have brought British officer George Clayton to Montreal after the British surrender of Fort William Henry. Captain Chevaz is assigned to bring Clayton to Quebec. Acting conspiratorially, he claims that he is willing to surrender to British General Amherst. Clayton's daughter Nora and a French priest, Joseph Savatfor, are leaving for Crown Point to negotiate with Amherst. Fr. Savatfor is, however, unveiled as a traitor and Major Rogers and his Rangers set out for Quebec to release Clayton.

The British are attacking Quebec. During the battle Rogers encounters Captain Chevaz. In a final combat in an abandoned church, Rogers kills Chevaz. Captain Clayton is saved and Nora shows her gratitude to Rogers.

"The Counterfeiters"

Directed by George Waggner. Written by Anthony Ellis. Produced by Adrian Samish.

Cast: *Salomon Buckett* John Day, *Weeks* Chester Statton and *Giles Kingby* Edwin Jerome.

In Portsmouth, New Hampshire in 1760, Rogers, Hunk and Langdon are sent to collect money from the governor to be brought to Crown Point for payment of the troops.

In a tavern, when they pay for their meals, it is revealed that the money is fake. Henderson, an old friend of Hunk who has a printing shop, is asked about the falsifications. The paper quality leads to another printer, Salomon Buckett. In Buckett's house the counterfeiters are revealed. Hunk and Langdon are captured by the renegades but saved by Rogers.

"The Witch"

Directed by Thomas Carr. Written by Sloan Nimbley. Produced by Adrian Samish.

Cast: *Reba Morris* Judith Barnett; *Jacob Browning* Robert E. Griffin.

French soldiers track Major Rogers in the woods. He is wounded but manages to escape. Meanwhile a woman and her daughters meet an Indian witch doctor in the forest. The women misunderstand the witch, who wants to help, and run away from her.

The witch finds the wounded Rogers in the forest and heals him. It turns out that she is a white captive who has been living with the Indians for 10 years. Missing Rogers, Amherst at Crown Point sends Hunk and Langdon to search for him. Some settlers go after the witch because they believe she has bewitched one of the daughters of the woman she previously met in the forest. The leader of the settlers is Jacob Browning, who previously has shown cowardliness by abandoning his wife during the same incident when the witch was captured.

Browning recognizes Rogers and plans to capture him, knowing the French have set a £1,000 bounty on him. The witch goes to the sick girl and heals her. Browning and his men continue to accuse her of being an evil woman, and they plan to execute her by drowning. She is, however, saved by Rogers and his two friends. Browning is revealed as the coward he is.

"The Break Out"

Directed by Jacques Tourneur. Written by Gerald Drayson Adams. Produced by Adrian Samish.

Northwest Passage (MGM TV series, 1958-59)—Studio shot of the general cast: *Left to right:* Hunk Marriner (Buddy Ebsen), Robert Rogers (Keith Larsen), and Langdon Towne (Don Burnett).

Northwest Passage—Robert Rogers (Keith Larsen, *left*) and Hunk Marriner (Buddy Ebsen) ready for a wet reception.

Cast: *Nathan Hill* Sandy Kenyon, *Ben Smith* Bing Russell, *Zach Miller* House Peters, Jr., *George Quill* Adam Williams and *Captain Hugo Marten* Bruce Gordon.

On a scouting trip, Rogers and his friends are attacked by the French and brought to a French prison. The situation in the prison camp is terrible: the captives are suffering from starvation and yellow fever. Not to reveal their real identities, the new captives claim they all are named Smith.

During daytime the prisoners are brought to work on a road construction project in the wilderness. During the night they dig a tunnel for their escape.

The French camp commandant suspects that Rogers is among the captives and offers the prisoners freedom if they reveal him. The plot doesn't work, and during the night the captives leave through the tunnel. Although hunted by the French, they manage to escape them.

"The Vulture"

Directed by Jaques Tourneur. Written by Gerald Drayson Adams. Produced by Adrian Samish.

Cast: *Sir Martin Stanley* Bruce Cowling; *Lady Kate* Marva Stevens.

In Portsmouth, crafty seamen shanghai drunks at bars. Langdon is in town to paint a "civilized" Indian girl from the Mohawk Valley whose husband, Martin Stanley, is an Indian agent. Martin dislikes Major Rogers.

Rogers and Hunk arrive at Portsmouth to raise funds for the Rangers. During a drinking party Rogers and his friends get into trouble at a tavern. Langdon and Hunk are knocked down and brought as captives to a ship. Rogers, however, is saved by the tavern's waitress. It turns out that a companion of Martin is the leader of the villains who have carried away Langdon and Hunk.

During the night Rogers enters the ship and frees his two friends. In the end, Rogers makes up with Martin, in the presence of his wife. Martin has been the real organizer of the plot. It turns out that Martin's Indian wife has long mistrusted him.

"The Secret of the Cliff"

Directed by George Waggner. Written by Gerald Drayson Adams. Produced by Adrian Samish.

Cast: *Colonel Gironix* Maurice Marsac, *Audrie Boney* Taina Elg and *General Montcalm* Albert Carrier.

The British Army under General Wolf is planning an attack on the French stronghold of Quebec. Captain Stanton has been sent to scout for a way to climb the cliffs to reach the Plains of Abraham, but the French capture him. Rogers, Hunk and Langdon are sent to free Stanton at Quebec. In the woods they run into a woman, Audrie Boney, who claims she is a British Agent. She accompanies them to Quebec.

At Quebec, Audrie visits her French mother. Colonel Gironix, who is chief of espionage, visits her to obtain information about the British plans. Rogers, dressed as a French soldier, arrives and claims that he has escaped from captivity at Fort Pitt. During a party he meets with General Montcalm, who wants to learn about his escape.

Audrie reveals the false identity of Rogers. Hunted by French soldiers, he escapes. Audrie returns to Rogers and his friends and helps them free Captain Stenton. During their mission, the French attack, but they escape. Audrie decides to stay in Quebec. Rogers and his friend bring Stanton back to Crown Point where he can explain how to climb the cliffs of Abraham.

"Stab in the Back"

Directed by Alan Crosland, Jr. Written by Anthony Ellis. Produced by Adrian Samish.

Cast: *Mr. Dureh* Luis van Rooten, *Emilie Direh* Lisa Montenl and *Gay Perro* Paul Picerni.

Hunk finds a British dispatch messenger who has been stabbed in the back with a knife. Back at the fort it is concluded that it is an Algonquin knife, but Rogers suspects that the knife does not belong to the Indians.

Young Emilie, who turns the head of Langdon, visits the fort. Another British messenger is found with a knife in his back. General Amherst is upset and orders the capture of the guilty. Four Frenchmen dressed as Rangers arrive at the fort. Emilie's father is conspiring with the French.

Langdon, in love, defends Emilie against Amherst. The general fears that another dispatch messenger sent on a forest trail to Fort Number Four to inform about a planned attack on Montreal might be in trouble, and he sends Rogers and his Rangers after him.

In the woods the French collaborators capture the dispatch carrier. Emilie's father arrives to warn the French against the advancing Rangers. The messenger is threatened with torture if he does not give away his dispatch, but Rogers and the Rangers save him. Emilie's father is killed during the fight. Emilie writes Langdon to explain her trust and love for him.

"Surprise Attack"

Directed by Jaques Tourneur. Written by Gerald Drayson Adams. Produced by Adrian Samish.

Cast: *Natuja* Lisa Gaye, *Black Wolf* Larry Chance and *Mary Brook* Madge Meredith.

While hidden, Langdon is drawing sketches of Chief Black Wolf's Algonquin village. He is, however, captured by the Indians.

The warriors at the village have for a long time been a threat to the British, and General Amherst sends Rogers and his Rangers to strike against the place.

With some other white captives Langdon is imprisoned in the village and threatened with torture. Rogers captures an Indian woman, Natuja, who in reality is an adopted white, and brings her to the village using her as a cover with the purpose of freeing Langdon.

Rogers beats Black Wolf in a duel, but the Indians take him prisoner. When Black Wolf is going to torture and burn the captives, Natuja becomes hesitant and goes for help. She runs into the Ranger company in the woods and guides them to the village. At dawn they attack the village. In a final combat between Rogers and Black Wolf, Natuja saves Rogers.

"The Hostage"

Directed by Jaques Tourneur, Written by George Waggner. Produced by Adrian Samish.

Cast: *Jean Louis* Bobby Clark.

Montreal, in 1760, is under attack by the British. Rangers are sent in to clean up the town.

Some young French children, under the leadership of Jean Louis, find Major Rogers, who is wounded. The children are escaping the warfare by hiding in abandoned buildings. Rogers makes good friends with them. One is a little girl who is unable to speak. He also meets with a friendly French priest.

French coureurs de bois track Rogers and capture him. In prison, Jean Louis sneaks up to Rogers and Rogers sends him after help. The British are close to overtaking the city. The priest is visiting Rogers to heal and help, but he is also imprisoned. Rogers, however, escapes and joins his Rangers, who have been led to him by the little mute girl. The Rangers win the battle of the city and Rogers expresses his gratitude to the children for their help, especially to Jean Louis and the little girl.

"Vengeance Trail"

Directed by Alan Crosland, Jr. Written by Gerald Drayson Adams. Produced by Adrian Samish.

Cast: *Joe Waters* Paul Fix, *Kisheewa* Rod Dana and *Acacita* Joseph Vitale.

At Bear Creek, Rogers surprises Joe Waters when Waters is killing a Mohican. Waters explains that the reason for his outrage is that the Mohicans are joining the French side in the war against the British. Joe Waters also hates the Mohicans because they burned his farm and captured his son years earlier.

In the Mohican village, through Chief Kisheewa, they find out that the French are trying to win over the Mohicans to join the Algonquins against the British.

Acacita, a young warrior who has blue eyes, turns out to be Joe Waters's son, who years earlier was captured by the Mohicans during the raid on Waters's farm. A big problem stems from the fact that Acacita's Indian stepfather is the man whom Waters killed. It is decided, however, that Acacita will help Rogers in peace talks with Chief Kisheewa.

Hunk Marriner brings Waters to Crown Point. On their route, Waters knocks down Hunk, and for vengeance he returns to the Mohican village. He wounds Kisheewa and fights with his son. He is in trouble, but Acacita saves his life. After discussions the Mohicans decide to stay out of the war, and a regretful Waters seeks reconciliation with his son.

"War Signs"

Directed and written by George Waggner. Produced by Adrian Samish.

Cast: *Will Martin* Joe Maross, *Johnny Martin* Peter Votrian and *Ruth Martin* Mary Lawrence.

In a settlement on the frontier, Will Martin accuses his own 13-year-old son Johnny of cowardice. This causes Johnny to run away.

In the woods Rogers and his Rangers see signs of Hurons on the warpath. They run into Johnny, who is on his way to Crown Point to become a Ranger. Rogers becomes good friends with young Johnny and persuades him to return to his family settlement to help defend it against the Hurons. Johnny and the Rangers arrive at the Martins' settlement, and Rogers persuades Martin to rethink his position toward his son.

The Hurons attack the blockhouse. Johnny proves himself in battle while his father turns out to be the real coward. The Hurons are forced to retreat and after the fighting, father and son regain respect for each other.

"The Deserter"

Directed by Alan Crosland, Jr. Written by Gerald Drayson Adams. Produced by Adrian Samish.

Cast: *Lila Jason* Carole Mathews, *Steve Warner* John Benardino, *Tom Jason* Burt Douglas, *Betty Jason* Carolyn Craig, *William Jason* Roy Gordon, and *Bailiff Ramkin* Stuart Randell.

A Ranger, Tom Jason, deserts from Crown Point. Tom is a good friend of Hunk Marriner, who believes that he must have a good reason for leaving.

Tom is on his way to take care of his wife and their newborn child. He visits his father William Jason, a rich landowner by whom he has been repudiated, to obtain some money inherited from his mother for the support of his wife and child. His father refuses to help him and he leaves. During the visit he loses his Ranger knife.

The father is found dead with Tom's knife in his back. Tom is arrested for murder. It turns out that William's wife, Tom's stepmother, is having a love affair with a bond servant, Steve Warner. Rogers visits the stepmother and questions Warner about the murder. Warner's story does not convince Rogers about Tom's guilt.

The sheriff and Warner leave for the cabin where Tom's family lives. They expect that Tom will turn up, and their plan is to arrest him. Rogers and Hunk are following at a distance. When Tom appears, Rogers questions him about the incident. Convinced of Tom's innocence, Rogers brings up evidence of the stepmother's and Warner's conspiracy against Tom, and Steven Warner is shown to be the real murderer.

Rogers and Hunk bring Tom back to Crown Point with a promise to change the charge against him from desertion to "absence without leave."

"The Long Rifle"

Cast: *Judd Ramsey* Dean Havens, *Martha Ramsey* Jeanne Baird and *Eli Dillon* Douglas Kennedy.

A gunsmith, Judd Ramsey, invents a new formula for gunpowder, one more powerful than what the British army is using. Hoping to become rich on his invention, he and his wife Martha leave for Crown Point to sell the gunpowder to Amherst's army.

At a tavern they meet with Hunk and Langdon. Judd and Hunk are old friends, and Hunk volunteers to speak to Major Rogers and ask him to assist Judd in selling the powder to Amherst. Rogers talks to Amherst but he turns down the offer.

Not giving up, Rogers arranges a shooting contest between Hunk and a competing gun trader to prove the superiority of Judd's gunpowder. The night before the contest, Hunk is lured by Eli Dillon, the rival gun trader, to participate in a drinking party.

In the morning Amherst and Colonel Benson, who is responsible for the purchase of army supplies, oversee the contest. Hunk, with a bad hangover, has problems concentrating during the game. Everything goes well, however, with a little cold water that Langdon pours over Hunk to prove to the army officers that the gunpowder also works well under wet conditions. The deal is closed and Judd is also offered companionship by his competitor.

"The Fourth Brother"

Directed by Alan Crosland, Jr., Written by Gerald Drayson Adams. Produced by Adrian Samish.

Cast: *Dan Wade* Gene Nelson, *Joan Paget* Marcia Henderson, *Fred Paget* Grant Withers and *Frank Wade* Lee Van Cleef.

Dan Wade returns from Boston to set up a fur trading station. His three brothers have bad reputations as backwoods thieves in the area.

Wade meets Joan, who is a grown daughter of a local trader, Fred Paget, and they fall in love. Because a wagonload of valuable pelts has been stolen, Fred Paget asks Crown Point to send in some Rangers to investigate. Major Rogers and his companions arrive to see Paget. Paget accuses the Wade brothers of the crime. Rogers looks up Wade to search for pelts but finds nothing. He leaves Hunk and Langdon to spy on the suspects.

Joan's father is angry about her meeting Dan Wade, even though she assures his innocence. Therefore she leaves her father.

Hunk and Langdon disclose the treachery of the other Wade brothers. Dan arrives and announces that they have captured Joan. This initiates a hunt after the renegades who are captured. Dan gets his Joan.

Notes: "...this well-produced series sets its sights firmly on action with little time wasted on dialogue. Actual pursuit of the Northwest Passage takes second place to the Ranger's commando tactics during the French and Indian wars.... Impressive color photography by Harkness Smith."—Edward Buscombe *The BFI Companion to the Western*

"...**Northwest Passage** left the lineup on September 8, 1959 after only 26 episodes had been shot. Nobody involved with the project is to be faulted as **Northwest Passage** was a well produced and acted series and was chock full of exciting action sequences."—Neil Summers *The Official TV Western Book Vol. 3*

The Pathfinder (Columbia, 1952)

Produced by Sam Katzman. Directed by Sidney Salkow. Screenplay by Robert E. Kent, based on the novel by James Fenimore Cooper. Photography in Technicolor by Henry Freulich. Music by Mischa Bakaleinikoff. Running time: 78 minutes.

Cast: *Pathfinder* George Montgomery, *Welcome Alison* Helena Carter, *Chingachgook* Jay Siverheels, *Col. Duncannon* Walter Kingsford, *Chief Arrowhead* Rodd Redwing, *Col. Brasseau* Stephen Bekassy, *Lokowa* Elena Verdugo, *Captain Bredford* Bruce Lester, *Eagle Feather* Chief Yowlachie, *Uncas* Ed Coch, Jr., *Togamak* Russ Konklin, *Ka-Letan* Vi Ingraham and *Matron* Adele St. Maur.

The story: Pathfinder is a white man, raised by the Indians. In 1754, a friendly Mohican village is attacked and wiped out by murderous Mingoes allied to the French. The loss of his friends persuades Pathfinder to ally himself with the English.

Pathfinder is sent on a dangerous mission to find out the secret defense of the key French fortress town St. Vincente. To cover his identity, he hires himself to the French as a scout. Since Pathfinder does not speak French, Welcome Alison, who poses

The Pathfinder (Columbia, 1952)—A wounded Mohican brings a message about the Mingo attack on his village to Colonel Duncannon (Walter Kingsford, *left*) and Pathfinder (George Montgomery).

as a French girl stranded by an Indian attack, is sent with him. Pathfinder's Mohican friend Chingachgook is also accompanying them on their mission.

Welcome is recognized by her former fiancé, Colonel Brasseau, a renegade who has gone over to the French, when she and Pathfinder try to obtain the French defense plans. The scout and the girl he has come to love are sentenced to be executed as spies. The espionage work of Pathfinder for the English has simplified a successful campaign, and when the English attack and defeat St. Vincente, Pathfinder and Welcome are saved.

Notes: This version of Cooper's *Pathfinder* has nothing in common with the original story. It is a Hollywood fiction, and except for Pathfinder and Chingachgook, nothing from Cooper's novel can be recognized.

This was straightforwardly explained in the original pressbook:

"The greatest Indian-fighter of them all in our frontier's most savage history! ... The screenplay for '**The Pathfinder**' retains the same principal characters and the same locale and settings as the James Fenimore Cooper novel. However, the story on the screen has been varied somewhat from the story of the novel. Please bear this in mind when effecting tie-ups concerning the book because no attempt should be made to infer that the picture follows the novel exactly. It does not; '**The Pathfinder**' merely is based upon the famous novel."

"There's plenty of action but not much of script in this cheap adaptation of the yarn about frontier skirmishes on the Great Lakes during the French and Indian War."—Brian Garfield *Western Films—A Complete Guide*

THE MOST DANGEROUS MARKSMAN IN ALL THE WEST!

...The love story of the greatest Indian-Fighter of them all...told with all the turbulence and terrific excitement of the Fenimore Cooper masterpiece that inspired it!

A man—a woman —and a wilderness to win!

COLUMBIA PICTURES presents

THE **PATHFINDER**

starring GEORGE MONTGOMERY

The Wide-Open West in Color by **T**ECHNICOLOR

with Helena Carter Screen Play by ROBERT E. KENT · Based on the novel by JAMES FENIMORE COOPER
Produced by SAM KATZMAN · Directed by SIDNEY SALKOW

The Pathfinder (1952)—From the pressbook.

The Pathfinder (Hallmark Home Entertainment, 1996)

Produced by Leather Stocking Productions. Directed by Donald Shebib. Based on James Fenimore Cooper's novel *The Pathfinder*. Running time: 94 minutes.

Cast: *Pathfinder* Kevin Dillon, *Chingachgook* Graham Green, *Mabel Dunham* Laurie Holden, *French General* Stacy Keach, *Guard on Ship* Ralph Kussmann, *Arrowhead* Russell Means and *Lt. Zale* Charles Powell.

The story: During the outbreak of the French and Indian War, a young woman from Boston, Mabel Dunham, is guided by Chingachgook and Pathfinder to meet with her father, Sergeant Major Dunham, at Fort Oswego. Chingachgook is a Mohican Chief and Pathfinder is a white who has been raised among the Mohicans.

Mingos of the Tuscarora tribe attack the party on their route, but Chingachgook and Pathfinder repel the attackers. With the help of a young sea captain, Jasper Wester, who brings canoes, the party reaches the safety of the fort.

Both Pathfinder and Jasper are in love with Mabel. A Lieutenant Muir at the fort accuses Jasper of being a spy. An expedition is sent out by ship on Lake Ontario. On board the ship, Muir's conspiracy against Jasper, who commands the ship, continues. Muir, as military commander, orders the imprisonment of Jasper. A monstrous storm breaks out, and to save the ship, Pathfinder releases Jasper to deal with the situation. After the storm the ship returns to the fort.

The French are planning for an attack on the fort. Lieutenant Muir orders the troops out of the fort, intending to leave the fort without protection for the French to take over.

In the woods French and Mingos ambush the English troop. During the battle, Lieutenant Muir shows his true face and shoots Sergeant Major Dunham. The English, however, manage to escape their attackers and return to the fort.

The weakened fort has already been taken by the Mingos, and when the troops return they are again ambushed. This results in a violent fight. During the fighting Pathfinder challenges Muir and kills him. In the last minute Jasper arrives with reinforcements by ship and the fort is saved. Mortally wounded, Sergeant Major Dunham dies, but before he dies he turns over Mabel to the man she loves. She chooses Jasper, even when she in reality she loves Pathfinder. Pathfinder and Chingachgook leave for Kentucky in the West.

The Pathfinder (Sledopyt) (1987)

Produced by Zinovii Genzer. Directed by Pavel Lyubimov. Screenplay by Pavel Lyubimov based on the novel by James Fenimore Cooper. Photography by Anatoli Grishko. Music by Yuri Saulsky. Running time: 91 minutes.

Cast: Yuri Avsharov, Andris Zagars, Anastasiya Nemolyayeva, Emmanuil Vitorgan, Andrei Mironov, Tatyana Augskap, Kirill Avenirov, Alexander Glazun, Sergei Kovalyov, Alla Plotkina, Igor Rogachyov, Yevgeni Yevstigneyev, and Georgi Yumatov.

A Russian adaptation of Cooper's story.

The Pioneers (Monogram, 1941)

Produced by Edward Finney. Directed by Al Herman. Screenplay by Charles Alderson, loosely based on James Fenimore Cooper's novel. Photography by Marcel Le Picard. Music by Frank Sanucci. Running time: 58 minutes.

Cast: *Tex* Tex Ritter, *Slim* Lloyd "Arkansas Slim" Andrews, *Suzanna* Wanda McKay, *Doye* Doye O'Dell, *Wilson* George Chesebro, *Ames* Del Lawrence, *Benton* Post Park, *Carson* Karl Hackett, *Jingo* Lynton Brent, *Pete* Chick Hannon, *Sheriff* Gene Alsacre, *Judge* Jack C. Smith, *Warcloud* Chief Many Treaties, with Art Dillard, Charles Soldani, Red Foley and His Saddle Pals and White Flash the Horse.

The story: Frontiersman Tex and his companion Slim are hired to guide a settlers' wagon train in their search for new land. Problems start when a gang of villains is stirring up Indians in an effort to prevent the settlers from taking up residence on valuable land.

Notes: Not much of James Fenimore Cooper's story can be recognized in this one. In action sequences, a lot of stock footage was utilized.

Plymouth Adventure (MGM, 1952)

Produced by Dore Schary. Directed by Clarence Brown. Written by Helen Deutsch from the novel by Ernest Gébler. Running time: 104 minutes.

Cast: *Captain Christopher Jones* Spencer Tracy, with Gene Tierney, Van Johnson, Leo Genn, Dawn Addams, and Lloyd Bridges.

The story: Christopher Jones is captain of the ship *Mayflower*. With 100 pilgrim passengers he will cross the Atlantic for the New World. Since he does not care too much about their cause, he plans to leave them there and return to England directly.

The voyage becomes troublesome, with diseases, shortage of water and a monstrous storm. The courageous behavior of the pilgrims softens up Jones, and when they reach land in the New World he offers them continued support from the ship, even if this means he has to go against his own mutinous crew to do so.

Notes: " ...uplifting, enlightening, educational—and a most entertaining picture."—*Hollywood Citizen News*

"...an inspiring bit of America."—*The Hollywood Reporter*

"Magnificent! An engrossing, stirring and suspenseful motion picture."—*Boxoffice*

Pocahontas (Thanhouser, 1910)

Length: 1,000 feet.

Cast: Anna Rosemond, Frank H. Crane and George Barnes.

The story: Pocahontas saves the life of Captain John Smith and eventually marries John Rolfe, with whom she goes to England.

Pocahontas (Buena Vista, 1995)

A Walt Disney cartoon. Running time: 78 minutes

Pocahontas—A Child of the Forest (Edison, 1908)

Directed by Edwin S. Porter. Photography by Edwin S. Porter. Filmed in New York City, N.Y. Length: 1,050 feet.

The story: Pocahontas saves Captain Smith from Kunder-Wacha, a hostile who thinks she belongs to him. Then she persuades her father, Powathan, to let her marry Captain Smith.

Pocahontas and John Smith (Universal, 1924)

Directed by Bryan Foy. Length: one reel.

Comedy from the series Hysterical History Comedy.

Pocahontas, the Legend (Goodtime Entertainment, 1995)

Produced by Steven Leviten, Paul Bronfman and Mark Prior. Directed by Daniele J. Suissa. Written by Donald Martin and Daniele J. Suissa. Running time: 99 minutes.

Cast: *Pocahontas* Sandrine Holt, *Sir Edwin Wingfield* Tony Goldwyn, *John Smith* Miles O'Keeffe, *Kocoum* Billy Merasty, with Becky Butler, George Buza, Kenneth Charlette, Desmond Ellis, David Hemblen, Bucky Hill, Samaya Jardey, Patrick Mark, Shawn Mathiesen, Billy Oliver, Mark J. Richardson, Mona Staats, Gordon Tootoosis and Billy Two Rivers.

The story: When British settlers arrive in Virginia in the early 1600s, Powhatan Chief Kocoum looks upon them with suspicion. His cousin, Princess Pocahontas, is more positive about the newcomers, especially about the handsome John Smith. Some time after their arrival, a number of the settlers become ill, and Smith goes to the Powhatan village to trade rifles for medicine. The Indians are unwilling to help and Smith is captured and sentenced to death. Pocahontas, however, saves him when she claims him in accord with her rights as princess.

Among the whites, Smith has an enemy in Sir Edwin Wingfield, who accuses him of being a traitor. Smith obtains some medicine that he sends to the settlement with a note that explains his situation. The medicine and the note never reach the settlers because Wingfield intercepts them. The situation between the Indians and the settlers gets worse and Kocoum urges his chiefs to go on the warpath against the intruders.

Smith escapes, but when he arrives at the white fort he is arrested as a traitor. He is released when another settler proves his innocence. Wingfield continues his conspiracy and tries to have Kocoum kidnap Pocahontas. The plan fails, however, and Smith rescues her. During the attempt, Kocoum is wounded. Using his wound as evidence, he tries to convince the chiefs that the whites are hostile. Pocahontas claims the opposite; to prove who is right, they perform the truth test, which involves holding one's hand over a fire. Kocoum does not pass the test, and he is killed.

The chiefs offer the settlers peace on condition that John Smith is sent back to England. Pocahontas can only see her love sail away.

Notes: This made-for-TV film was produced in Canada.

"**Pocahontas, the Legend** scores poorly on the historical accuracy meter.... This is classic noble-savage love story, complete with stilted dialogue, easy-reading plot lines, and native American drum thumping."—*TVgen*

The Prairie (Screen Guild, 1948)

Produced by Edward Finney. Directed by Frank Wisbar. Screenplay by Arthur St. Clair, based on the novel by James Fenimore Cooper. Photography by James S. Brown, Jr. Music by Alexander Steinart.

Cast: *Ellen Wade* Leonore Aubert, *Paul Hover* Alan Baxter, *Abiram White* Russ Vincent, *Asa Bush* Jack Mitchum, *Ismael Bush* Charles Evans, *Esther Bush* Edna Holland, *Eagle Feather* Chief Thundercloud, *Abner Bush* Fred Coby, *Jess Bush* Bill Murphy, *Gabe Bush* David Gerber, *Enoch Bush* Don Lynch, *Luke* George Morrell, *Matoreeh* Chief Yowlachie, *Running Deer* Jay Silverheels, *Annie Morris* Beth Taylor and Frank Hemingway.

The Story: The story centers on a family that moves into the newly opened Louisiana Territory. Hardships are ahead with starvation and threatening Indians.

Joining the family is a young girl, Ellen Wade, whose parents the Indians have killed. The two sons in the family fight for her affection, but she prefers Paul Hover, an Army cartographer, who more than once has helped out the family with their problems.

The President's Lady (20th Century–Fox, 1953)

Produced by Sol C. Siegel. Directed by Henry Levin. Screenplay by John Patrick, based on the novel by Irving Stone. Photography by Leo Tover. Music by Alfred Newman. Running time: 96 minutes.

Cast: *Andrew Jackson* Charlton Heston, *Rachel Donelson Robards* Susan Hayward, *Jack Overton* John McIntire, *Mrs. Donelson* Fay Bainter, *Lewis Robards* Whitfield Connor, *Moll* Ruth Attaway, *Colonel Stark* Ralph Dumke, *Mrs. Stark* Nina Varela, *Mrs. Robards* Margaret Wycherly, *Charles Dickinson* Carl Betz and *Mrs. Phariss* Gladys Hurlburt.

The story: In 1798, Andrew Jackson, a young lawyer, arrives in Nashville, Tennessee, to work for his friend Jack Overton. He meets Rachel Donelson Robards and there is an instant attraction between them.

Rachel is having a tough time with her husband, so her mother is sending her down the Mississippi to visit with her sister in Natchez. Andrew saves Rachel when Indians attack them on the river. As Andrew and Rachel share excitement they become closer, and when Rachel receives a message with information that Lewis has divorced her, she agrees to marry Andrew.

The couple settles down on a small farm in Nashville. They soon find out that the Robards's divorce act has been delayed, and Andrew is accused by Lewis of having stolen another man's wife. This causes Andrew to fight for her honor, and he kills Lewis in a duel.

Indian trouble arises and Andrew organizes a militia and goes to war to fight the Creek Indians. During Andrew's absence, Rachel takes care of the farming work on her own. When the war is over, Andrew leaves for Washington to become a senator. At his return, Andrew once more has to stand up for Rachel's honor and in a duel he kills Charles Dickinson, and is wounded.

The War of 1812 breaks out, and Andrew fights against the British and wins one

of the war's greatest victories in New Orleans. After the war, Andrew returns to the Congress in Washington, and where he runs for presidency. Rachel, who is sick, dies in her husband's arms just before his White House victory.

Notes: "...rarely embellishes the memory of a brave and simple person who sat out the slings and arrows of outrageous fortune at home, and did little else."—H.H.T. in *The New York Times*

"...Whatever liberties were taken by the book and script were kept to a minimum, something not usually the case in biographies. That taste was appreciated by everyone who admired 'Old Hickory.'"—*The Motion Picture Guide*

The Pride of Lexington (Republic, 1911)

The story: Depicts the patriots' rebellion at Lexington and an Indian attack in the Mohawk Valley.

A Priest of the Wilderness: Father Jogue's Mission to the Iroquois (Kalem, 1909)

Directed by Sidney Olcott. Length: 735 feet.

Priscilla and the Pequot War (Kalem, 1911)

Length: 925 feet.

Cast: Irene Shannon.

Prisoners of the Mohicans (Pathé, 1911)

Directed by Joseph Golden. Screenplay by Anthony Coldeway, based on the fiction of James Fenimore. Cooper. Length: 1,000 feet.

The story: Mohicans capture a white girl who had earlier helped a poor, starving Indian. This man shows his gratitude by rescuing her from the Mohican camp and returning her to her parents.

Puritans and Indians (Kalem, 1911)

Length: 970 feet.

The Quakers (1913)

No information available.

Rachel and the Stranger (RKO, 1948)

Produced by Richard H. Berger. Directed by Norman Foster. Screenplay by Waldo Salt, based on the story "Rachel" by Howard Fast. Photography by Maury Gerstman. Songs by Roy Wegg and Waldo Salt. Running time: 92 minutes.

Cast: *Rachel* Loretta Young, *Big Davey Harvey* William Holden, *Jim* Robert Mitchum, *Davey* Gary Gray, *Parson Jackson* Tom Tully, *Mrs. Jackson* Sara Haden, *Mr. Green* Frank Ferguson, *Gallus* Walter Baldwin, *Mrs. Green* Regina Wallace, and *Jabez* Frank Conlan.

The story: In Ohio, around 1800, Big Davey Harvey is still in love with his dead wife. He buys during a visit to a neighborhood settlement bondwoman Rachel for $22 to take care of his household and look after his nine-year-old son.

Big Davey mostly ignores Rachel, and his young son has no faith in her. A friend of Big Davey, the trapper Jim, who soon shows an interest in Rachel, visits the Harveys. Jim wants to take Rachel from Big Davey, whose interest in her has grown since the arrival of Jim. While the men are quarreling about the matter, Rachel makes her way out in the wilderness. Both men and young Davey become worried about Rachel's disappearance, since they fear that she can fall into the hands of Shawnees, who are on the warpath. They search for

Opposite, top: The President's Lady (20th Century–Fox, 1953)—Rachel Donelson Robards (Susan Hayward, right) takes farewell of her mother Mrs. Donelson (Fay Bainter) when she is about to leave with Andrew Jackson (Charlton Heston). Bottom: Rachel (Susan Hayward) and Andrew Jackson (Charlton Heston, right) prepare for a rest at an inn.

Rachel and the Stranger (RKO, 1948)—Rachel (Loretta Young) goes her own way into the wilderness. *Left to right:* Davey (Gary Gray), Big Davey Harvey (William Holden), and Jim (Robert Mitchum, *on horseback*).

Rachel and find her and bring her back to the farm.

The Indians attack the farm. During the combat, Rachel shows that she has learned how to handle a gun. Amid flaming arrows and war-whoops, Big Davey and Rachel achieve a deep feeling for each other. The Indians are beaten and when danger has passed, Jim makes up his mind to continue his wandering. Big Davey and Rachel are finally united as a happy couple.

Notes: "Norman Foster has directed the first part of the film at too leisurely a pace, but by the time the Indians arrive the action rips along. The principals are all attractive and pleasant ... it all adds up to a good evening's entertainment."—Jack Thompson in *The New York Sunday Mirror Magazine*

"...this romantic adventure dealing with pioneers who wrested the Ohio wilderness from nature and marauding Indians, has the necessary complements of fine story spinning, subdued and natural characterization and excellent moviemaking.... Mr. Fast's tale has been transferred to film fairly faithfully..."—A.W. in *The New York Times*

"Lots of comedy, warmth, action, and human interest ... an amiable western with more than something extra. Mitchum gives one of his rare performances that doesn't appear to be under the influence of torpor."—*The Motion Picture Guide*

Rachel and the Stranger—Lobby card: Rachel (Loretta Young) is in trouble when Shawnee Indians attack the Harvey settlement.

Revolution (Goldcrest-Viking/WB, 1985)

Produced by Irwin Winkler. Directed by Hugh Hudson. Screenplay by Robert Dillon. Photography by Bernard Lutic in System 35 Widescreen Technicolor. Filmed in England and Norway. Music by John Corigliano. Running time: 125 minutes.

Cast: *Tom Dodd* Al Pacino, *Sgt. Maj. Peasy* Donald Sutherland, *Daisy McConnahay* Natassja Kinski, *Mrs. McConnahay* Joan Plowright, *Mr. McConnahay* Dave King, *Sgt. Jones* Steven Berkoff, *Corty* John Wells, *Liberty Woman,* Annie Lenox, *Ned Dobb* Dexter Fletcher, *Young Ned* Sid Owen, *Lord Hampton* Richard O'Brien, *Merle* Eric Milota, *Betsy* Felicity Dean, *Amey* Jo Anna Lee, *Cuffy* Cheryl Miller, *Israel Davis* Harry Ditson, *Bella* Rebecca Calder, *Abby* Theresa Boden, *Corporal to Sgt. Peasy* Jesse Birdsall, *Ben* Cameron Johann, *Ahab* Danny Potts, *Sgt. Marley* William Marlowe, *Capt. Lacy* Stefan Gryff, *Gen. Washington* Frank Winsor, *Lord Darling* Paul Brooke, *Tonti* Skeeter Vaughan, *Honehwah* Larry Sellers, *Ongwata* Graham Green, *Iroquois Indians* Denis Lacroix, Joseph Runningfox and Harold Pacheco, *Sgt. Malin* John Patrick, *Dr. Sloan* Malcolm Terris, *Clowski* Steve Kliegerman, *Bill* Adrian Rawlins, *Capt. Cray* Nanning Redwood, *Carrie Cray* Kate Hardie, *Roger Otis* Richard Hicks, *Marcel* Tristram Jellinek, *Pierre* Lex Van Delden and *Chaplain* Jonathan Adams.

The story: Scottish trapper Tom Dodd lives in the colonies with his son Ned. Tom

Revolution (Goldcrest-Viking/WB, 1985)—Father and son during the Battle of Brooklyn Heights: Tom Dodd (Al Pacino) with young Ned (Sid Owen).

just wants to be left alone with his fur trade, but his boat is confiscated by the patriots and, against his will, he is forced into the battle against the British. From time to time his way is crossed by Daisy, the well-bred daughter of loyalist McConnahay, with whom he falls in love. Daisy does not share her family's beliefs and she joins the rebels.

Tom is injured during the battle of Brooklyn Heights but recovers, being nursed by Daisy. Dobb deserts with the boy and returns to New York, which the British Army has seized. Tom is forced to take part in a grotesque "fox hunt" in which British officers set dogs on him. Ned is enrolled by force by the British as a drummer boy under the command of Sgt. Major Peasy, and follows the army on a campaign to Canada.

Tom follows the British Army and effects a rescue of his son. Some friendly Huron Indians tend to Ned's badly injured feet and legs. When Ned has recovered, he and his father become army scouts at Valley Forge, where Daisy is apparently killed fleeing from Peasy. Three years later, however, she and Tom are reunited after the battle at Yorktown, in which Tom and Ned get their revenge on Peasy.

Ned makes his way North to marry and settle down and Tom and Daisy decide to become a couple.

Notes: Not since the silent film period had a film company made an attempt to take up the full scope of the American Revolutionary War in a production. **Revolution** picked up the thread, but did not emphasize historical characters. American

Revolution—The final battle at Yorktown: Tom (Al Pacino) goes after enemy Sgt. Maj. Peasy, accompanied by son Ned (Dexter Fletcher) and Huron scouts.

producer Irwin Winkler decided at an early stage not to do a straight historical film. He explained that he did not want to tell a story about Washington and Franklin, but wanted to do a film about common people in a wartime situation. He soon realized that for the stage settings it would be difficult to do the film in America. In England he found what he was looking for, and also hired a British director, Hugh Hudson, to do the film.

Hudson had gained fame for directing **Chariots of Fire** and **Greystoke**. In addition to the filming in England, Hudson brought his crew for some scenes to the cliffs of Lofoten in Northern Norway. Except for the spectacular natural settings he found in Norway, similar to those of Virginia in the 18th century, some favorable tax benefits also contributed to the choice of Norway for settings.

The finishing of the film was made under deadline pressure, which partly depended on an ambition to meet the schedule for Academy Award nominees, and also to have the film ready for a Christmas opening.

Commercially the film became a disaster. Following the tradition of other movies dealing with the American Revolutionary period, the film also had problems satisfying critics. During the silent film period the Revolutionary War epics were accused of being too anti–British during a time when America was England's ally during wartime. The criticism of **Revolution** was different. Possibly because it was a British film, American critics accused it of being too plain in its history, of focusing too much on human relations rather than glorifying the American Revolutionary heroes.

"The film makes a noble attempt to present history in a realistic, nonheroic light, but Hudson is done in by a dull script and some ludicrous casting ... filmgoers want their history bigger than life and rejected Hudson's attempt to put it all in realistic perspective."—*TVgen*

"**Revolution** fails on several levels.... There is little reason for anything in this hodgepodge..."—*The Motion Picture Guide*

"Only a half-dozen or so movies have dealt more than superficially with the Revolutionary War; thanks to this megabomb, it'll be 2776 until we get another one..."—Leonard Maltin's *Movie and Video Guide*

A more balanced analysis of the film was delivered by William Schoell in his book *The Films of Al Pacino*:

"...**Revolution** might have emerged as a classic. Hugh Hudson knew what he wanted, but this time the talented director couldn't quite get his vision on the screen.... All that hard work, fine acting by Pacino, great period detail—what a picture **Revolution** could have been."

For Al Pacino, his role in this movie is one of the few for which he has been negatively criticized. His Brooklyn accent failed to fit in a film dealing with the Revolutionary period. His slow acting throughout the story has also been questioned. After this hard criticism, it would be four years before Al Pacino would make another movie.

Roanoak (Public Broadcasting System. TV mini-series, 1986.)

Produced by James K. McCarthy and Timothy Marx. Directed by Jan Egleson. Screenplay by Dina Harris and James K. McCarthy. Music by Paul Chihara. Running time: 180 minutes.

Cast: *John Smith* Victor Garber, *Amadas* Patrick Kilpatrick, *Wanchese* Joseph Runningfox, *Wingina* Will Sampson, *Ralph Lane* Adrian Sparks, *Manteo* Tino Juarez, *Tirctought* Eddie Benton-Banai, *Ascopo* Sherry Blakey-Banai, *Appomosiscut* Victoria Racimo, *Cossine* Ralph Brannan, *Walter Raleigh* J. Kenneth Campbell, with Paul Guilfoyle, James Eckhouse, Giancarlo Esposito and Hallie Foote.

The story: The story deals with the first contact between English explorers and Algonquin-speaking Indians on Roanoak Island between 1584 and 1590. Sir Walter Raleigh orders an expedition to find a suitable location for a colony that can be used as a base for striking against Spanish treasure ships.

Later John White returns from the voyage and declares that they have found the right location at the outer banks of North Carolina. He also brings two Indians, Manteo and Wanchese, who have learned English, to use their knowledge of the area. The Indians experience the difference between the white culture and their own. Manteo adjusts, but Wanchese becomes an enemy to the whites.

A flagship, *The Tiger*, is sent to settle the colony. On the journey the ship runs aground in a storm and much of the food intended for the settlers is lost. A colony is established at Roanoak Island, and the settlers survive the winter by trading for goods with the neighboring Indians. The Indians become tired of feeding the helpless settlers. A conflict escalates, and when a supply ship promised for the early spring does not arrive, the conflict develops into war. Later, Sir Francis Drake, arriving from Spanish plundering, saves the settlers and takes them home to England.

John White persuades Raleigh to finance one more attempt for a colony in America, this time at Chesapeake Bay under White's command. Due to a dispute with the ship captain the colonists are again dropped at Roanoak instead of Chesapeake Bay. White returns to England to inform Raleigh of the situation. When he returns a couple of years later, the colony is deserted and there are no signs of the colonists.

Notes: This three-hour TV mini-series was produced for the PBS network and aired in 1986 as part of the American Playhouse series. The intention with the series was to document the settling of Roanoak Island on the coast of North Carolina by the English. The colony would later disap-

Roanoak (Public Broadcasting Systems, 1986)—Cultural exchange: Amadas (Patrick Kilpatrick, *left*) inspects the trading treasures held by John White (Victor Garber, *center*) as they engage in barter with Wingina (Will Sampson, *right center with headdress*).

Roanoak—Wanchese (Joseph Runningfox) contemplates the English society.

pear, and what really happened is still a mystery.

To be as correct as possible, historians David Beer Quinn and Alison Quinn were brought in on the project. In Indian roles Ojibwas from Minnesota were hired, and they were allowed to use their living Algonquian language, with their speech subtitled on the screen.

"In contrast to recent commercial docudramas on early American history, **Roanoak** raises important historical issues and is worthy of classroom analysis, especially if used in conjunction with some of the primary sources which are readily available."—Karen Ordahl Kupperman in *Film and History*

The Scarlet Coat (MGM, 1955)

Produced by Nicholas Naytack. Directed by John Sturges. Screenplay by Karl Tunberg. Photography in Cinemascope and Eastmancolor by Paul C. Vogel. Music by Conrad Salinger. Running time: 101 minutes.

Cast: *Major John Boulton* Cornel Wilde, *Major John Andre* Michael Wilding, *Dr. Jonathan Odell* George Sanders, *Sally Cameron* Anne Francis, *Ben Potter* Bobby Driscoll, *General Robert Howe* John McIntire, *Benedict Arnold* Robert Douglas, *Peter* Rhys Williams, *Nathanael Green* John Dehner, *Sir Henry Clinton* Paul Cavanagh, *Mr. Durkin* Ashley Cowan, *Col. Winfield* John O'Malley and *Col. Jameson* James Westerfield.

The story: In 1780, Washington gives the command of Fort West Point on the highlands of the Hudson to his war experienced friend General Benedict Arnold. Major John Boulton is an American espionage agent who is trying to find out how American military intelligence is leaking to the British. General Howe asks Boulton to desert to the British to find out about the matter.

In British-held New York, Boulton meets with Sally Cameron, a young Tory woman, who in reality turns out to sympathize with the patriots. John learns that the most important information source for the British is an agent at West Point with the cover name "Gustavus."

John and Sally start a love affair. He acquires a rival for Sally in British Major John Andre. However, a respectful friendship develops between Andre and Boulton.

Andre is a link between the British and the American spy "Gustavus" in carrying espionage information. "Gustavus" is unveiled as being General Benedict Arnold. Arnold escapes when he is supposed to be arrested. The Americans, however, catch John Andre, and he is sentenced to death for espionage. John Boulton tries to save his friend from hanging, claiming he had entered the American lines only as a soldier

The Scarlet Coat (MGM, 1955)—A spy behind the British lines: American Major John Boulton (Cornel Wilde, *left*), British Major John Andre (Michael Wilding), and Tory Dr. Jonathan Odell (George Sanders).

and not as a spy. In spite of Boulton's efforts the sentence of Andre is executed.

Notes: "Rather talky historical actioner with too much time spent on friendship and romance."—*Halliwell's Film Guide*

The Scarlet Letter (MGM, 1926)

Directed by Victor Sjostrom. Screenplay by Frances Marion, based on the novel by Nathaniel Hawthorne. Photography by Hendrik Sartov. Length: nine reels.

Cast: *Hester Prynne* Lillian Gish, *The Rev. Arthur Dimmesdale* Lars Hanson, *Roger Prynne* Henry B. Walthall, *Giles* Karl Dane, *The Governor* William H. Tooker, *Mistress Hibbins* Marcelle Corday, *The Jailer* Fred Herzog, *The Beadle* Jules Cowles, *Patience* Mary Hawes, *Pearl* Joyce

Coad, *Sea Captain* James A. Marcus, *Indian* Chief Yowlachie and *Townswoman* Polly Moran.

The story: In New England in 1645, a colony of British Puritans are living under strong religious rules. Their leader is the young Rev. Arthur Dimmesdale. Dimmesdale falls in love with Hester, a young indecent girl of the community.

Service calls Dimmesdale to leave for England. Before leaving he asks Hester for marriage, but she reveals to him that she already was married to an older doctor before coming to America.

When Dimmesdale returns a year later to the colony, he finds out that Hester has borne his child and has been forced by the community to wear the letter "A" (for

The Scarlet Letter (MGM, 1926)—*Top:* A forbidden love affair: Hester Prynne (Lillian Gish) and the Reverend Arthur Dimmesdale (Lars Hanson). *Bottom:* The Reverend Dimmesdale (Lars Hanson) facing his "guilt," his illegitimate child with Hester Prynne (Lillian Gish).

The Scarlet Letter—The Puritans' victim, Hester Prynne (Lillian Gish), alone with her child.

Adultress) on her dress. Hester has refused to reveal who the father is.

Dimmesdale persuades the community to allow Hester to keep and baptize her illegitimate child, even if she has to accept social isolation. A few years later Hester's husband arrives, and Dimmesdale, tortured by guilty conscience, confesses in public his "sins" and dies in front of the congregation.

Notes: The Scarlet Letter was brilliantly directed by a Swede, Victor Sjostrom (Seastrom). The initiative for choosing him as director came from leading actress Lilian Gish herself. At the time the movie was made she was probably the most celebrated and well-paid actress in Hollywood. D.W. Griffith discovered her in 1912 at the same time as Sjostrom entered the film industry.

Gish liked the Swedish director immensely, and they become lifelong friends. She expressed her appreciation for Sjostrom in her biography by Albert Bigelow Paine:

"I knew that we must have a Swedish director. The Swedish people are closer to what our Pilgrims were ... than we present day Americans ... He got the spirit of the story exactly ... I never worked with anybody I liked better than Seastrom."

At its time the film was religiously controversial, and was condemned by the church and women's movements. Lillian Gish personally managed to persuade church and women's groups all over America not to boycott the making of the movie. With Gish's personal guarantees that the story would not be religiously offensive, MGM selected Frances Marion to do the

The Scarlet Letter—Tortured by a guilty conscience, Dimmesdale (Lars Hanson) dies in front of the congregation in the arms of Hester (Lillian Gish).

script under supervision by Gish. Marion's final script is dated December 30, 1925, and filming began on January 25. Filming finished two months later on March 25. One of the reasons the filming went so smoothly was probably because Sjostrom got along so well with the actors, especially Gish. Sjostrom also had the opportunity to work with Swedish actor Lars Hanson in the male lead role as the Rev. Arthur Dimmesdale.

Sjostrom and Gish received good notices for the film, and for Lillian Gish, even though she was a celebrated Griffith actress, **The Scarlet Letter** was a peak in her career.

"...an American classic ... Seastrom brought with him to the picture the Scandinavian talent of 'darkness' the stark tragedy of the story, the grim settings, the pastoral elements that helped make the picture so elemental."—*The Motion Picture Guide*

"...Lars Hanson, who plays the lead opposite the star (Lillian Gish), handles the role with a great finesse.... [T]he direction of Victor Seastrom is pretty nearly perfect and the composition in some of the scenes bespeaks the highest art in picture photography."—*Variety August 11, 1926*

About Lillian Gish:

"...here Miss Gish reveals substantial dramatic power; she proves that her Dresden china fragility is backed by Bessemer steel strength ... the scarlet letter of shame, as she wears it, appears as a red badge of courage."—Robert E. Sherwood in *Life*

"Her beauty lies in her fragility, in her excessive weakness, in her tragic representation of a dying creed and a decadent mysticism.... The gentle flow of her manner, the music of her frail, ethereal body, are the flow and serenity of a religious Christian life."—Seymour Sterns in *Greenwich Village, 1926*

The Scarlet Letter (Darmour/ Majestic, 1934)

Directed by Robert G. Vignola. Screenplay by Leonard Fields and David Silverstein, based on the novel by Nathaniel Hawthorne. Photography by James S. Brown. Running time: 70 minutes.

Cast: *Hester Prynne* Colleen Moore, *Arthur Dimmesdale* Hardie Albright, *Roger Chillingworth* Henry B. Walthall, *Gov. Billingham* William Farnum, *Bartholomew Hockins* Alan Hale, *Abigail Crackstone* Virginia Howell, *Pearl* Cora Sue Collins and *Samson Goodfellow* William Kent.

The story: Adaptation of the early American classic novel by Hawthorne of a woman forced by the Puritan community to wear a letter on her chest because of her illegitimate pregnancy.

The Scarlet Letter (1973)

Directed by Wim Wenders. Running time: 90 minutes.

Cast: Senta Berger, Lou Castel, Hans-Christian Bleach, Yella Rottlander, Yelina Samarina and William Layton.

Notes: Absorbing German version. Filmed in Spain.

The Scarlet Letter (A WGHBH/ Boston Production for PBS, 1979)

Produced and directed by Rick Hauser. Adopted for television by Allan Knee and Alvin Sapinsley, based on the novel by Nathaniel Hawthorne. Music by John Morris. Running time: 240 minutes.

Cast: *Hester Prynne* Meg Foster, *Arthur Dimmesdale* John Heard, *Roger Chillingworth* Kevin Conway, *Mister Wilson* George Martin, *Governor Bellingham* C.K. Alexander, *Sexton* Ralph Drischell, *Pearl*

(at 5) Jessica Ruth Olin, *Mistress Bellingham* Margo Skinner, *Mistress Hibbins* Penny Allen, and *Pearl (at 7)* Elisa Erali.

The story: In a New England British settlement in the early 1600s, Puritans are forcing Hester Prynne to wear a scarlet letter "A" for adultery on her chest—condemned for her passion—after having giving birth to a child with an unknown father.

Proud, courageous and defiant, Hester chooses to assert her independence against the social pressure against her. Enduring the public punishment, Hester grows stronger as the years pass. Her lover, the Reverend Arthur Dimmesdale, lives undetected in the community, tormented and suffering from the burden of the black secret of his soul. Hester's husband Roger Chillingworth, thought to be lost at sea, returns and coldly plans for his revenge.

Notes: One of the many film versions of Nathaniel Hawthorne's well-known novel.

Critics were favorable:

"...A completely fruitful, totally fascinating dramatization of a masterpiece generally regarded as the first great American novel..."—*Los Angeles Times*

"An impeccable rendering ... outstanding performances..."—*TV Guide*

"Four hours of overwhelmingly enjoyable literate entertainment ... an 'A-Plus'..."—*The Christian Science Monitor*

The Scarlet Letter (Lightmotive/ Allied Stars/Cinergi/Moving Picture, 1995)

Produced by Roland Joffe and Andrew G. Vajne. Directed by Roland Joffe. Screenplay by Douglas Day Stewart, freely based on the novel by Nathaniel Hawthorne. Photography by Alex Thomson. Music by John Barry. Running time: 135 minutes.

Cast: *Hester Prynne* Demi Moore, *Arthur Dimmesdale* Gary Oldman, *Roger Prynne* Robert Duvall, *Mituba* Lisa Jolliff-Andoh, *John Bellingham* Edward Hardwick, *Horac Stonehall* Robert Prosky,

Thomas Cheever Roy Dotrice, *Harriet Hibbons* Joan Plowright, *Major Dansmuir* Malcolm Storry, *Goodman Mortimer* Jim Bearden, *Goody Mortimer* Larissa Lapchinski, *Goody Gotwick* Amy Wright, *Johnny Sassamon* George Aguilar, *Brewster Stonehall* Tim Woodward, *Elisabeth Cheever* Joan Gregson, *Meredith Stonehall* Dana Ivey, *Pearl* Bella Bruce, *Margaret Bellingham* Diane Salinger, *Mary Rollings* Jocelyn Cunningham, *Sally Short* Francis Swift, *Moskeegee* Sheldon Peters Wolfchild and *Metacomet* Eric Schweig.

The story: In 1666, Hester Prynne arrives at the colony New Jerusalem in Massachusetts. She is a free spirit, trapped in a harsh and puritanical colony, and while awaiting the arrival of her husband, she meets the young Reverend Dimmesdale, whose ambition is to build a bridge between the whites and the Indians in the area.

Hester's attraction to Dimmes-

The Scarlet Letter (Light Motive/Allied Stars/Cinergi/Moving Picture, 1995)—*Top:* Accused adulteress Hester Prynne (Demi Moore) refuses to admit that she has committed any crime in the Puritan society. *Bottom:* Hester Prynne (Demi Moore), forced to wear a scarlet "A" for adulteress, in a passionate scene with the Reverend Dimmesdale (Gary Oldman).

dale is developing into a love affair when Hester believes that Indians have killed her husband, Roger Prynne. Hester becomes pregnant, and when she does not agree to reveal who is the father of the child, she is sent to jail. After pressure from the Reverend Dimmesdale and some women of the colony, she is released from the jail but is forced to wear a scarlet "A" as a sign of adultery.

Roger Prynne, who was not killed but kept a prisoner by the Indians, arrives at the colony and finds out about Hester's relation to Dimmesdale. The betrayed Prynne, acting dominant and violent, accuses his wife of witchcraft. He attacks Dimmesdale to get his revenge but finds out that he has attacked and killed the wrong person, and therefore takes his own life.

To clear Hester from all accusations, Dimmesdale reveals that he is the father of the illegitimate child. When he is about to be hanged, the Indians attack the settlement, which saves Dimmesdale's life. Hester, Dimmesdale and their daughter leave the colony to start a new life together in the Carolinas.

Notes: "Hokey adaption of Nathaniel Hawthorne's classic novel throws in everything from witch hunts to Indian attacks to controversial happy ending—all to no avail. Moore is woefully miscast as Hester Prynne (though she sure fills a Puritan frock)..."—*Movie and Video Guide*

"The film bears little resemblance other than caricature to its literary precursor, and trivializes its sophisticated study of the dynamic of moral."—*1996 Motion Picture Guide Annual*

"The film version imagines all of the events leading up to the adultery, photographed in the style of those 'Playboy's Fantasies' videos.... The movie has removed the character's sense of guilt, and therefore the story's drama."—*Chicago Sun-Times*

"In the movies, literary classics are not sacrosanct, nor should they be. But director Roland Joffe's **"The Scarlet Letter,"** starring Demi Moore and Gary Oldman, takes this free license and bombs with it..."—*Washington Post*

Seven Cities of Gold (20th Century–Fox, 1955)

Produced by Robert D. Webb and Barbara McLean. Directed by Robert D. Webb. Screenplay by Richard L. Breen, John C. Higgins and Joseph Petracca, based on the novel by Isabelle Gibson Ziegler. Photography in CinemaScope, De Lux Color by Lucien Ballard. Music by Hugo Friedhofer. Running time: 103 minutes.

Cast: *Jose* Richard Egan, *Capt. Portola* Anthony Quinn, *Father Junipero Serra* Michael Rennie, *Matuwir* Jeffrey Hunter, *Ula* Rita Moreno, *Sergeant* Eduardo Noriega, *Galves* Leslie Bradley, *Juan Coronel* John Doucette, *Lt. Faces* Victor Juncos, *Pilot Vila* Julio Villareal, *Schrichak* Migual Inclan, *Dr. Pratt* Carlos Masquis, *Father Vizaino* Pedro Galvan, *Capt. Rivera* Angelo De Stiffney, *Pilot Perez* Richard Adalid Black, *Blacksmith* Fernando Wagner, *Miscomi* Guillermo Calles, *Axajui* Eduardo Gonzales Pliego, *Atanuk* Yerye Beirute, and *Kukura* Anna Maria Gomez,

The story: There is a legend that the Indians have seven cities filled with gold. This story brings Spanish captain Portola and his men to Mexico in 1769. As guide they bring with them Father Junipero Serra, who has his own intention of establishing a series of missions in the area.

After several setbacks they decide to establish a base station in a place which today is San Diego. Captain Portola's companions, Jose and Father Serra, are left behind with a group of soldiers while he travels north in his search for the gold.

Indians under leadership of Matuwir attack Jose's group. Matuwir is wounded during the struggle and Serra gives him medical attention. The Indians abandon their hostile attitude and Serra even tries to convert them to his faith. Jose starts a love affair with Matuwir's sister Ula.

Captain Portola returns after an unsuccessful expedition. The situation is starting to become troublesome because they are running out of supplies. Ula wants to marry Jose, but when he does not approve of this, it angers the Indians and a new

attack on the whites is prepared. To save the others, Jose sacrifices himself and gives his life.

Captain Portola is on his way to leave the place with his men when finally Spanish ships arrive with supplies and the group is saved.

Notes: "Some good action, more than a bit of humor and a strong performance by Quinn who plays the proud Spanish Captain as though he was born to it, which incidentally, he was. Quinn was born in Mexico in 1915 of Irish-Mexican ancestry."—*The Motion Picture Guide*

"The scenery is occasionally handsome, but more often it is obviously fake. This does not help the illusion of this pious and slow-moving film. Robert D. Webb's direction is wholly pedestrian."—*The New York Times*

"Where '**Seven Cities**'scores best is in the believable development of the part both the Church and the military played in the establishment of California under early Spanish rule..."—*Variety*

Seven Seas to Calais
(Adelphia Compagnia/ MGM, 1963)

Seven Seas to Calais (Adelphia Compagnia/MGM, 1963)— Pirate Francis Drake (Rod Taylor).

Produced by Paolo Moffa. Directed by Rudolph Maté and Primo Zeglio. Screenplay by Filippo Sanjust, George St. George and Lindsay Galloway. Photography by Guilio Gianini (Cinemascope, Eastmancolor). Music by Franco Mannino. Running time: 99 minutes.

Cast: *Sir Francis Drake* Rod Taylor, *Malcolm Marsh* Keith Michell, *Queen Elizabeth* Irene Worth, with Hedy Vessel, Basil Dignam, Anthony Dawson, Gianni Cajafi, Mario Girotti, Esmeralda Ruspoli and Marco Guglielmi.

The Story: In 1577, England rules the high seas. To prevent Spain from overtaking its sea dominance, Queen Elizabeth secretly finances pirate Francis Drake's raids against the treasure ships of Spain. After some adventures on their long route to America, Drake lands with his ship in California, and he names the country "New Albion." Drake makes a triumphant return to England, and showing her appreciation, Queen Elizabeth makes him a knight.

Later Drake saves Queen Elizabeth from a Spanish plot to have her replaced by Mary of Scotland.

Opposite: Seven Cities of Gold (20th Century–Fox, 1955)—*Top:* Father Junipero Serra (Michael Rennie, *right*) and Spanish officer Jose (Richard Egan, *left*) win the friendship of Matumir (Jeffery Hunter, center) after having healed his battle wounds. *Bottom:* A present for building a "civilization." Clocks are brought to Father Serra (Michael Rennie, *right*) for his Indian Mission Church.

Seven Seas to Calais—The secret alliance: Pirate Francis Drake (Rod Taylor) and Queen Elizabeth (Irene Worth).

Notes: A minor Italian produced pirate story about the adventure travels of Sir Francis Drake filmed in major Cinemascope format.

"Ho-Hum swashbuckler with a background of schoolboy history."—*Halliwell's Film Guide*

Shehaweh (Les Productions de CERF/Telefilm Canada/Canadian Broadcasting Corp. TV-mini series, 1992)

Produced by Louise Gendron. Directed by Jean Baudin. Photography by Pierre Mignot. Music by Richard Gregorie. Five episodes.

Cast: *Shehaweh* Marina Orsini, *Jeanne Mance* Monique Mercure, *Nicholas* Denis Bernard, *Maisonneuve* Pierre Curzi, with Maurice Barrier, Olivia Brunnaux, René Richard Cyr, Annie Galipeau, Paul Guers, Louis Laparé and Marie-Renée Patry.

Episode 1

At 13 years of age, the Indian girl Shehaweh is captured when a hostile tribe attacks her village. Humiliated and wounded she is brought to L'Hôtel-Dien de Ville-Marie (Montreal).

Jeanne Mance, who will be her protectress, takes care of her, and in unconscious condition Shehaweh is baptized as Maria. "Untamed" Shehaweh resists adjusting to the white civilization. It is decided that she will be brought to France for her adaptation.

Episode 2

In France, Shehaweh has difficulties adjusting to the frivolity of the life around Louis XIV's court. She misses her previous life close to nature with her people. After disobeying rules, she is taken to a home for misfits and the insane.

The lack of women in the American colony causes Ambassador Filles du Roy to recruit potential wives in France to be brought to the colony. This opens an opportunity for Shehaweh, and with two friends she returns to New France after two years in France.

Episode 3

When they arrive in New France, the women find the king's mandate for them clear: they have 15 days to choose their husbands. Jeanne Mance opposes forcing Shehaweh into marriage, and suggests as an alternative that she serve three years in a religious community. Shehaweh, however, refuses the alternative and chooses to marry a French trapper, Nicholas Lac.

Episode 4

After two years of marriage with Nicholas, Shehaweh's longing for her people and the death of Jeanne Mance cause her to leave her husband and return to her people.

She persuades Ambassador Frontenac to take her to the land of her people. The return turns out to be a nightmare; the village has been destroyed and all of her relatives have been killed.

Episode 5

Shehaweh starts to realize that the white man's world holds nothing for her, and that her only future is to live with her own people. Her final decision to do so comes when she meets with the Iroquois warrior Gaientohoa, with whom she falls in love.

Song of Hiawatha (Hallmark Home Entertainment, 1997)

Produced by Danny Danylkiw. Directed by Jeffrey Shore. Screenplay by Earl Wallace, based on Henry Wadsworth Longfellow's poem. Photography by Curtis Petersen. Music by Reg Powell. Running time: 114 minutes.

Cast: *O Kagh* Graham Green, *Mudjekeewis* Russel Means, *Hiawatha* Litefoot, *Minnehaha* Irene Bedard, *Nokomis* Sheila Tousey, *Chibiabos* Adam Beach, *Bertrand* Michal Rooker, *Marcel* David Strathairn, *Tagoo* Gordon Tootoosis, *Sparrow Song* Tina Louise Bomberry, *Mondamin* Peter Kelly Gaudreault, *Mishe-Mokwa* Mike Kanentakeron, *10-year-old Hiawatha* Adrian Jamieson and *Pearl Feather/Megissongwan* Flint Eagle.

The story: A white hunter, Bertrand, an Indian guide, O Kagh, and a French priest, Marcel, travel to a village of the Chippewa tribe to learn more about their great war chief Hiawatha, of whom they have heard rumors.

Bertrand is a greedy fur trader whose real intention is to trade guns for pelts with the tribe. When arriving in the village of the Chippewa, Hiawatha is not present, but through Hiawatha's grandmother Nokomis and tribal elder Ingoo, they will, through a series of stories framed in flashback, learn about Hiawatha's growing from a young warrior to the people's mightiest leader.

It turns out that myths and religious visions surround Hiawatha's life, and that he has gained appreciation by bringing corn and medicine to his starving and sick tribesmen. He also has managed to bring peace between his tribe and hostile neighbor nations.

Hiawatha meets his love in Minnehaha, a Dakota woman, whom he brings home and marries. When she dies and Hiawatha realizes, through a vision, that problems will arise with the arrival of the white man, he leaves the tribe as the mythic person he is.

Notes: Graham Green, Academy Award nominee for his role in **Dances with Wolves**, Russell Means, who played Chingachgook in **The Last of the Mohicans**, and Litefoot, who played in **The Indian In the**

Cupboard, were natives cast in the major roles of the movie. Irene Bedard, the voice of Disney's **Pocahontas**, was featured as Dakota maiden Minnehaha.

The Spirit of '76 (Continental Producing Company, 1917)

Produced by Robert Goldstein. Directed by George Siegmann. Screenplay by Virginia Tyler Hudson. Film length: 12 reels.

Cast: *Catherine Montour* Adda Glaeson, *Lionel Esmond* Howard Gaye, *George III* Jack Cosgrove, *Walter Butler* George Cheseborough, *George Washington* Noah Beery, *Cecil Stuart* Jane Novak, *Lord Chatham* William Freemann, *Marquis de Lafayette* George Smith, with Babe Lawrence, Dark Cloud and Jack McCready.

The story: Catherine Montour, a mixed-race Indian, uses her influence with the British King George III to conspire against the Americans and to become queen of the colonies. She plots with her love interest, Lionel Esmond, to obtain her goal, but discovers when they are about to be married that they are brother and sister.

In the meantime, she has fallen out of favor with King George, and the American Revolution has dashed her hopes for an American monarchy.

A number of historical events are featured, including Patrick Henry's speech before the Virginia House of Burgesses, Paul Revere's ride, the signing of the Declaration of Independence, Washington at Valley Forge and Lord Chatham's death. The highlight is a massacre in the Mohawk Valley.

Notes: Producer Robert Goldstein was involved in D.W. Griffith's production of **The Birth of a Nation**. This inspired him to make a similar film about the American Revolution, and he formed the Continental Production Company to do it. He hired George Siegemann, a member of Griffith's stock company, as director, and he also hired one of Griffith's players, Howard Gaye, for the lead role.

Just before America entered World War I, **The Spirit of '76** was finished. It was scheduled to open in Chicago on May 17, 1917, and it was advertised to contain massive and beautiful sets and an all-star cast with hundreds of extras.

The story of the American War of Independence in this picture was told in an anti–British way, especially in sequences which deal with the Wyoming Valley massacre on the Susquehanna River in Pennsylvania, in which British soldiers commit atrocities against patriot women and children. This probably would have been acceptable—had not America been about to enter the war in Europe on the side of the British.

At its opening in Chicago, a city with a huge German population sometimes accused of anti–British propaganda, the critics were generally favorable:

" ...the picture contains a number of splendid moments... The photography and tinting is fine throughout. Many of the sets are elaborate.... The picture gives opportunity for elaborate patriotic display ... we understand the fear that the picture might cause a feeling of resentment against England."—Genevieve Harris in *Motography*

"Contrary to the opinion of Chicago censors it contains nothing that would dampen the fervor of America at war now. Instead, it inspires patriotism. It has some truly wonderful moments and should cause the red blood of American to tingle."—*Exhibitor's Trade Review*

New York critics were also mainly positive at its opening:

"All in all the opening of this historical photo drama was most successful.... It will draw patronage because of its historical interest and those who see it will feel well repaid, although we can't help wondering what a Griffith would have done with the material."—R.W. Baremore in *New York Times*

However, when the film opened on November 28, 1917, in Los Angeles, federal officers seized it and charged producer Robert Goldstein with violation of the Espionage Act.

In the charge is was said:

"The Spirit of '76, designed to arouse antagonism, hatred, enmity between the American people and the people of Great Britain, at a time when the defendant well-knew the government of Great Britain ... was an ally of the United States in prosecution of a war against ... Germany."

The court found that the **Spirit of '76** was anti–British and Goldstein was sentenced to a ten-year prison term.

When the war in Europe ended, Goldstein was released after serving only one year of his sentence. In 1921 the film reopened in Chicago. This time it was received more enthusiastically. Critics were generally favorable. The only negative reaction was by Edward Weitzel in *Moving Picture World:*

"...Robert Goldstein ... has ground out a crude concoction of fact and fiction, purposing

to deal with some of the most momentous episodes in American history, and filled it with astonishing and mirthful anachronisms..."

Unfortunately **The Spirit of '76** is a lost film so it cannot be viewed today. It may seem from present point of view that Goldstein did little, if anything, wrong; wartime periods are, however, politically sensitive, and the First World War years were no exception.

Squanto: A Warrior's Tale (Walt Disney, 1996)

Produced by Kathryn Galan. Directed by Xavier Koller. Screenplay by Darlene Craviotto. Photography by Robbie Greenberg. Running time: 99 minutes.

Cast: *Squanto* Adam Beach, *Epenow* Eric Schweig, *Sir George* Michael Gambon,

Squanto: A Warrior's Tale (Walt Disney, 1996)—Upon his return to England, Sir George (Michael Gambon, *left*) presents two exotic specimens of primitive life in the New World, Epenow (Eric Schweig) and Squanto (Adam Beach, *second from right*), to Harding (Alex Norton, *second from left*).

Squanto: A Warrior's Tale—In England, Native American captives Epenow (Eric Schweig, *left*) and Squanto (Adam Beach) are forced to perform in public "entertainment."

Thomas Dermer Nathaniel Parker, *Brother Daniel* Mandy Patinkin, *Harding* Alex Norton, *Brother Timothy* Stuart Pankin, *Brother Paul* Donal Donnelly, *Nakooma* Irene Bedard, *William Bradford* Tim Hopper, *Pequod* Leroy Peltier, *Captain Hunt* Mark Margolis and *Pocknet* Mark Abbott.

The Story: In the early 1600s, English explorers arrive in Eastern Massachusetts, expressing an interest in taking up trade with the Algonquins. In reality their purpose is to capture Indians and bring them back to England as slaves.

Warrior Squanto and his friend Epenow are captured, taken to Plymouth in England and put on display as "savages." Squanto is thrown into a bear pit. In the fight with the grizzly, Squanto calms the beast, and he and Epenow get an opportunity to escape. Epenow is caught, but Squanto steals a boat and escapes. During a storm at sea he is injured and stranded on

a beach, where cloistered monks find him unconscious.

The monks nurse him back to health and there is an exchange of cultural traditions between Squanto and his rescuers. Later Squanto and Epenow escape the English by boarding a ship at Plymouth bound for the New World.

When it arrives in Massachusetts, the Algonquins destroy the British ship. Squanto finds out that the English have destroyed his village. Despite his travails, Squanto makes peace between the Pilgrims and the Indians. As a result the Indians and the Pilgrims are united in the first Thanksgiving dinner.

Notes: The story in **Squanto** deals with some events that would lead up to the first Thanksgiving. Disney's **Squanto** is fictional and not real history. During the time the English arrived in Plymouth, Massachusetts, some 2,000 Indians lived in the area.

The arrival of the British reduced the Natives' numbers by infectious diseases and warfare. By 1614, John Smith had discovered the Algonquian Patuxent tribe ("Squanto's tribe"). When Smith left for England, he left Thomas Hunt to deal with the natives. Hunt captured 20 Indians (including Squanto) who were brought to Malaga in Spain to be sold as slaves. It is not known what happened to Squanto during this time. He turned up in London in 1617 and later was brought back to America, where the English employed him as a guide in New England. He died in 1629 from an arrow wound.

Swiss director Xavier Koller, who in 1991 won the Academy Award for best foreign film with his **Journey of Hope**, directed this Canadian production. Most of the shooting was done at the Fortress of Louisbourg in Nova Scotia.

"...'**Squanto**' is the kind of superficial, tided-up, idealized history that might appeal to younger viewers. No thoughtful person will be able to take it seriously."—*Chicago Sun-Times*

"...But the narrative is hopelessly muddled, the dialogue is stiff, the characters are all cartoons (especially the villains) and the stunts get sillier as the film goes along."—Chris Hicks in *Desert News*

"...Squanto has its moments of suspense and humor. It is kind of sweet, very corny, emphatically skin-deep, and superficially politically correct film(Noble, yes, savage, no, English bad, Indians good).... The acting is OK but many faces are not convincingly Indian."—Edwin Jahiel in *The News-Gazette*

The Swamp Fox (Walt Disney TV Show, 1959–61)

Produced by James Pratt. Photography by Philip Lathrop. 8 episodes @ 52 minutes.

Cast: *General Francis Marion* Leslie Nielsen, with Myron Healey, John Sutton, Robert Douglas, Henry Daniell, Slim Pickens, Tim Considine and Richard Erdman.

The story: Reflects the guerrilla fighting of General Francis Marion against the British in South Carolina in 1780.

Tecumseh (Defa, 1972)

Directed by Hans Katzert. Screenplay by Rolf Römer and Wolfgang Ebeling. Photography by Wolfgang Braumann. Music by Gunter Fischer.

Cast: *Tecumseh* Gojko Mitić, with Eileen Annakatherin Burger, Rolf Römer, Leon Niemczyk and Mieczyslaw Kalenik.

The story: In the early 1800s the westward movement of white settlers causes unrest among the Indian nations. The Indians realize that their existence is threatened, and this escalates an Indian-white conflict.

American Governor Harrison of Indiana tries to negotiate treaties with the Indians to prevent a general uprising. The whites, however, continuously break the treaties, Shawnee Chief Tecumseh unites the Indian nations for a general uprising against the Americans. In contrast to his general dislike for the whites, Tecumseh has a love affair with a white woman, Eileen.

Tecumseh and some of the tribes ally themselves with the British against America in the War of 1812. The enemy, however, is superior, and on October 5, 1813, Tecumseh is killed at the battle on the Thames.

Notes: This movie is one of the series of Indian movies which were released by the East German production company DEFA between 1966 and 1983. The leading actor in all 12 films was Gojko Mitic, a Yugoslavian. He had started his movie career in West Germany's Karl May–based Winnetoue movies in 1963. The DEFA series of Indian movies made him an East German star.

Tecumseh is ambitious in the sense that it tries to create an historically accurate movie. The film highlights the political activities by Tecumseh to unite all Indian tribes east of Mississippi.

Tecumseh the Last Warrior (Turner Pictures, 1995)

An American Zoetrope production in association with Daniel H. Blatt Productions. Produced by Lynn Raynor. Directed by Larry Elikann. Teleplay by P. F. Edwards and Daniel H. Blatt, based on the book *Panther in the Sky* by James Alexander Thom. Photography by Eric Van Haren Noman. Music by David Shire.

Cast: Jesse Borrego, David Clennon, David Morse, and Tantoo Cardinal.

The story: This TNT network TV feature from its Native American series is about the life of Shawnee Chief Tecumseh.

Ten Gentlemen from West Point
(20th Century–Fox, 1942)

Produced by William Pearlberg. Directed by Henry Hathaway. Screenplay by Richard Maibaum, George Seaton and Brian Hecht; suggested by a story by Malvin Wald. Photography by Leon Shamroy. Running time: 102 minutes.

Cast: *Dawson* George Montgomery, *Carolyn Bainbridge* Maureen O'Hara, *Howard Shelton* John Sutton, *Major Sam Carter* Laird Cregar, *Henry Clay* John Shepperd, *Florimond Massey* Victor Francen, *Bane* Harry Davenport, *Schully* Ward Bond, *General William Henry Harrison* Douglas Dumbrille, *Maloney* Ralph Byrd, *Benny Havens* Joe Brown, Jr., *Shippen* David Bacon, *Mrs. Thompson* Esther Dale, *Chester* Richard Derr, *Jared Danforth* Louis Jean Heydt, *Capt. Sloane* Stanley Andrews, *Capt. Luddy* James Flavin, *Letty* Edna Mae Jones, *Senate President* Charles Trowbridge, *Grandpa* Tully Marshall, *John Randolph* Edwin Maxwell, *William Eustis* Edward Fielding, *Wood* Morris Ankrum, *Sersen* Selmer Jackson and *Tecumseh* Noble Johnson.

The story: This story is set in the early 1800s. The new Military Academy at West Point is facing political opposition. To destroy the academy, its opponents hire a ruthless commandant, Major Sam Carter, hoping this will ruin the reputation of the school.

Carter drives the first class into the ground; only ten cadets remain at graduation. Among them are young Dawson, eager to serve his country. Another is a rich boy, Howard Shelton, and they both are after lovely Carolyn Bainbridge. At the end, Dawson wins her heart.

The young cadets prove themselves to Major Carter by warding off an Indian attack. This convinces the opponents that the academy is worthwhile.

Notes: "...Henry Hathaway's direction is uncommonly uneven for a man of his talent.... But when he has something meaty to work with such as the cannon ride sequence or the murderous game of Indian lacrosse ... Mr. Hathaway really gets drive and punch into his scenes." *New York Times*

Tomahawk (CBC TV-series, 1957-58)

Directed by Pierre Gauvreau. 26 episodes @ 26 minutes.

Cast: Jacques Godin, Rene Caron, Percy Rodriquez and Julien Besette.

The story: Pierre Radisson explores the wilderness of the Canadian Northwest. Exciting adventures for young viewers.

L'ultimo dei Mohicani (The Last of the Mohicans) (Italcaribe Eguiluz, 1965)

Produced by Angel Ampuero. Directed by Matteo Cano. Screenplay by Manual Gijon and Vinicio Marimucci. Music by Angelo F. Lavagnino. Photography by Carl Carlini.

Cast: Jack Taylor, Paul Muller, Barbara Loy, Sara Lezana, Daniel Martin, José Marco, Luis Inpuw, and José Manual Martin.

An Italian-French co-production of Cooper's novel.

Unconquered (Paramount, 1947)

Produced and directed by Cecil B. DeMille. Screenplay by Charles Bennett, Frederick M. Frank and Jesse Lasky, Jr., based on the novel by Neil H. Swanson. Photography in Technicolor by Ray Rennahan. Music by Victor Young. Running time: 147 minutes.

Unconquered (Paramount, 1947)—Christopher Holden (Gary Cooper) and Abby Martha Hale (Paulette Goddard) try to escape from captivity by Indians.

Cast: *Capt. Christopher Holden* Gary Cooper, *Abby Martha Hale* Paulette Goddard, *Martin Garth* Howard Da Silva, *Gayasuta* Boris Karloff, *Jeremy Love* Cecil Kellaway, *John Fraser* Ward Bond, *Hannah* Katherine DeMille, *Capt. Steel* Henry Wilcoxon, *Lord Chief Justice* Sir C. Aubrey Smith, *Capt. Simon Ecuyer* Victor Varconi, *Diana* Virginia Grey, *Leach* Porter Hall, *Dave Bone* Mike Mazurki, *Pontiac* Robert Warwick, *Col. George Washington* Richard Gaines, *Mrs. Fraser* Virginia Campbell, *Sir William Johnson* Alan Napier, *Lt. Fergus McKenzie* Gavin Muir, *Mrs. Pruitt* Nan

Unconquered—Pontiac's warriors: Fire and destruction.

Sutherland, *Sioto* Marc Lawrence, *Everlyn* Jane Nigh, *Lt. Hutchins* Lloyd Bridges, *Jim Lovat* Jack Pennick, *Venango Scout* Raymond Hatton, *Chief Killbuck* Chief Thundercloud and *Mulligan* Charles B. Middleton.

The story: In 1763, Martin Garth, a powerful trader, tries to stop the westward movements of settlers by secretly trading guns to different Indian tribes.

Abby Hale, young English girl unjustly accused of a crime, is sentenced to 14 years' slavery in North America. In a slave auction Garth attempts to purchase Abby for himself, but the highest bid comes from Captain Christopher Holden, a Virginia patriot militiaman, whom Abby had met aboard the ship from England. After having purchased the girl, Holden frees her.

Hoping to drive the colonists back to the sea for good, Martin Garth plays an important role in the historic "Pontiac Conspiracy" in which 18 Indian tribes pledge their allegiance to the great Ottawa Chief. Holden is aware of Garth's role in the conspiracy because of his marriage to Hannah, daughter of one of the Indian chiefs. Jealous of Abby, Hannah arranges to have the young woman captured by the Indians. At the last minute Holden rescues Abby from a slow death by torture at the hands of Seneca Chief Gayasuta, by frightening the Indians with exploding gunpowder.

Holden is unjustly accused of desertion, and in a court-martial he is sentenced to death. Abby, however, helps him to escape. The pair sets off to the safety of Fort Pitt, but they find it already besieged by the Indians. Holden obtains reinforcements and saves the fort from the Indians. After killing Garth in the fort's stable, Holden is finally reunited with Abby for good.

Notes: "...**Unconquered** is a most enjoyable piece of semi-history, even at repeated viewing. There's something about DeMille's treatment of historical subjects and/or events that is always satisfying."—Homer Dickens in *The Films of Gary Cooper*

"In some ways **Unconquered** is better than anything Mr. DeMille has done. Although some scenes are improbable to the point of absurdity, the picture, in the main, sticks closer to the main current of history than has been the case with most of his productions."—*Baltimore Sun*

"...**Unconquered** is the type of film which, contradictorily, doesn't stand analysis and yet will get and interest the customers.... The redskins are ruthless scalpers and the British colonials naive and brave, patriotic and full of skullduggery..."—*Variety*

Variety also commented on DeMille's fame in bringing in female bath scenes into his movies, as also in this production:

" ...there is even a characteristic DeMille bath scene, albeit a bit on the road-company side, as she [Paulette Goddard] takes a primitive tub, but none the less, the trademarked absolutions take place."

Washington at Valley Forge
(Kalem, 1908)
Length: 905 feet.

Washington at Valley Forge
(Universal, 1914)
Directed by Francis Ford. Screenplay by Francis Ford and Grace Cunard. Length: four reels.

Cast: *The Spy* Francis Ford, *Betty* Grace Cunard, *Betty's brother* Harry Schumm, *Washington* Peter Leon, *Lafayette* Ernest Shields and *The innkeeper* Harry Edmonson.

The story: The film opens with some attention to historical topics including the Minute Men, Paul Revere's Ride, Lafayette's arrival, and leading up to Washington's army's winter encampment at Valley Forge.

At Valley Forge, Washington is staying at an inn. Betty, the innkeeper's daughter, is in love with a man who, unknown to her, is a British spy. The Hessians plan to attack Washington's force. Betty overhears their plans and also learns about a plot to kill Washington when he is asleep.

To save Washington, Betty persuades the general to change rooms with her. During the night the spy goes to kill Washington but the fatal stab, intended for the general, is given to Betty instead. Mortally wounded, Betty exposes the spy, who is arrested.

Notes: Francis Ford, the older brother of famous director John Ford, directed and played in the picture.

"The portrayer of Washington appears to be too youthful and lacking in the strength and dignity with which we associate in our mind a picture of 'the father of our country.'"—*Variety, March 6, 1914*

Washington Under the American Flag (Vitagraph, 1909)

Cast: Joseph Kilgour and William Shea.

Washington Under the British Flag (Vitagraph, 1909)
Produced and directed by J. Stuart Blackton. Screenplay by Charles Kent. Length: 990 feet.

Cast: *George Washington* Joseph Kilgour, with William Humphrey, Charles Kent, James Young and Clara Kimball Young.

When Broadway Was a Trail (Shubert/World, 1914)
Directed and story by O.A.C. Lund. Length: five reels.

Cast: *Priscilla Elliot* Barbara Tennant, *Henry Minuet* O.A.C. Lund, *Peter Minuet* Edward Roseman, *Salvation Kibbens* Lindsay J. Hal, *Standish Hope* Alec B.

Francis and *Mistress Hibbens* Mary Neverro.

The story: In 1626, Henry, son of Peter Minuet, governor of New Amsterdam, travels to Salem, Massachusetts, where he meets Priscilla Elliot and falls in love with her.

A member of the colony, Salvation Hibbins, is also in love with Priscilla and he wants to marry her. When she refuses, he accuses her of practicing witchcraft. She is defended by Henry, which results in both being banned from the colony.

They leave for New Amsterdam, but Henry's family also has difficulties accepting Priscilla. Turning his back on his family, Henry marries Priscilla and the two leave for the wilderness to start a life on their own.

When the Redskins Rode
(Columbia, 1951)

Produced by Sam Katzman. Directed by Lew Landers. Screenplay by Robert E. Kent. Photography in Super Cinecolor by Lester White. Music by Mischa Bakaleinikoff. Running time: 78 minutes.

Cast: *Prince Hannoc* Jon Hall, *Elisabeth Leeds* Mary Castle, *George Washington* James Seay, *Christopher Gist* John Ridgely, *Morna* Sherry Moreland, *Chief Shingiss* Pedro de Cordoba, *John Delmont* John Dehner, *Gov. Dinwiddie* Lewis L. Russel, *Appleby* William Bakewell, *St. Pierre* Gregory Gaye, *Znueau* Rusty Wescott, *Davey* Milton Kibbee and *Duprez* Rick Vallin.

The story: In 1753, just before the outbreak of the French and Indian War, Elisa-

When the Redskins Rode (Columbia, 1951)—The expedition to Fort LeBoeuf: Christopher Gist (John Ridgely, *left*), George Washington (James Seay) and Prince Hannoc (Jon Hall).

When the Redskins Rode—The attack on the Delaware village: Shingis (Pedro de Cordoba) saves Morna (Sherry Moreland) from being killed by a Wyandot.

beth Leeds, a French spy, tries to win over the Delawares to the French side with attempts to seduce Delaware Chief Shingiss's son Hannoc.

The French send allied Indians to raid English settlements on the frontier. George Washington goes to Fort Le Boeuf to protest to the French. The Delawares decide to remain neutral in the conflict. When Washington and his party deliver his protest, the French imprison them. Hannoc and Ranger Captain Gist, however, free the prisoners.

French-allied Wyandot Indians attack the Delaware village, which causes Shingiss to side with the British in the conflict. Shingiss and his warriors arrive just in time to support Washington against an attack on Fort Necessity by a force of French and Indians from Canada. Hannoc promises to join the British during the war and later to return to his love interest, Morna, in the Delaware village.

Notes: "A heavy dosage of action but lacking in plot development."—*The Motion Picture Guide*

"Weak story of Indian warfare in early colonial times will appeal to moppets but adults are more apt to be amused than entertained by the proceedings...

...For what appears to be a modest budgeter, producer Sam Katzman draped the picture with good physical values."—*Variety*

Winners of the Wilderness (MGM, 1927)

Produced by Irving Thalberg. Directed by W.S. Van Dyke. Screenplay by John Thomas Neville. Photography by Clyde de Vinna. Running time: 68 minutes.

Winners of the Wilderness (MGM, 1927)—French Captain Dumas (Roy D'Arcy) is waiting in the forest with his regulars and Canadian coureurs de bois to attack Braddock's advancing army.

Cast: *Colonel Sir Dennis O'Hara* Colonel Tim McCoy, *Renee Contracouer* Joan Crawford, *General Contracouer* Edward Connelly, *Captain Dumas* Roy D'Arcy, *Mimi* Louise Lorraine, *George Washington* Edward Hearn, *Timothy* Tom O'Brien, *General Edward Braddock* Will R. Walling, *Governor Dinwiddie* Lionel Belmore, *Pontiac* Chief Big Tree and *Woman* Jean Arthur.

The Story: During the French and Indian War, Sir Dennis O'Hara, an Irish officer attached to Washington bluecoats under the generalship of Edward Braddock, is sent to spy on the French about their plans to conquer the Ohio Valley.

Dressed in a mask and cape, he steals the treaty that the French and the Indian tribes under Chief Pontiac are about to sign. During the flight, he meets the turncoat General Contrecouer's daughter Renee and falls in love with her.

In the forests O'Hara encounters Pontiac and wins the fight that follows, but spares Pontiac's life.

Later, at a ball given by the French, he wins the affection of Renee. Followed by trouble, O'Hara finds himself challenged by the French officer Captain Dumas to a duel, an event which never occurs.

Under the command of General Braddock, British troops set out to attack the French Fort Duquesne. Braddock's forces are defeated by a handful of French regulars and Pontiac's Indians. During the combat O'Hara is captured and turned over to the Indians by Captain Dumas to be shot. Renee pleads for his life, but Dumas is implacable. Pontiac, however, remembers O'Hara's kindness during their earlier encounter and spares him his life. In a subsequent sword fight, O'Hara vanquishes Dumas. O'Hara and Renee are able to escape, and as soon as they are safely behind British lines the two of them are wed.

Notes: In the 1920s MGM produced a series of good western movies. One of these was **Winners of the Wilderness**, although the film was not a "real" western, with its French and Indian War setting.

MGM executive Louis B. Mayer, even with his unerring instinct for a good picture, didn't like westerns. Associate Thal-berg, however, knew how to mount a successful film, and he made sure **Wilderness** would make it. At the time MGM had a corporate strategy to make the best outdoor dramas in the industry.

A lot of historical research was done by scriptwriter John Thomas Neville to make the story as historically correct as possible. A major source of information came from George Washington's own descriptions of the battle (Washington was a colonial military aid to Braddock during the campaign). Colonel Tim McCoy was brought in by MGM to do the lead role of the movie.

McCoy did 16 westerns for MGM between 1926 and 1929. **Winners of the Wilderness** was the second entry. With the coming of sound movies, the studio had to

Winners of the Wilderness—Pontiac's (Chief Big Tree) victory over the British.

cut down on the budget targets. This economizing was unfortunate, because the McCoy westerns kept a very high standard for the period, and stood up well to many for the years to come.

Critics were positive:

"McCoy's finest silent film, and in fact, perhaps the finest film he ever made ... a powerful, compelling drama, with brilliant direction, and superb dramatic interplay between Tim McCoy and Joan Crawford."—Jon Tuska in *Views & Reviews* (Vol. 3, 1971)

"Colonel Tim McCoy, a handsome soldier and a fine actor, mostly because he doesn't act. He is natural at all times. Joan Crawford the lady sought and Roy D'Arcy up to his usual deviltry."—*Film Daily*

"The costumes of the period offer a pleasant contrast to the interesting sequences ... in which are seen such historical figures as Washington and Braddock. The latter's disastrous defeat is the film's high light and is carried out with realism..."—*Motion Picture News*

Wolfe and Montcalm (The Chronicles of America Picture Corporation, 1924)

Adapted and directed by Kenneth Webb. Adapted from *The Conquest of New France*, by George M. Wrong.

Cast: *General James Wolfe* Arthur Hohle, *Marquis de Montcalm* Juan De La Cruze, *Governor-General Vaudreuil* Bradley Barker, *William Pitt* Stanley Walpole, *Lord Anson* J. Moy Bennett, *Brigadier-General Murray* Gordon Standing and *Brigadier-General Monckton* Maurice Baird.

The story: In September 12, 1759, General James Wolfe on board the British flagship *Sutherland* is in command of the expedition against Quebec.

In Quebec the French Governor Vaudreuil is jealous of General the Marquis de Montcalm, who has been sent from Paris to cooperate with him. Montcalm believes that the English are preparing an attack on the Foulon, but is met with disagreement from Vaudreuil. On the night of the 12th,

the British keep up a constant bombardment. Meanwhile Wolfe, with 1,700 picked men has prepared to strike. With his first division, nicknamed the "Forlorn Hope," Wolfe opens the way for his main force to go up the Foulon Road. Governor Vaudreuil's lack of understanding of the seriousness of the French situation prevents the mobilization of a strong defense by the French and on the Plains of Abraham, on September 13, the French are defeated. During the battle, General Wolfe is killed and the French suffer the serious loss of Montcalm.

During the winter, the British have to withdraw their fleet from the St. Lawrence because of the ice, leaving the army isolated at Quebec. The troops suffer from disease and privations during the bitter winter, and when spring comes, of 8,000 men but half remain to bear arms.

The French forces now concentrate at Montreal, the last stand in the tragedy of France's lost cause in North America. On September 8, 1760, Vaudreuil surrenders and the French menace to England's American colonies comes to an end.

Wolfe, or the Conquest of Quebec (Kalem, 1914)

Directed by Kenean Buel. Length: five reels.

Cast: *General James Wolfe* Guy Coombs, *His mother* Helen Lindroth, *Katherine Lowther* Alice Hollister, *Lt. Arlieig of the Royal Americans* Jere Austin, *Marquis de Montcalm* Arthur Donaldson, *Mignon Mars* Anna Nilsson and *Hubert Mars* Harold Livingston.

The story: General Wolfe attacks Quebec, and Montcalm's forces have to surrender. Both generals expire. Included is a love affair between a Royal American officer and a French Canadian girl.

Young Daniel Boone (Monogram, 1950)

Produced by James S. Burkett. Directed by Reginald LeBorg. Screenplay by Clint Johnston and Reginald LeBorg. Photography in Cinecolor by G. Warrenton. Music by Edward J. Jay. Running time: 71 minutes.

Cast: *Daniel Boone* David Bruce, *Rebecca Bryan* Kristine Miller, *Helen Bryan* Mary Treen, *Capt. Fraser* Damien O'Flynn, *Charles* Bryan Don Beddoe, *Col. von Arnheim* John Mylong, *Little Hawk* William Roy, *Col. Benson* Stanley Logan, *Pvt. Haslet* Herbert Naish, *Walking Eagle* Nipo T. Strongheart, *Lt. Perkins* Richard Foote and *Sentry* Stephen S. Harrison.

The story: In 1755, after General Braddock's defeat by the French, Philadelphia merchant Bryan and Hessian officer von Arnheim are following a party of raiding French-allied Indians who have captured Bryan's two daughters.

British scout Daniel Boone and his Indian companion, Little Hawk, track and rescue von Arnheim and Bryan when Indians attack them. They also manage to free Bryan's daughters from the Indians. During their escape in the wilderness they take protection in an abandoned fort for the night. The younger sister Rebecca is attracted to Daniel, and Helen finds affection in von Arnheim's military courtesy.

A Captain Fraser, who in reality is a spy and French officer, arrives at the fort

Young Daniel Boone (Monogram, 1950)—Daniel Boone (David Bruce) is captured by French spy, Captain Fraser (Damien O'Flynn).

Young Daniel Boone—Daniel (David Bruce) has to fight French-allied Indians. Chief Yowlachie plays his adversary here.

and claims that his purpose is to safeguard von Arnheim back to British lines.

Shawnee Indians attack the fort, but the attack is repelled. Fraser, whose right identity has been unveiled, assembles French-allied Indians and captures the party. Daniel manages to slip away, and outlasts his Indian persecutors in the wilderness when they believe they have finished him. Daniel returns and rescues his captured friends and kills Fraser.

Later, back in safety behind British lines, Daniel and Rebecca decide to make their way to Kentucky together.

Notes: "A good film for action though the story isn't much ... the cast is little more than adequate. Some nice color camera work adds to the film's quality; all in all, an entertaining picture that children will probably enjoy."—*The Motion Picture Guide*

Young Dan'l Boone (Fox TV— Frankel Prods., 1977-78)

Produced by Jimmy Sangster. Four episodes @ 52 minutes.

Cast: *Daniel Boone* Rick Moses, *Rebecca Bryan* Devon Ericson, *Peter Dawes* John Joseph Thomas, *Hawk* Ji-Tu Cumbuka and *Tsiskwa* Eloy Phil Casados.

The story: This TV series was an attempt to depict the early life of Daniel Boone before he became a legend on the frontier.

Daniel explores the Tennessee frontier, together with a young English boy, Peter Dawes, and Hawk, an ex-slave. Involved in the adventures are also Boone's Indian friend Tsiskwa and his young love interest, Rebecca Bryan.

Young Dan'l Boone (Fox TV—Frankel Prods., 1977-78)—
Top: Daniel Boone (Rick Moses) and young Peter Dawes
(John Joseph Thomas). *Bottom:* A disgraced British officer
who has turned pirate (Paul Shenar, *right*) and his aide
(Clive Revill), in a plot to steal furs from Daniel Boone and
Hawk and then take young Peter hostage.

Notes: This TV mini-series
was a failure. The idea behind the
series was to recapture some of
the popularity 20th Century–Fox
experienced with its Fess Parker–
Daniel Boone series a decade earlier. The series had some realistic
exterior scenes shot in Tennessee.

Disagreements between members of the production team and
the fact that stories dealing with
early American history were not a
popular theme at the time it was
released contributed to the failure
of the series.

The Young Rebels (Col-TV for ABC, 1970-71)

Produced by Peter Gayle. 17
episodes @ 52 minutes.

Cast: *Jeremy Larkin* Rick Ely,
Isak Poole Lou Gossett, *Henry
Abington* Alex Henteloff, *Elizabeth Coates* Hilarie Thompson
and *Lafayette* Philippe Fourquet

The story: Set during the
American Revolution in the year
of 1777. Four teenagers in
Chester, Pennsylvania, members
of the fictional "Yankee Doodle
Society," harass the British occu-
pying forces behind their lines.

The leader of the rebel
fighters is Jeremy Larkin, son of
the mayor in Chester; and Isak
Poole, a former slave, aids him.
Parts of the team are also Jeremy's
girlfriend Elizabeth Coates and
Henry Abington, the "intellectual
capacity" in the group.

Together the group of young-
sters do everything to make life
complicated for the British. They
steal their cannons, double-cross
their war plans and carry misin-
formation. The 20-year-old
French nobleman, General Marquis de Lafayette, frequently

appears as an ally to help the young "rebels."

Notes: ABC premiered the series on September 20, 1970. To give it some authenticity, a few of the scenes were shot at historical sites in Boston and its surroundings. The series was generally well received by viewers.

"The Young Rebels" was no earth shaking television series but it was well written and photographed. The young attractive leads did their best to make it a success, but unfortunately the audience it was targeted at were tuned in to **Lassie** and **Hogan's Heroes** on CBS."— Neil Summers in *The Official TV Western Book, Vol. 4.*

Opposite: The Young Rebels (ABC TV series, 1970–71)—*Top:* "The Young Rebels" meet with George Washington at Valley Forge; *left to right:* Elizabeth (Hilarie Thompson), General Washington (Myron Healey), Henry (Alex Henteloff), Jeremy (Rick Ely), and Isak (Lou Gossett) in "The Father of His Country" episode. *Bottom:* Jeremy (Rick Ely, *left*) takes leave of his fellow Yankee Doodle Society members in the "To Hang a Hero" episode. Isak is played by Lou Gossett (*center*).

Index